Private Lucius S. Moseley, age 19 (courtesy of the Moseley family)

Heavy Marching

Heavy Marching

The Civil War Letters of
Lute Moseley, 22nd Wisconsin

Lucius S. Moseley

Edited by
Sara DeLuca

Foreword by
Robert Lucius Moseley

THE UNIVERSITY OF WISCONSIN PRESS

Publication of this book has been made possible, in part,
through support from the Anonymous Fund of the College of Letters and
Science at the University of Wisconsin–Madison.

The University of Wisconsin Press
728 State Street, Suite 443
Madison, Wisconsin 53706
uwpress.wisc.edu

Gray's Inn House, 127 Clerkenwell Road
London ECIR 5DB, United Kingdom
eurospanbookstore.com

Printed in the United States of America
This book may be available in a digital edition.

Library of Congress Cataloging-in-Publication Data

Names: Moseley, Lucius S., author. | DeLuca, Sara, 1943– editor.
Title: Heavy marching : the Civil War letters of Lute Moseley, 22nd Wisconsin /
Lucius S. Moseley ; edited by Sara DeLuca ; foreword by Robert Lucius Moseley.
Description: Madison, Wisconsin : The University of Wisconsin Press, [2023] |
Includes bibliographical references and index.
Identifiers: LCCN 2022039131 | ISBN 9780299342708 (hardcover)
Subjects: LCSH: Moseley, Lucius S.—Correspondence. | United States. Army.
Wisconsin Infantry Regiment, 22nd (1862-1865) | Soldiers—Wisconsin—Beloit—
Correspondence. | United States—History—Civil War, 1861-1865—Personal narratives.
Classification: LCC E537.5 22nd .M 67 2023 | DDC 973.7/475092—dc23/eng/20221107
LC record available at https://lccn.loc.gov/2022039131

For the family of

LUCIUS S. MOSELEY,

generations past and present
and those yet to come

We have shared the incommunicable experience of war. We have felt, we still feel, the passion of life to its top . . . In our youths, our hearts were touched by fire.

—OLIVER WENDELL HOLMES JR.

Neither party expected for the war the magnitude or the duration which it has already attained. Neither anticipated that the cause of the conflict might cease with or even before the conflict itself should cease. Each looked for an easier triumph, and a result less fundamental and astounding. Both read the same Bible and pray to the same God, and each invokes His aid against the other. It may seem strange that any men should dare to ask a just God's assistance in wringing their bread from the sweat of other men's faces, but let us judge not, that we be not judged.

—ABRAHAM LINCOLN, Second Inaugural Address,
March 4, 1865

Contents

Contents

Illustrations

Foreword

Robert Lucius Moseley

My keen interest in our nation's history began in elementary school, soon after I discovered the joy of reading. I recall the excitement of opening an illustrated book on the Civil War, a special birthday gift from my aunt Lillian Baer. To this day that book remains one of the most memorable gifts I have ever received.

During my boyhood in the early 1960s, prior to the escalation of the Vietnam War, kids grew up playing army in the woods and collecting toy soldiers. I remember playing with my blue and gray Civil War soldiers in the living room of our home while my mother entertained her bridge club. I also remember collecting Civil War trading cards. I was fascinated by the battles that had been so consequential in determining the future of our country. A visit to Gettysburg with my parents further stoked the fire. When I became an adult, the Ken Burns television series on the Civil War rekindled my interest.

I was also influenced by my family's prized piece of Civil War memorabilia, passed down through the years—a drinking gourd, engraved by my great-grandfather, *L. S. Moseley, Co "B," 22d Reg. Wis. Vol.* This was such a treasured object that my siblings and I were not allowed to touch it. Because it was light and fragile, my parents kept the gourd hidden away in a closet and brought it out only on rare occasions.

Today that drinking vessel is prominently displayed in a glass case in my living room, along with a typewritten transcription from "Lute" Moseley's letter dated June 24, 1864, offering his thoughts on the reelection of Abraham Lincoln:

About the presidential election. I think "Old Abe" will be elected, and certainly hope he will. He will have my vote. If they let the soldiers vote he will be elected sure. The only hope the rebels have is that we elect some other man in his place. I think they will give in if we put him in again. I sincerely hope you will all at home do your utmost for his support. You will, won't you, Father?

My great-grandfather's Civil War letters were shared among many descendants over the years. We do not know who did the painstaking work of transcribing them on a manual typewriter for easier reading or what became of the original handwritten letters. My mother, Esther, recognized their historical value and became interested in having them published, but she passed away before she could accomplish the task. We are grateful that this history, so influential within our family, can now reach other readers. We feel privileged to share it with all who seek to understand a period during which Americans sacrificed so much for concepts of honor, freedom, and national unity.

Preface

Preparation of this remarkable collection of Civil War letters for publication represents a long, meandering, and serendipitous journey for me, and also for Lucius S. Moseley's descendants.

"History is a pact between the dead, the living and the yet unborn." I came across that quotation attributed to the philosopher Edmund Burke when I was a high school student in rural northwestern Wisconsin. It resonated, deeply. I loved writing and I loved first-person history—the unfiltered personal telling that bears witness to life as it is being lived and thus preserves human experience for future generations.

During the 1990s, a collection of letters written by my maternal grandmother and her four daughters was entrusted to me. Those intimate writings from the 1920s through the 1950s, in which four sisters and their mother shared the details of their daily lives, their hopes and joys and frustrations, revealed the strong foundation I had known as a child on a Wisconsin dairy farm. I knew these places, these people, this farming culture that was passing into history. I felt compelled to preserve the letters in a form that could be shared more broadly. I finally got down to business and found it to be engrossing and rewarding work—but work I expected I would never have to do again.

When my husband and I moved to Atlanta, Georgia, in early retirement, I met a vivacious woman, Esther Baer Moseley, who also loved letters and diaries and the joy of storytelling, which created an entrance into other times and places, other lives. She had shared her own adventures as an Army Air Corps evacuation nurse during World War II in a self-published memoir titled *Lady, Don't Stop Here*. When I met her in 2006, Esther (known to friends and family as "Essie") was working with a treasure of Civil War letters written by her late husband's grandfather, hoping to digitize, organize, annotate, and publish them. Ironically, the young Civil War soldier, Lucius S. Moseley (Lute) was from my home state of Wisconsin and had served in the Wisconsin 22nd Volunteer Infantry from August 1862 until June 1865. Letters to his family in Beloit, Wisconsin, were filled with detailed accounts of military drilling, exhausting marches, tedious waiting and watching, deadly battles, bitter conflicts between his company's officers, fears for friends and family, for his own survival, and always . . . always the longing for more news from home.

Essie asked for my assistance with her project; she died in 2009, before we had made much progress. I moved back to Wisconsin, and the Moseley letters moved with me, but they remained boxed, nearly forgotten, for eleven more years. Then, during the long confining winter of 2020–21, I contacted Essie's family and received their permission to continue this work.

It has been an absorbing and rewarding journey. Lucius Moseley's letters took me on a journey through time and across regions I had known only in present tense. I came to know this farm boy who was born a hundred years before my time, followed him as he became a soldier, became a man. I felt his innocence and pride, his doubts and grievances, high hopes and deep despair . . . all the tides of life brought into sharp relief against the extraordinary background of war.

I would have loved to have held his writings in my hand. Unfortunately, the original letters have been lost to time as have the diaries and scrapbooks. Even after making numerous inquiries, I have not found them archived in any Wisconsin libraries or museums. However, a Moseley descendent—no one in the family is certain who that was—took time and care to transcribe Lute's letters on a manual typewriter several decades ago, preserving them for future generations. Whoever did that job made careful work of it, retaining spelling and grammatical errors, odd and inconsistent punctuation, abbreviations, and archaic expressions. Judging from the quality and style of type, the work was done some time during the mid-twentieth century. It must have been a difficult task. Soldiers' letters were often written in cramped script, utilizing margins and all available space on paper, which could be expensive and often difficult to obtain in the field. Pens might be leaky, pencils stubby, writing faded. During our discussion in 2008, Esther Moseley speculated that these challenges may help explain why a family member discarded the original letters, preferring a transcription that would remain legible and accessible in future years. Or possibly the handwritten letters were lost or left behind during one of many household moves. Whatever the case, we can be grateful that Lucius Moseley's words have been preserved.

In copying the letters on a computer keyboard, I have been faithful to the original transcription, adding corrected spelling of proper names and titles [in square brackets] for clarification. Since Lute's misspellings remained quite consistent, I felt it necessary to indicate the correction only in the first instance. Some abbreviated names have been supplied in full [also bracketed] where I could be certain of identities. Archaic expressions, unusual capitalization, errors in punctuation and grammar have been left as originally transcribed. Words underlined in the letters are rendered here using italics for emphasis. I have omitted some brief letters, and portions of letters, that were repetitive or of interest primarily to Lute's family in Beloit. Omissions have been indicated with ellipsis points.

Lute mentioned many comrades in his letters, often local boys, well known in the community. Because most of these names (including dates of enlistment, mustering out, or separation due to death or disability) can be found in the roster of Wisconsin 22nd Volunteer Regiment officers and staff and the soldiers of Company B—included in appendix A—I have not consistently provided notes. Nor have many well-known persons, locations, and events been further identified. I have not attempted to furnish comprehensive background regarding military strategies, troop movements, skirmishes and battles, protracted disputes between the regimental officers, or the wider scope of political, economic, and social upheaval during this tumultuous period, all of which have been detailed in countless publications. This is primarily the personal journey of one Union soldier, unique in the telling yet representative of so many young men on both sides of the conflict, who fought with valor and determination, certain that God was on their side.

I thank the family of Esther Moseley, especially her son Robert and his wife, Sheila, for permission to publish this collection and for providing additional documents, maps, and photos. I deeply appreciate my too-brief friendship with their mother, Esther Moseley, who, like my own family elders, understood the importance of preserving personal and family history, contributing to the larger narrative that we all share. I gratefully acknowledge the research assistance and encouragement provided by Fred Burwell,

who for many years served as archivist at Beloit College (the same institution where Lucius Moseley studied before enlisting in the army in 1862,
and where my granddaughter recently earned her history degree—more
serendipity). I am also grateful to several research librarians at the Wisconsin Historical Society. Special thanks to Dennis Lloyd, Jacqueline Krass,
Sheila McMahon, Jessica Smith, Jennifer Conn, Mary Sutherland, and all
at the University of Wisconsin Press who helped to guide me through the
editing and publication process.

I thank my husband for his patience and support—technical and otherwise. Thanks also to Susan Mitchell, Sandra Stevermer, Larry Smetak, Paul
Lentz, and others who assisted with research, proofreading, and cheering
me on in this work.

Heavy Marching

Introduction

As for style of writing, if one has anything to say, it drops from him simply and directly as a stone falls to the ground.

—HENRY DAVID THOREAU

Lucius "Lute" Selden Moseley did indeed have a lot to say during three years of service in the Civil War as a foot soldier in Company B, 22nd Wisconsin Volunteer Regiment. He wrote as often as possible to his mother, father, and brother in Beloit, Wisconsin, and the words seemed to fall from his pen freely and candidly . . . "directly as a stone." He sometimes apologized for having little of interest to share, yet the letters were filled with keen observations, solemn reflections, petty irritations and major grievances, irony, humor, and growing compassion, punctuated by raw, almost dispassionate, reporting on the horrors of war.

Not yet twenty years old at the time of his enlistment, the young soldier wrote to his father, mother, and younger brother in an intimate style, less guarded than many older men whose letters to their wives were filled with financial and other domestic concerns as well as reassurances that all was well, or surely would be when the war might soon be over. While Lute Moseley was articulate and better educated than many infantrymen, he was not writing for publication or with the purpose of recording history for posterity. He did not feel the need to glorify or justify the war, to present himself, his comrades, and commanders as brave and heroic in military campaigns about which he often had limited knowledge. He was simply sharing his daily experiences, observations, and emotions with loved ones who were eager for news. He needed to write the letters as much as his family needed to receive them, and he freely expressed a deepening appreciation for the home he so dearly missed.

Just three weeks after he was mustered into service, Lute wrote from Nicholasville, Kentucky, on November 29, 1862: "I don't believe I could stand it two weeks without a letter from you, so when you feel like doing your absent boy a favor: the greatest one I know you can do him is to write." There would be many periods of two weeks and more when letters were neither written nor received. Mail delivery was often disrupted due to sudden troop movements, long marches, isolated locations, destruction of railroads, property, and lives. When the mail did come through, it felt like a lifeline to writer and recipient alike.

Lucius Selden Moseley was born in Indiantown, Bureau County, Illinois, on February 26, 1843. He was the second in a family of four children born to Selden Devotion Moseley, a native of Wyndham, Connecticut, and Harriet (Gage) Moseley, from Bedford, Massachusetts. During the early 1830s, prior to their marriage, Lute's father and mother, along with other colonists, traveled with teams of oxen, by way of the Ohio River, and settled near Dixon, Illinois. Here they married and lived for several years. Early in 1843, Selden Devotion Moseley made a trip to Rock County, Wisconsin, and selected a homesite where his family settled later that spring. Selden worked as a drayman, operating the first horse-drawn delivery service in Beloit. He also had a blacksmith shop and, later, a lumberyard that prospered modestly, but through litigation from a contract to build a schoolhouse, Selden lost all he had accumulated. He later engaged in farming near Beloit and died there in 1884; his wife, Harriet, died two years later. Their daughter Cornelia, born in 1845, died at the age of three; another daughter, Harriet, born in 1840, died in 1857, at seventeen. Their sons, Lucius and Edwin, grew to manhood in Beloit.[1]

The city of Beloit, located on the Rock River in southern Wisconsin, had become a manufacturing and trading center by midcentury; the population of 4,100 was recorded in the 1860 census. Young Lucius was educated in the Beloit public schools and, for an additional three years at the Preparatory Department affiliated with Beloit College, where he expected to continue his studies. His plans were interrupted in August 1862, when he felt compelled to enlist in the army, as did many young men at that time.[2] Their reasons were varied, including community pride, national patriotism, opportunity for travel and adventure, and a chance to prove themselves as men. While few were staunch abolitionists, most believed in the importance of saving the Union, and those issues were inextricably linked.

Financial considerations were also significant for sons of struggling pioneers. Beginning in July 1861, a bounty of $100 was paid for a three-year enlistment as a means of enticing volunteers. Union privates were paid $13 per month (increased to $16 per month in May 1864), and soldiers frequently arranged for allotments to be sent home to their families. "Lute," as he was known to friends and family, allotted $10 from each monthly payment to go to his father; however, he later apologized many times for requesting that some of that money be returned to him so he could supplement meager rations or purchase other necessities. He also wrote and asked for paper, postage stamps, envelopes, a diary, a pen, tobacco, and other small comforts, many of which did not always arrive.

Like so many of his comrades, Lute enlisted in the army for what he expected would be a few months, a year at most, putting down the Southern rebellion and returning home victorious. He was full of enthusiasm on August 31, 1862, when he wrote to his younger brother Edwin, from Camp Utley in Racine[3]: "I like camp much better than expected. There is always something to cheer us or divert our minds from anything that tends toward the blues. I do not know how many times I have heard the boys say they wished the folks at home could see us ... It is very hard for me to write in such a crowd and confusion, but when I get home I will talk enough to make it up."[4]

Wisconsin had been admitted to the Union just thirteen years before the outbreak of war. The population was fewer than 800,000, but the state had played an active role in the debate over states' rights and slavery. When the Civil War broke out in the spring of 1861, Wisconsin swiftly mobilized militia companies and sent them to the armies of the Union.[5]

Lute Moseley's regiment became part of Coburn's Brigade, fighting in the Western Army.[6] This brigade consisted of the 85th Indiana, 33rd Indiana, 19th Michigan, and 22nd Wisconsin. They stayed together throughout the war, which was unusual, since the assignment of regiments to a brigade was not often permanent.[7] Coburn's men became a cohesive unit, spending much of their time performing reconnaissance or guard duties, constructing fortifications, building bridges, and foraging for food and supplies. While they fought in several skirmishes, they were also engaged in major battles at Thompson's Station, Tennessee, at Resaca and Peachtree Creek in Georgia, and at Averasboro, North Carolina.

Throughout the war, Lute reported on rations, health, and weight—a theme found in so many soldiers' letters to loved ones whether they were Union men fighting the "War of the Rebellion" or Confederates fighting the "War of Northern Aggression." Weight was frequently mentioned, particularly when a soldier was adding pounds, indicating that food was adequate and health maintained. Lute did write about suffering from scurvy, dysentery, being tormented by rats and flies and lice, but generally he tried to reassure the family that he was doing well under trying circumstances.

And trying circumstances they were, from the very beginning. The winter of 1862–63 in Kentucky was cold and wet; contaminated water as well as inadequate diet, shelter, and sanitation added to the soldiers' misery. Disease began claiming many young men of Coburn's Brigade. Lute reported to his parents on losses in the 22nd Regiment. On December 28, 1862, he wrote from Camp Baird near Danville, Kentucky: "There have been 30 out of the regiment that have died already—five died in one night. There are a great many sick, and when we left Racine we had 96 men and now there are not over 50 men that are fit for duty." He sometimes included assurances, especially when addressing his mother, that he was upholding the family's values. Early in his service, he assured her: "You may doubtless want to know how your son behaves when he is away from home. I give you my word I am steady and try to do as well as if I were under the eyes of my parents."

Few regretted leaving Danville when they marched off through mud and slush to Louisville on January 26, 1863. In early February they embarked on a long journey down the Ohio River to the mouth of the Cumberland, then up that river to Nashville for rendezvous at Fort Donelson. By this time, the brigade was harboring a number of fugitive slaves who had sought protection with the troops; the 22nd Wisconsin, in particular, had earned a reputation as "the abolition regiment" which caused conflict with Kentucky officials and delayed the transport. From Nashville, the brigade marched on to Brentwood, Tennessee, a region seething with activity by Rebel cavalry and guerrillas, all of which required the men to be in a constant state of readiness for possible attack.

Lute was among approximately 1,200 officers and enlisted men who were captured in the disastrous battle at Thompson's Station on March 5, 1863.[8] After spending several weeks in the notorious Libby Prison in Richmond, Virginia, they were released according to an exchange agreement with the Confederate government. Lute wrote from a hospital on April 19, 1863: "We have indeed seen hard times . . . I am now in the hospital, have been since we came here [to St. Louis] but I am going back tomorrow . . . I am poor as a snake, but I have gained since I got back to America. I feel like fighting them as long as I live. We all got as lousy as we could be and our hips are all worn from lying and sitting on the floor so much."

The paroled troops, who were sent to Camp Gamble near St. Louis, took an oath that they would not "take up arms nor in any way aid or give comfort to the Union cause" until the exchange was made official three months later. They moved on to Nashville, then Murfreesboro, Tennessee, for many months of drilling, guarding, foraging, waiting and watching, or as Lute expressed it, "pursuing the monotonous duties of a soldier's life." Morale sank very low. The men of the 22nd Wisconsin felt dishonored not only by their surrender at Thompson's Station but also by the bitter disputes among their officers, which they felt were keeping them sidelined. Lute complained often of incompetent leadership, lax discipline, and demoralized men within Company B and the entire regiment. The ongoing conflicts between Col. William Utley and Lt. Col. Edward Bloodgood were particularly consequential for all who served with them. On July 2, 1863, Lute wrote to his "dear ones at home": "The ol Col. [Utley] and Lt. Col. [Bloodgood] have been at swords points and each watching for an opportunity to prefer charges against the other. Some of the commishioned officers were on one side and some on the other . . . Now how this will terminate, no one knows, but certainly it is the biggest kind of disgrace." The disputes continued for many months, leading to Bloodgood's trial by court-martial and dismissal from service.[9]

In spring 1864, the soldiers welcomed reorganization of the regiment and orders to move out. They could only guess at their destination and what might lie ahead. Lute wrote to his family on April 29, from an island in the Tennessee River: "We came to this island on a pontoon bridge. We draw rations tonite, and in the morning we muster for pay and then go on. I don't know how far and I don't care."

Where they were going was south, through the rugged north Georgia terrain, building fortifications, engaging in several skirmishes and battles of the Atlanta Campaign, joining 62,000 men in blue, who would cut a swath of destruction through Georgia on Sherman's March to the Sea. They would continue marching and fighting through the Carolinas, on to Washington, DC for the celebratory Grand Review before being mustered out on June 12, 1865. It would be a long road home.

When he joined the army in August 1862, Lute Moseley could not have imagined the physical and emotional challenges that lay ahead. He occasionally admitted to feeling homesick or "having the blues." Although he begged his parents not to worry, sometimes boasting that he and the Beloit boys were "feeling bully," he also shared some darker moods. On October 14, 1862, he wrote: "It was just two months ago today that I enlisted. I curse that day. If I was back in Beloit I would remain there contented." A year later, October 23, 1863, Lute was feeling more than discouraged: "A man thinks he is enlisting to put down the rebellion, but not so, only to gratify some big Man's ambition, and at the same time to fill their pockets."

On July 2, 1884, Lute wrote from Marietta, Georgia: "I hope I shall be spared, but lots of young men, as anxious to live as I, have had to fall." By that time he had witnessed more violence and tragedy than most people know in one lifetime. When he wrote of bloody battles, casualties, burying the dead, Lute's tone was usually reportorial and restrained. Conversely, he expressed himself openly about many lesser events. In a letter dated February 8, 1863, from a camp near Nashville, Lute reported: "We were camped in an awfully muddy place and it was so near the city we couldn't get straw so I stole an armful of hay from the mules. To tell you the truth I felt as mean and sick as I ever did."

When victory was close at hand, Lute wrote proudly from Raleigh, North Carolina: "We can stand most anything now," and on April 21, 1865: "I am not sorry I enlisted and, too, that I have stayed until the war is ended."

Lute frequently asked family to excuse his "poor letters" and admitted that he sometimes "wrote because I have nothing else to do, so I sit down and record what I happen to think." What Lute happened to think about could range from the humorous to the heartbreaking. So many contradictions—hope and discouragement, pride and regret, brotherly love, petty irritations, harsh judgments—it's all there on the page. A particularly painful issue, in the context of the present day, is the outspoken prejudice of Northern troops toward the enslaved people that they were supposedly fighting to free. Lute's comments on the subject seem to be fairly representative of Wisconsin soldiers who had little experience or knowledge of "negros" or of the injustices they suffered.[10] Apparently Lute's understanding and compassion deepened over time. In December 1862, Lute wrote from Nicholasville, Kentucky, where the regiment was harboring several "contrabands": "Because we are making such work of their niggers we are hated pretty badly . . . We have a lot in our regiment, they are lazy and will sauce you and call you anything they can think of. I will never fight or say a great deal to free them if they don't get free in this enterprise." September 5, 1863, from Murfreesboro, Tennessee: "How thankful I am to have my pen to communicate with you and my absent and far off friends. I often think of

those poor negros leaving their families to go and help in this great struggle, for few can either read or write." And on November 29, 1863, from
Murfreesboro:

> I was on guard down at the depot a few nights ago, and there was a train came
> in from the front loaded with negro women and children. I never knew what
> want was. If they weren't a pitiful looking lot of humans, I never want to see
> any that are. I had a loaf of bread and some coffee and I gave it to them . . . I
> remember the negro that gave me the corn cake at Tullahoma. They came
> from Alabama and say there isn't ¼ enough to eat there. Some of them were
> real smart.[11]

On the other hand, Lute's assessment of the "Rebs," and the South in general, remained quite constant. His disparaging remarks sometimes verged
on the comical. Early in his term of service, he began comparing the land-
scape, the soil, the crops, and the people of the southern states with his
beloved home state. Everything southern, including the border states that
remained in the Union, suffered in the contrast. On January 15, 1863, writing from Camp Baird in Danville, Kentucky, he made this observation: "The
country thru this part of the states is, to a northern boy at least anything but
inviting. Nothing but hills and rocks. Until he thinks it is not the country
but the union we are fighting for, he feels like complaining and wonders
why so much blood is shed over so poor a country, while there are so many
hundreds of nice prairie unoccupied in the west."

On October 3, 1863, Lute wrote about foraging for provisions, shooting
livestock and "making the old reb that owned them yoke up his oxen and
take them to camp . . . he owns a large farm and lots of cattle and negros,
but can't read or write—a fair sample of all the inhabitants of Tennessee."
October 17, 1863: "I hav'nt seen one southern person that would talk anything but negros. Over two thirds of them can't read or write and half of
them can't change a dollar bill and take out 15 cents." And from Atlanta,
September 11, 1864: "You certainly don't know how much you have to be
thankful for, that our lot was cast in the North instead of this part of the
world."

As in wars of any era, in any location the world over, each side demon-
ized the other. Yet, when they had the rare chance to lower their defenses,
the soldiers must have recognized the enemy as men much like themselves, swept up in powerful events and purposes. We find ironic details in

many Civil War letters, describing butchery on the battlefield, followed—
or preceded by—an unofficial truce, with Confederate and Union soldiers
chatting casually, sharing coffee, trading tobacco and newspapers. Lute
Moseley wrote of fraternizing with Confederates when they were camped
on opposite sides of the Chattahoochee River in Georgia, July 16, 1864:

> We have great times talking with the Johnnies. Our skirmish line is right on
> the edge of the river, and theirs is as close on the other side. The river is not
> as wide as the Rock River but is deep, swift and muddy. We go in swimming
> on our side and they on theirs, at the same time. The day I was down there,
> there were 100 of each on the banks, talking and trading. We would swim
> over to them and trade anything we had for tobacco. One of them gave me a
> piece. They are very generous and talkative. Not a shot is fired from either side
> the whole length of our corps.

It is stunning to read the words of the same young man, written five
days later, recounting the battle at Peachtree Creek: "They came on till they
were so near we could almost shake hands with them. Then our men
poured a deadly volley into them, just mowing the rascals, and you bet they
began to get back over the hill again, covering the ground with their dead
and wounded."

That a tenderhearted, home-loving boy like Lute Moseley could be con-
ditioned to engage in action such as this, and then rejoice in it, is one of the
abiding tragedies of war. When death becomes so commonplace, the senses
can be numbed to horror, which may be beneficial to survival. But as the
war drew to a close and Lute could see that victory was at hand, he did not
feel like celebrating. He was not pleased about participating in the Grand
March in Washington, DC, feeling it was a show put on for the "big men"
at the expense of exhausted troops who were eager to return home and "get
right with the world."

By April 16, 1865, the future was looking brighter and Lute expressed
"strong hopes of returning soon" to "your kind and loved society, which I
must confess, I have at time nearly despaired of." On that same day the
soldiers of the 22nd Wisconsin received the news that President Abraham
Lincoln had been assassinated at Ford's Theatre in Washington, DC. Accustomed as he was to rumors that flourished in an absence of reliable information, Lute responded with doubt. "I don't believe it yet. There is a report
this afternoon that it is not so. I hope it will prove untrue, surely."

This time the news was all too true. President Lincoln, overwhelmingly supported by Union soldiers in the November 1864 election, was assassinated on April 14 and died the following day, April 15, 1865, before Confederate surrenders were official. Harvey Reid, of Company A, 22nd Wisconsin wrote: "Such deep, universal sorrow as pervaded this army when the sad truth became known, is without a parallel."[12]

More than three million soldiers served in the Civil War, and each represents a personal story, but most of these reminiscences remain untold and lost to history. The diaries and letters that have been preserved reveal unique journeys of men who sacrificed so much in an overwhelmingly destructive conflict. Their writings also expose the common threads that weave a narrative richer and fuller than statistics and official documents can supply. Letters such as those written by Lucius Moseley can bring the past to life and help us realize how little human nature has changed through time and circumstance, and how far we still need to travel in pursuit of a peaceful and just society.

Missing, faulty, and inconsistent records of Civil War deaths, especially within the Confederacy, have resulted in varying calculations. Many present day historians estimate that at least 750,000 people lost their lives in the American Civil War, more than all other American wars from the American Revolution through the Vietnam War combined. Total 1860 population (North and South combined, including the enslaved) was about 31 million people, one-tenth the size it is now. If the war were fought today, a proportionate number of deaths (nearly 2.5 percent) would total eight million.[13] Such loss is staggering to contemplate. The further cost in terms of wealth and property and human suffering, is, of course, impossible to measure.

Was it all worthwhile? The question continues to be debated. Bruce Catton, a Civil War historian, took the positive view that the war did accomplish something important:

> It gave us a political unity in the sense that it kept the country from fragmenting into a number of separate, independent nations . . . The geographic unit that made the wealth and prosperity of later days was preserved. Beyond that, the country made a commitment during the war; a commitment to a broader freedom, a broader citizenship for all our people, regardless of their color,

their race, their religion, their national origins; regardless of anything. We are fated to continue the experiment in peaceful democracy, and I don't think any people were ever committed to a nobler experiment that that one.[14]

NOTES

1. Biographical information is based on William Fiske Brown's *History of Rock County: Its Villages, Towns, Citizens, and Varied Interests from the Earliest Times Up to Date*, vol. 2 (Chicago: C. F. Cooper, 1908), 969–71.

2. "War fever" had taken hold at Beloit College and throughout the community, soon after the attack at Fort Sumter in April 1861. President Lincoln called for seventy-five thousand military volunteers to put down the rebellion. Alexander Randall, Wisconsin's governor, issued a proclamation calling for soldiers and funds: "All good citizens, everywhere, must join in making common cause against a common enemy." Fred Burwell, "Fridays with Fred: A Call to Arms Reaches the College," Beloit College, April 14, 2011, https://beloit.edu/live/news/613/fridays-with-fred-a-call -to-arms-reaches-the-college/.

3. Camp Utley was named after Colonel William Utley, a former Wisconsin legislator and successful army recruiter, appointed by the governor to lead Wisconsin's 22nd Regiment. While he was a charming and charismatic speaker, Utley lacked previous military experience, a deficit that would have serious consequences for him, his fellow officers, and the entire regiment. Richard H. Groves, *Blooding the Regiment: An Account of the 22nd Wisconsin's Long and Difficult Apprenticeship* (Lanham, MD: Scarecrow Press, 2005), 25–26.

4. By the summer of 1862, Camp Utley was humming with activity as one of four training camps—in Milwaukee, Fond du Lac, Madison, and Racine. The 22nd Wisconsin Regiment consisted of ten companies, organized locally. The men of Company B were recruited in Beloit; many were well acquainted with their fellow soldiers prior to enlistment in the Union army.

5. Between 1861 and 1865, Wisconsin would send more than 91,000 young men, in 56 regiments, to fight in the Civil War. More than 12,000 never returned; 3,802 were killed in action, and 8,499 died from disease, exposure, and other causes. "Wisconsin's Involvement in the Civil War," Wisconsin Historical Society, accessed July 12, 2022, wisconsinhistory.org/Records/Article/CS3355/.

6. Col. John Coburn (1825–1908), from Indianapolis, was a lawyer, a state representative, and a judge during the 1850s. He was a commissioned colonel of the 33rd Indiana in September 1861 and became brigade commander of the 22nd Wisconsin. After the war, he served four terms as a U.S congressman from Indiana. "Coburn, John," U.S. House of Representatives, History, Art & Archives, accessed April 20, 2022, https://history.house.gov/People/Detail/11148/.

7. A Union regiment was usually made up of ten companies, with approximately one hundred men each; a full regiment would include around one thousand officers and men. Numbers varied, usually decreasing as the war progressed.

8. This was also known as the Battle of Spring Hill. The final report of casualties among officers and men of the 22nd Wisconsin listed 2 dead, 29 wounded, and 129

captured or missing, making a total of 160. Casualties in the whole expedition totaled 1,446, and most of the captured men became prisoners. *War of the Rebellion: Official Records of the Union and Confederate Armies* (Washington, DC: Government Printing Office, 1880–1901), ser. 1, vol 23, 75 (cited hereafter as *War of the Rebellion: Official Records*).

9. Petitions by fellow officers, intervention by Edward Salomon, Wisconsin's governor, and approval by President Lincoln restored Bloodgood to duty in January 1864. Colonel Utley resigned in July 1864, citing ill health. *Semi-Weekly Wisconsin News*, Milwaukee, WI, January 2, 1864; Harvey Reid, *Uncommon Soldiers: Harvey Reid and the 22nd Wisconsin March with Sherman*, ed. Frank L. Byrne (Knoxville: University of Tennessee Press, 2001), 167–68.

10. According to the 1860 census, the black population in Wisconsin numbered only 1,171; this meant that black people comprised fewer than one-fifth of 1 percent of the state's total population. Frank L. Klement, *Wisconsin in the Civil War* (Madison: Historical Society of Wisconsin, 2001), 93.

11. "After the Emancipation Proclamation took effect in 1863, the War Department created a bureau specifically to recruit black troops. Racism remained widespread in the Union army throughout the war, but numerous letters from white troops reveal a drastic change in racial attitudes after 1863." Tom Robotham, *The Civil War Album* (New York: Smithmark, 1992), 176.

12. Reid, *Uncommon Soldiers*, 245.

13. Guy Gugliotta, "Civil War Toll Up by 20 Percent," *New York Times*, April 3, 2012; Bob Zeller, "How Many Died in the American Civil War?," January 6, 2022, https://www.history.com/news/american-civil-war-deaths.

14. Bruce Catton, *Reflections on the Civil War*, ed. John Leekley (New York: Doubleday, 1981), 225, 226.

CHAPTER 1

Drilling for War

August 31, 1862–February 9, 1863

I try to be a man and act my part.

—Lucius S. Moseley, October 9, 1862

Wisconsin 22nd Volunteer Infantry Regiment—Organized at Racine, Wisconsin, and mustered in September 2, 1862. Left State for Cincinnati, Ohio, September 16, thence moved to Covington, Kentucky, September 22. Attached to 2nd Brigade, 1st Division, Army of Kentucky, Department of the Ohio, to November, 1862.

Service: March from Covington to Georgetown, Lexington, Sandersville, and Nicholasville, October 7–November 13, 1862. Duty at Nicholasville till December 12. Moved to Danville, Kentucky, December 12 and duty there till January 26, 1863. Moved to Louisville, Kentucky, thence to Nashville, Tennessee, January 26–February 7, 1863.

—Frederick H. Dyer, *A Compendium of the War of the Rebellion*, vol. 3, *Regimental Histories* (Des Moines, IA: Dyer, 1908), https://www.loc.gov/item/09005239/; hereafter Dyer, *Compendium*.

August 31, 1862—from Camp Utley

Dear Eddie,[1]

Having a few minutes of leisure I thot that I could not employ them better than to write a few lines to you altho I hav'nt much to say. I received your kind letter Sat., and I assure you it was a welcome one to me. We are to be mustered into the U.S. service today. I expect we have guards all around the camp, so you see we are not allowed to go to the city without a written pass from the Colonel. After we are mustered we will receive our uniforms and then I expect we will be able to get a furlough. I expect next Saturday. They have six men in the guardhouse already, only one from our company. There was an attempt made last night to tear down the Sutler's tent,[2] although it failed they made two of the men walk from one tree to another all day to pay for their trouble.

Our camp is beautifully situated about 1½ miles from town on the lake shore.[3] There are boats passing all the time. The other day I got a pass and went on the lake, and was gone all afternoon, so you see there is some enjoyment for us poor soldiers. The boys are all well and seem satisfied except that little Knill boy who had to go on guard last night. He says he is going to go home, but that is not for him to say. As far as I am concerned, I like camp much better than I expected. There is always something to cheer us or divert our minds from anything that tends toward the blues.

I do not know how many times I have heard the boys say they wished the folks at home could see us. It is really quite amusing to see the different maneuvers that so many men will think up. Well Eddie, I guess you will think my letter is quite monotonous, for so it is. It is very hard for me to write in such a crowd and confusion, but when I get home I will talk enough to make it up. I want you to write immediately and let me know how the folks are, besides the pony, pigs, dog and kitten must not be forgotten. I want to hear from them all.

The other night there were five little girls came up to our camp and sang for us. I tell you if I didn't cheer them at the end of each song.

There is a band getting up in our regiment at the expense of the boys, and if it succeeds I shall play either the drum or cymbals. You needn't say anything about it there tho at present. Now I will pause till next time.

Yours with affectionate regards, Lute

NOTES

1. Edwin Devotion Moseley, born on October 21, 1848, was more than five years younger than Lucius ("Lute"), who was born on February 26, 1843.

2. The sutler was a civilian merchant who was authorized to sell provisions to soldiers, usually from a tent or the back of a wagon. He could provide a variety of dry goods not supplied by the army, and his visits were welcomed, especially in remote outposts.

3. Camp Utley was created out of a seventy-five-acre lot between Sixteenth Street and College Avenue in Racine, Wisconsin. Col. William Utley, for whom the camp was named, recruited and trained men from Racine, Rock, Green, and Walworth

Counties. Details regarding facilities at Camp Utley are found in Groves, *Blooding the Regiment*, 22.

❧

Cincinnatti [Cincinnati], Sept. 18, 1862, Thursday

Brother Eddie,

We started from Racine last Tuesday about noon and arrived in Chicago about six in the evening without any accident, saving running over a cow and a hog. At Chicago I met a large number of boys I knew. We had to change cars there. After that we were not permitted to leave the train until we reached here. We ran over another cow on the way. We reached here last evening about ten and then marched near two miles to the market square where the city had provided a supper for us. After we had finished that they marched us to a large hall where we are now. We have full access to a large library and reading room, which makes it very pleasant. Last night we slept on the floor. I never slept more soundly in my life, nor was I in better health in my life. It is very hard to work for Uncle Sam, but there is something about it I like after all.

Yesterday we were within about 100 miles of here when we received a telegraphic dispatch to hurry on with all possible dispatch for they expected there would be an attack on the city immediately. So all the haste that could be made to hurry us on. I tell you that began to come right down to reality. But there was not a man that turned a hair. We were all desirous of hurrying up all we could. I did not feel the least fear. But there was not attack made yet, nor will there be on this place right away, altho the rebel scouts are within 5 miles of us. They say there is a large force of rebels about 24 miles from here. Our army have pickets stationed all along up to Lawrenceburg [Indiana] about ten miles down the river. There are over 80,000 of our troops around here. Before our troops reached the inhabitants, all turned out with such weapons as they had to defend the place. They have all gone home now. There was hardly a single log house along the road, but where women and children and men could be seen, swinging handkerchiefs, hats or something of the kind. They would bring out pails of water, baskets or apples and the like every time we stopped. Yesterday at Lawrenceburg, a place we came thru, they shot 5 sesesh spies.[4] We have good news from McClellan which makes the boys feel in good spirits.[5] We all want a share, and I believe we would do good service now, although we all feel we need more drilling.

I tell you Ed, it seems rather queer to leave a good quiet home in the north and come down here where it is all war and commotion. Altho if it were not for the privations of a home and its influences, I should rather be here than threshing rye for John Bannister. I tell you Ed I wish you were old enough to be here with me. I think of you often too, and hope you grow up to be a good man. Be good to father and mother, you will not always have them with you. Write me a long letter and tell me anything you think I would like to hear. How is father getting along? I heard he was sick and I am very anxious to hear, if he is sick, let me know and also how is mother. . . .

Have you got any other colts home yet? How are the colts? Are they well of their lameness yet? How much did Dr. Winters charge for his services? Tell father to pay him out of the money I left with him. I have allotted $10 per month to be paid to father of my wages. I want him to use it in his law suit. He will receive it from the paymaster of Beloit, once in two months. Is there any news in regard to his suit? Tell mother and father to write. You don't know how good a letter is to us here. Send me your pictures. I sent you a bill, it is one of the enemies. I don't know but it would be a curiosity to you.[6]

I had the misfortune to lose the little knife of mothers. I am sorry. As soon as I get your letter, I will write again.

From your true brother, Lute

Direct your letters to: L.S. Moseley, Co. B, 22nd Reg., Wis. Vol.

NOTES

4. *Sesesh*, a term that Lute used in many letters (spelled both with and without the capital S), referred to secessionists. As a soldier, he usually referred to the Confederate military. The term could also be applied to anyone sympathizing with the cause of secession from the Union.

5. Maj. Gen. George B. McClellan, commander of the Army of the Potomac. A former railroad president, McClellan was able to build a strong army, but a series of retreats and strong disagreements with President Lincoln resulted in McClellan's removal from the command. McClellan would battle with Lincoln once again, after winning the Democratic nomination for the presidency in 1864.

6. The bill ("one of the enemies") was likely a Confederate States dollar bill, or "grayback," first issued before the outbreak of war, to keep sufficient currency in circulation. Like the Federal "greenback," it was not backed by hard assets. The "grayback," as well as other notes issued by individual states and corporations, became worthless when the Confederacy was defeated, resulting in tremendous losses to banks, businesses, and citizens.

∾

Cincinnatti, Sept. 20, 1862

Dear Mother,

We are ordered off for Louisville, Ky. in ½ hr., so you see I can't write much. I sent three shirts home because I don't want to wash them, nor get anyone to do it for me. I am glad to leave here. It is a very pretty place tho. We are going down on boats. The boys are all well. I am well and I hope you are well. Do not deceive me but let me know if you are sick. Write me a long letter and give my love to my good father, tell him to write me a letter and if he can spare it, have him put in two dollars. I am not strapped but have to purchase a few things I had not thot of, two will be plenty. Tell Eddie to take good care of the colties, which I have no doubt he will. I will write you again in a few days. Write to me and direct as before.

From your dutiful son, Lute

❧

Five miles from Cincinnatti (in Kentucky), Sept. 24, 1862

Dear Brother Eddie,

I have just returned from guard duty and have a few minutes to spare. I received your kind and brotherly letter last night. Yesterday they sent me over to the General's quarters to guard him and his.[7] They relieved me this morning. My rations for 24 hours consisted of 5 hard crackers and that was all. But this is an exception. We have a great plenty to eat, such as it is. The boys are all well. I hope I can always write the same. We moved our camp about ½ mile yesterday. We are now situated in a beautiful grove of beach. We have no tents yet and sleep on the ground with nothing but a blanket and the sky over us. Night before last it rained most all night. We were as wet as sop in the morning, but that did not hurt us. We built a large fire and dried out.

If you were to see this place you would think it was war times. There isn't a bit of fence around here. We go into their fields and dig their sweet potatoes. We press them into services as we call it. There are rifle pits each way as far as we can see. They employ every man that they can for $1.50 per day—including their board, to work on fortifications. There are over 200 I guess, in sight of our tent, digging entrenchments. They have cut down all of the timber so as to have a fair sweep at them. All the large orchards are right out near. About one mile west of here on top of a hill they have built a fort called Ft. Mitchell.

Last night when I was over to the Generals the teams came in from down the river. They had a sesesh prisoner with them. He had nothing but a pair of drawers, an old straw hat and an old coat on. I don't know if he had shoes on or not, as he was in a wagon and I could not see. He said he had five brothers in the Illinois Regiment.[8]

There is a large house burned down today in sight of here. They say it was burned by a company from our regiment that went on picket duty this morning. As to the truth I don't know. There were two companies around it while it was burning. They say they are going to burn another one tonight. Poly is on guard today.[9] He is feeling first rate. He and I are thick as ever. He is a right good boy.

You ask if I liked it here as well as Racine. To this I would say: I like it a great deal better only for the thot of being so far away, it takes so long to get letters. The climate is very good, not near as cold as Wisconsin. It is rough country, covered with timber.

22nd Wis. Regiment crossing the pontoon bridge at Cincinnati, September 22, 1862 (courtesy of Wisconsin Historical Society)

If it is convenient, send me some Beloit papers. The boys all notice how much mail each receives. Last night I had 3 letters. It was quite a feather in my cap . . .

I will close now. Your affectionate brother, Lute

NOTES

7. Lute did not name the general he referred to in this letter; possibly he meant Maj. Gen. William "Bull" Nelson, who was in Northern Kentucky at the time. Harry Searles, "William 'Bull' Nelson," American History Central, April 29, 2021, https://americanhistorycentral.com/entries/william-bull-nelson/.

8. "He said he had five brothers in the Illinois Regiment." If true, the "sesesh prisoner" was an example of brothers fighting on opposite sides of the War of the Rebellion (or War of Northern Aggression, a term used by those aligned with the Confederate cause). Loyalties were sharply divided in the Middle and Upper South, within government, communities, neighborhoods, and families.

9. "Poly"—or in later letters "Pole"—was Napoleon Perry from Beloit. He served with Lute in Company B of the Wisconsin 22nd Volunteer Regiment throughout three years of service.

Thurs., Oct. 9, 1862, 5 miles out of Cincinnatti

Dear Mother,

We are ordered off for Lexington. Our regiment left here yesterday morning, but we were left behind at the fort. We have expected to remain here and not join our regiment. We are all packed up and in a few minutes we will start. It is about 30 miles. The regiment is about 15 miles from here. We will have our knapsacks carried for us today and will probably over take them tomorrow. The boys are all well, at least those you are acquainted with. If we had stayed here I should have been promoted to gunner.[10] Now we have to go back to the regiment. I of course will have to go back into the ranks again. I have had command of the gun one week anyway. You would have laughed to see your boy commanding a company, or squad rather, of men. I did it and I did it well. Mother, the thing looks dark at time but I think if any poor boy without influential friends to help him gets a position, I will . . .

You may doubtless want to know how your son behaves when he is away from home. I give you my word I am steady and try to do as well as if I were under the eyes of my parents. I do not let that little book lie untouched, that I showed you. Mother, I love you and when I read your kind letters it starts the tears. I try to be a man and act my part. I have not been homesick, although it is hard to be deprived of the comforts of home. Do not worry about me, I am fine. Give my love to father and brother Eddie. Write soon.

Your affectionate son, Lute

NOTE

10. "Should have been promoted to gunner." Operating a cannon was a team effort requiring several soldiers. The gunner's responsibility was to judge the distance and position of the target and aim the weapon.

∿

Oct. 9, 1862

To my Father

Since writing that note to mother I have been to supper and now I am on guard. Yesterday they detailed Alex Anderson and I from our company to take charge of a rifle cannon at the 3 battery. Now I am sitting on guard duty top of the magazine, writing to you. Eddie says you are peddling. I do hope, father, you will be prospered and do well. I feel very anxious here about your school house affair.[11]

. . . I am well and not very homesick yet but there are some who feel very badley and would give all they are worth to get home. I thot of meeting many unpleasant hours before I enlisted. I am well, yes better satisfied than I expected to be.

What do you think of the war? Do you think there is any chance of it closing within a year? There is some talk among the boys that it will close, but we don't have a chance to know anything about the war affairs. We expect some to go farther south within a day or two. If we do I shall go with them, but I expect I could stay with the cannon if I wanted to. We are going to shoot it tomorrow I expect. It is one of the largest kind of siege rifle cannon, carrying a ball six miles. It takes 13 of us to work it. It is getting so dark I cannot see the lines, so I trust you will excuse this poor note. Hoping soon to hear from you.

I remain, as ever your loving son, Lute

NOTE

11. Lute's father, Selden Moseley, who operated a lumber yard, was involved in litigation over his contract to build a schoolhouse in Beloit.

∿

Covington, Ky, Camp Wright, Tues., Oct. 14, 1862

Dear brother Eddie,

We are 40 miles from Cincinnatti in Ky . . . The boys are all well except R.L. Adams and he is not very sick. We have not lost a man out of our regiment yet. We were three days on our way here. The first day we marched 8 miles, the second 15 and the third 17 miles, making it about 40 miles to state line. Tomorrow we are going to march 16.

There are lots of boys who gave out on the way, but ol Lute and Poly are good for it. 17 miles may not seem to you to be a long way to march, but with 40 pounds of cartridges and your knapsack on your back, your haversack filled with crackers, your canteen filled with warm water and a heavy musket you are obliged to carry in position all the time and dust flying so thick you can't see—it is little diferent from takeng your own natural gate, it is hard.

I suppose you remember it was just two months ago today I enlisted. I curse that day. If I was back in Beloit I would remain there contented. I don't want you to think I have the blues, I have'nt. I am not sick of soldiering, if they would let us do it properly. We do have to guard rebel property. We are now camped on rebel ground. He has two sons in the rebel army. We are not allowed to touch even a rail off his fence when we are nearly frozen to death. We are not allowed to touch even an apple in the orchard along the road. We have to stand guard all night to keep others from touching the afore said property. Good heavens, I ask, when will this rebellion be crushed out. I did not expect when I enlisted to fight against my own people.[12]

We like our Captain [Thomas P. Northrop from Beloit] first rate. Tell Mrs. Northrop I am obliged to her for her kind rememberence of me in mother's letter. Tell her I will take care of her man. He was sick in Cincinnatti and Polly [Poly] and I went to see him. He was lying on a board in the hospital. We stold some hay, put it in a tick and put it under him. So was John Teague, he had the mumps. We fixed him up with hay too.

I guess I have already spun my letter out so long you are tired of reading it. Write soon. We have to drill 8 hours every day now. Paper is not scarce here. The suttler has plenty and he has his own prices for it. This is enough for now.

From your loving brother, Lute

NOTE

12. The border state of Kentucky did not secede from the Union although it was partially a slave state, and citizens were bitterly divided in their loyalties. Wisconsin soldiers expected that they had come to Kentucky as friends and defenders but were often treated as the enemy. James M. McPherson, *Ordeal by Fire: The Civil War and Reconstruction* (New York: Alfred A. Knopf), 153, 154.

Camp, near Lexington, Oct. 29, 1862[13]

Dear brother Eddie,

I was glad to receive a letter from you, Mother and Mrs. Miller. We are in camp on the fair grounds of Lexington. It is a beautiful place. The country here is the best I ever saw, but the inhabitants are so different—I cannot bear them. There is one great lack of water, it is scarce, and what there is, is very poor. I should like to get to our well and drink all I wanted.

We are expecting to march to Franklin—18 miles from here, today or tomorrow, maybe.

Our mail will come more regularly now. They have got the cars to running from here to Cincinnatti. The rebels destroyed the bridges when they were thru here. Last night was the first mail we have received for quite a number of days. I believe I told you that it snowed the other night. Has it snowed there yet? Mother said if I wanted anything to let her know. I need a pair of gloves very badley.

You say father thinks I am homesick. I want you to distinctly understand that I ain't. I would like to see you and my friends, but if I were home now, knowing what I know, I would enlist again. I don't like the way we are used—the way the thing is managed, but that isn't for me to dictate . . .

George Dates is pretty homesick. I understand his father has offered $100 for a substitute.[14] Don't tell anyone I wrote that, it will all come back and make the boys mad . . . Send me some stamps every time you write. The money you sent me is no good here, they take nothing but Kentuck money here.[15] No other news so I will close.

All my love, Lute

NOTES

13. The Army of Kentucky, under the command of Maj. Gen. Gordon Granger, was reorganized at Lexington with Gen. Absalom Baird commanding the third of three separate divisions. The First Brigade of the Third Division, under Col. John

Coburn, consisted of the 33rd and 85th Indiana, the 19th Michigan, and 22nd Wisconsin. It was commonly called Coburn's Brigade, though at various times it would be commanded by other officers. These four regiments served together until the end of the war. *War of the Rebellion: Official Records*, Series 3, vol. 16, part 2, 993.

14. In autumn 1862, Governor Salomon reluctantly ordered military conscription for counties that had not met their volunteer quotas. The announcement of a military draft lottery for healthy men between the ages of 18 and 45 resulted in widespread protests as well as the controversial practice of draftees hiring substitutes or paying $300 to opt out of military service. Since $300 was an impossible sum for many, this led to complaints of "the poor man fighting the rich man's war." Klement, *Wisconsin in the Civil War*, 27–31.

15. Kentucky, which declared neutrality at the start of the war, remained a house divided throughout four years of battle. Protracted war and economic uncertainties led to hoarding and a shortage of legal currency. Merchants, firms, and organizations began issuing their own tokens and paper as mediums of exchange.

Nicholasville, Ky, Nov. 16, 1862

Dear Home, Father, Mother, and Eddie,

I am seated on the sutler's wagon writing to you. It is a very convenient place to write as it is raining very hard. I am glad to see it for several reasons. There is scarcely any water for us to use here as it has not rained in a long time. Also, if it were not raining we would have to go out on Battalion review.

We are not allowed as much freedom as the negroes, for when it comes Sunday they can have the time to spend as they wish but we as a general thing only work harder.[16]

We are now camped at Nicholasville, 15 miles from Lexington. The church bells are now ringing. One of them sounds almost exactly like the one I used to ring. It makes me homesick. I wish I could spend just one night in my old bed.

We have all got to wear regulation hats which are wide brims with a tall tapering crown. I look like an ol cat. They say tonight we won't get our pay this month so you can send me a little money, not over $5. We had our regular weekly inspection today. The mail has come and I got a letter from you.

I have been quite unwell for the two or three days, had a little fever, but am quite alright now. We are not suffering. How did you hear we were not allowed ammunition? A worse lie could not have been told. Every man has

40 rounds and is obliged to carry them at all times. I don't believe there is a man in the regiment but would fight as quickly for our good ol Col. [Utley] as he would himself. He is liked by all the regiment. I don't like some things about him. He gets mad and swears at us once in a while. That does not look well in him, I think. Capt. Northrop has not resigned but we think he may.

The band is playing for the meeting. The Capt. is going to preach his farewell this morning and I want to hear him so I will close. Give my best regards to all who may inquire.

Your dutiful son, Lute

NOTE

16. Runaway slaves who escaped to Union lines often became paid camp labor-ers. As "contrabands of war," they were sometimes recaptured and returned to their masters. When Colonel Baird's Third Division was encamped near Nicholasville, there were about two hundred black men within the Union lines. To avoid further difficulties involving local citizens and runaway slaves, the acting provost marshal (Lt. Col. Alexander B. Crane of the 85th Indiana) issued orders that no one was to go out of the town. *History of the Eighty-Fifth Indiana Volunteer Infantry* (Bloomington, IN: Cravens Brothers Printers and Binders, 1902), 10.

∽

Camp Granger, Nicholasville, Ky, Nov. 29th, 1862

. . . I have just returned from meeting. Our chaplain [Caleb D. Pillsbury of Beloit] preached an excellent sermon today, altho I don't think it was quite such a one as he had ought to've preached. His text was "Come ye home with me and eat bread." He spoke principally about home. Do you suppose, mother, I could stand and listen to such a discourse with dry eyes? Oh no, it started my feeling more than anything I have met yet. He said he presumed there was not a soldier there but what had a home, where loved ones were thinking about him. I almost felt certain that it was true in my case. Every Sunday I feel quite sure you are thinking about your soldier boy. I know there are but few hours, even, that pass but that I think of you and my good father and brother.

One day last week I was down in the city with the team, getting commis-sary stores. While we were loading, the 104th Ohio regiment were going by to the grave yard with a poor boy that had died. They were playing a funeral dirge with muffled drums . . . I can tell you that, as it was the first one I had seen, it was affecting.

As before there is no news, but I write at least once a week. I don't believe I could stand it two weeks without a letter from you, so when you feel like doing your absent boy a favor: the greatest one I know of you can do him is to write. Do not think I am home sick by what I write, for I certainly *am not*. I can put it in no stronger language than this. Mother, I know you feel anxious about me, knowing the influences I am under. I promise you to retain my character, and if I am permitted to return home again: to come back as good as I left . . .

∽

Nicholasville, Ky, Dec. 1, 1862

Dear Home, Father, Mother and Eddie,

It is raining and little and we are all 13 in number in our tent, as thick as is uncomfortable—at least to write. I am sitting against the center pole, writing on my knees. Poly is sitting directly in front of me, Austin is cooking some corn cakes over a little fire in one side of our tent. Yesterday George Dates and I went down to the mill and bot some injun meal [corn meal]. We cook it with a little water and salt. After it gets cold we slice it and fry it. We think it is dreadful good. Yesterday we had some potatoes and today some fresh beef. So you see we are now living first rate for us.

This morning we received marching orders. Where, I don't know. Yesterday the body of the first of our noble band that has died was shipped for his home. It made it seem solemn, I can tell you. There is not much show for one of us when we get in the hospital. I hope I shall not get sick but if I do I shall send for father to take care of me.

Mother said if her letters were not acceptable to me to let her know and she will not write again. Now I wish she would let me know what reason she has for thinking such a thing. I cannot ask you in any stronger language to write than I have.

Henry Hodge has been promoted to corporal and let me tell you it makes us boys dreadful mad. There have been three promotions since we left. No man stands any change of promotion without he is a cousin of the Cap's, or of the same religion. So all my fond hopes of promotion are blasted.

A few days ago there were three men out of company G, a Monroe company, coaxed four negroes out of the regiment, that had come in with us and sold them for $100 a piece. One was the orderly sargent, a corporal and two privates. They found them out and put them under arrest. The boys say they are going to shave their heads, take off their stripes and drum them out of camp, then transfer them to another regiment. They had a right to be hung or shot, coaxing negroes to run away from their masters, and then sell them.[17]

All the boys are in good spirits. George Dates has got over his blue spells. There seems to be a move in Washington. I hope it will be a good one. It still looks like we will be here our three years. It is a long time to wait.

Old man Smith is the greatest old woman we have in the regiment. He is always complaining and grumbling. The boys make sport of him. I would not have my father here with me for the best farm in Rock County, we have too much double quick to go on drill.[18]

I wish Eddie could have some of the nuts that lie on the ground here, walnuts and butternuts all over the ground. Write soon and long. Give my respects to all who may ask for me. Direct as before.

All my love, Lute

NOTES

17. Kentucky was a slaveholding border state but did not secede from the Union; Missouri, Maryland, and Delaware were also border states that held slaves and remained in the Union. West Virginia became the fifth such state when it gained statehood in 1863.

18. This was an example of father and son serving together in the same regiment. Harvey Smith was discharged due to disability on July 8, 1863; his son Frank was listed in the Roster of Wisconsin Volunteers, 22nd Regiment, Company B, as "absent sick at mustering out of Regt" in June 1865.

[Undated letter, early December, 1862, according to content]

Dear Family,

We had a man was acting a spy for us, returned a few days ago. He has been clear down to Cumberland Gap and all though this state. He said that there isn't food for soldiers or mules between here and the Gap to keep them for one day. The rebels have used it all up. He said there were a few rebels there, not enough to make any resistance. He said one regiment would stand them all. So I don't see as there is any great show for us fighting very soon. Many of the boys think they will move us soon, out of this state. Because we are making such work of their niggers we are hated here pretty badly. I hate the sight of them. We have a lot in our regiment, they are lazy and will sauce you and call you anything they can think of. I will never fight or say a great deal to free them if they don't get free in this enterprise.

Monday morning there was another boy died at the hospital, making one a night for four nights. Ed, thank you for writing to me often. I wish I could see you in your new suit, you must look some changed. There is some talk we may go to Lexington into a barracks to spend the winter. I hope we will because it is close to the railroad and we can hear from you oftener . . .

It is raining quite hard and I am glad to see it for two reasons. There is scarcely any water for us to use here and if it didn't rain we would have to go on Battalion review.

We are camped near Nicholasville (camp Coburn) [originally Camp Nelson], 15 miles from Lexington.[19] The church bells are now ringing. One of them sounds almost exactly like the one I used to ring. It makes me think of Beloit . . .

Day before yesterday I was on picket about two miles the other side of the city. In the morning I went up to an old man's house and he ask me to eat breakfast with him. I can tell you I was glad of the invitation. We had honey, warm biscuits, fresh pig pork, cake, milk, coffee, bacon and butter. I tell you, didn't I enjoy that meal. The first time I have sat down to a table since I left home, except once in Cincinnatti. You would laugh to hear people down here ask questions about the north. They don't know much.

Not much of interest. The ol Colonel [Utley] was arrested the other day because he would not give up the niggers. Don't know how he will come out.[20] When I was on picket the other night they got us all up in the middle of the night and had us load our guns. They told us that Morgan was coming with a large force. So we loaded them and went back to bed. We had been fooled too many times to scare us. I don't believe John Morgan is within 50 miles of here.[21]

Oblige your son and write often, Lute

NOTES

19. Camp Coburn was named for Colonel John Coburn, who served as brigade commander of the 22nd Wisconsin, 33rd Indiana, 85th Indiana, and 19th Michigan, longer than any other officer. The camp was located near Nicholasville, Kentucky, a terminus of the Kentucky Central Railroad and site of a large army depot.

20. Colonel Utley's defiance of Kentucky authorities with regard to protecting "contraband" black people resulted in altercations but was supported by most of the soldiers under his command. Groves, *Blooding the Regiment*, 51–58.

21. John Hunt Morgan, Brigadier General, C.S.A., was a cavalry leader who conducted raids on Union supply lines in Kentucky and Tennessee. At the time of this letter, "Morgan's Raiders" were near Alexandria, Tennessee. Morgan did not move his troops into Kentucky until late December 1862. Frank J. Welcher and Larry G. Ligget, *Coburn's Brigade* (Carmel, IN: Guild Press of Indiana, 1999), 41.

∾

Dec. 7, 1862

Dear Home,

As usual, I find myself seated on Sunday morning to write a short letter. Last night was the coldest night we have had yet, but it is pleasant today. Friday I was out on picket about a mile west of the city. It snowed nearly all day and at night if it wasn't cold, I never saw cold weather. There was a pond of water near where I was that froze over so hard the boys went and slid all over it in the morning. If I had to stay out so at home I would have thot it would have killed me, but here we think nothing of it.

Lt. Tracy was our officer. I like him first rate. He is so different from our other officers. While we were out I got 3 very nice chickens and Lt. said nothing to me about them. When I was out with Lt. Brown I killed a couple of geese and he made me pay for them. I wish I had gone in their company—Hogden's![22] I mean their boys get used to a great deal better than we do. I wrote about our company not having our rifles yet. We got up a petition asking for them and sent it to the Colonel [Utley]. The reply he gave us: "You have not served your 3 years yet." I threw down the paper, looked Lt. Calvert in the face and laughed. At Racine we told them if we didn't get our rifles we wouldn't get mustered in. The Colonel came to us, promised us on his word of honor as a man and soldier we would have our rifles. And now to have them laugh at us! It does not set well. There were 14 men transferred from other companys for the sake of being sharpshooters. They say they will desert if they can't be transferred back and that will leave our company very small for there is about 50 men not fit for service. There are a great many sick now. Last night another one died, making 7 in all. Only 3 of us are fit in our tent out of 12. I am writing it just as it is. There are a great many not expected to live.[23] Poly and me are healthy. Aus is about well again, but I am afraid George Dates will have a hard time until he is stout again. No one from Beloit has died yet.

They have promised us another blanket apiece. That should make us comfortable.

I want to tell you that the cut from the paper you sent me is every word of it true. We like the Colonel [Utley] first rate, only the way he uses us about our rifles. He is no military man. The Lt. Colonel always takes command of the regiment. He is a very smart man. His name is Bloodgood.[24] All for now. Write soon.

Love to all, Lute

NOTES

22. Lute referred to the following officers of the 22nd Wisconsin Regiment: Captain Perry W. Tracy, Company I; First Lieutenant George H. Brown, Company B (promoted to captain in 1863); Lieutenant William H. Calvert, Company B; Captain Warren Hogden, Company I.

23. During the early cold winter of 1862, the men of Coburn's brigade suffered from exposure and sickness, including measles, typhoid fever, diarrhea, and pneumonia. The 22nd Wisconsin's Chaplain Bradley reported that there were times when

Col. John Coburn (courtesy of U.S. Army Heritage and Education Center)

Col. William Utley
(courtesy of Wisconsin
Historical Society)

Lt. Col. Edward Bloodgood
(courtesy of Wisconsin
Historical Society)

there were hardly enough men who were well to take care of the sick. George S. Bradley, *The Star Corps; or, Notes of an Army Chaplain During Sherman's "Famous March to the Sea"* (Milwaukee: Book and Job Printers, 1865), 22.

24. Lt. Col. Edward Bloodgood from Milwaukee. His ongoing conflicts with Col. William Utley would have major consequences for the men under their command.

∽

Sunday, Dec. 14, 1862

Dear Home,

It is again Sunday afternoon and I will inform you of my where abouts. We started from Camp Coburn at Nicholsonville [Nicholasville] last Friday— marched 14 miles and camped at Camp Dick Robinson, a place where all the Sesesh and Union troops that have ever passed thru here have camped.[25] There is an immense quantity of harnesses, provisions and everything used by the army, left there by Bragg on his retreat out of the state.[26] The next day we marched 9 miles and camped at Danville, stayed there until morning and then we pulled up again and marched over here, about 1½ miles. We are expecting to stay here for some time. It is a splendid place in a grove. The town is about ½ larger than Beloit. We are on a hill or a knoll, so we can look right into the city.

I don't know if it will be news to you to hear that Capt. Northrop is coming back to Beloit, for very likely he will be there before this letter. He started day before yesterday. He says he is only going home on furlough of 30 days to regain his health, but that is a lie. He has resigned. He would not come out to see us or even let us know he was going, but went off down town to a tavern before 5 in the morning. He could have come out and waved his hand to us as he went by if he had not been ashamed to have seen us. Not one week ago today he had wanted John Kendall to write a letter to be published in the Beloit paper, stating that he had not resigned, nor was he going to. He would get mad if we should ask him if he was going to resign. He is a big liar. Over half the men in our company say now that he promised them offices to get them to enlist. I am glad he is gone if he couldn't use us better, even the sight of him makes me mad.

Lt. Calvin Bullock, the orderly Sargt., is not expected to live. He is at Nicholasville. Ira Nye, the next Sargt. is sick, so you see our company is left without many officers.

My health is good but I am the poorest boy you ever saw. George Dates never will get well I think, unless some of his friends come and take care of him and get him into some private home. He is left at the hospital at Nicholasville, a pretty poor place for a sick boy to get well.

They tell us that John Morgan [Confederate general John Hunt Morgan] is near here with a large force, that we will probably have a chance to fight soon. It doesn't frighten us much, we have been fooled too many times.

Now write soon and long. Something to laugh at would do me good. Father said if I need money to let him know. I do need some money, but I am afraid he hasn't it to spare. Northern or Eastern money are not good here. Indiana or Kentucky or greenbacks are good here. You ought to see my whiskers; you would hardly know me. You spoke of furlough. I asked Lt. Brown and he said yes, in three years.

Love, Love, Love to all, Lute

NOTES

25. Camp Dick Robinson was established on the farm of Richard Robinson in August 1861 by the Union officer and native William "Bull" Nelson. Many of Kentucky's first Union regiments were formed at the camp, and the site became a staging ground for early military campaigns.

26. As commander of the army of Tennessee, Confederate Gen. Braxton Bragg conducted operations in Kentucky and Tennessee. After his defeat by U.S. Grant at Chattanooga, Bragg was replaced by Joseph E. Johnston in December 1863.

Camp Coburn, Saturday, Dec. 20, 1862

Dear Eddie,

Thot I would write a short letter, as you seem to take such an interest in your soldier brother. You said you would make that box a present to me. Now Eddie you don't know how much I appreciate your kindness. I don't want you to go to such an expense for me. Keep an account of every cent you spend on me and when I get my pay, you must take it out.

. . . You said Alva Hodge was going to write to me. I will answer if she does. I dare not write to Ida Perry, she shows the letters around, there are six different boys in our company that write to her. Her letters are a little strong for me.

Ed, I miss you but it will be a long time before I see you. You are not old enough to join and I am glad. Stay at home with the old folks, that is the best place.

... How long we will stay here I cannot tell. It is likely they will keep marching us from one place to another as they did troops last winter. I do not fear any battles, altho they tell us to be ready for John Morgan will pounce in on us some time when we are not ready for him.

I suppose the noble Capt. Northrop is home and Lt. Calvert is playing sick and will soon be home. I don't believe there ever was a company of boys used and lied to as we have been. I am mad about it most of the time . . .[27]

They say Calvin Bullock is past all help and that he must die. His brother Bert is sick with the same fever.[28] George Dates is a little better, Silas Wright and George Perkins are both pretty sick. The Norwegian from our tent is not expected to live. The rest of the boys are good. I am good and gaining weight. Pole is fat as a moose and getting mean. I don't like him as well as at first. He doesn't think he can get sick. You spoke of sending a man down here to take care of the sick. It will be very expensive. I would be very glad to see someone from Beloit, but I hardly think it advisable. We can ask Dr. Bricknell what he thinks about it.[29]

Excuse the poor letter, Lute

NOTES

27. 2nd Lt. William H. Calvert and Cap. Thomas P. Northrop, both of Beloit. These two men resigned due to disability in January 1863.

28. Both Calvin Bullock and Bert Bullock survived the war and were mustered out in May and June 1865.

29. Dr. George W. Bricknell of Beloit served as 22nd Wisconsin Regimental Surgeon until his resignation on February 12, 1863, due to disability.

◌◦

Camp Baird, [Danville, KY,] Dec. 28, 1862[30]

Dear and much respected parents and brother,

Again I am permitted to pen a few lines to you. I have received three letters from you since I have written, but I have not been able to write. I thot I would write you a long letter Xmas but the night before there were three out of the company died, and that day they were buried. Their names were; Wm. Parker, grandmother was acquainted with him, George Secrist, Eddie knew him, and George Olson. There have been 30 out of the regiment that have died already. Five died in one night. They say Calvin Bullock is dead. Bert is very sick. They were left at Nicholasville. George Dates is about well. There are a great many sick. When we left Racine we had 96 men, now there are not over 50 men that are fit for duty.[31] My health is pretty good.

Thursday we had just finished burying our dead boys when we had orders to march to Mumfordsville [Munfordville], 55 miles from here. So in the morning we pulled up and started. We marched 15 miles and it rained as hard as it could. The mud was ankle deep and of the clay kind, so it stuck fast to our feet, making it anything but easy marching. The best of it was at night, the ground just as wet as a sponge, our clothes all wet and no way to dry anything. We went to a field and brot some cornstalks. They were rather rough, but we slept like pigs, never caught a bit of cold. It rained and thundered in the night as hard as I ever heard it. The water ran under our tent so hard we could drink anywhere in the tent. All the complaining there that I heard was; $10 for the next volunteer—a cow for the next man that enlists. If anyone said rather rough, some one would tell him "You [have] no business being a soldier." The worst of it was in the morning, they started us all back to Danville, Ky., and here I find myself—in the same place we started. They said that Morgan was fighting them down there and we were going down to help them out of their trouble, but old Morgan whipped them.[32] We were camped 4 miles from the battle field. Excuse the poor writing, for I have been so wet and tired that my hand is very unsteady.

Aus in on picket today. The sun is shining and all my things are drying out.

2nd edition,

I received letter No. 10 yesterday. It contained $5 greenback.[33] I did not expect so much, am sorry I sent for it.

I got my box Xmas eve about nine. If we had not come back I would never have gotten it. My boots are just right. You cannot tell how dreadful acceptable such a box is. I think it not advisable to send any more. I paid 25 cents to bring it up from Nicholasville, this is the end of the express. Nothing was more acceptable than that tea. They charge $2 a pound for it here. The box came thru safe and sound. The black current sauce fermented and worked out all along the seams of the can. It wet the corn and papers a little. That corn is very acceptable to me. We see no such things as that here.

I hope I will be permitted to return, and then if possible I will try to make your old age happy. I feel that I owe it to you. Those papers that you sent me, I had to lose, for we were ordered to march the next morning. I am sorry, I wanted to read them. I don't know what is going on.

On our march out a man from the 85th Indiana laid down on a log with his knapsack under his head. The officer ordered him back to his company. He said he couldn't go, and they left him. When the battery came up they saw him lying there, he was dead. That is the way they let men die. Major Murry was as drunk a man as I ever saw on our march down. He rode his horse over everyone and gave orders to the Colonel and the Doctors and even Gen. Baird.[34] I rather think they will make a fuss about it. He is always drunk.

Every day there are negros come to us and want to come into our regiment, but the ol Colonel [Utley] is afraid to let them come in. This morning there were three wanted to go with us. I don't want anymore, they are dishonest. You would laugh to see them come by here with their ol rusty clothes and a cane and a cigar. They put on more style than any white man I ever saw.

Your soldier son, Lute

NOTES

30. Camp Baird was named for Brig. Gen. Absalom Baird, who commanded the recently formed Third Division of the Army of Kentucky; the First Brigade was commanded by Col. John Coburn.

31. By the time the Wisconsin 22nd left Nicholasville on December 12, they had buried nine soldiers and had to leave many behind in the hospital. Groves, *Blooding the Regiment*, 60.

32. On December 24, John Hunt Morgan marched his troops through Munfordville and on to Elizabethtown, which he captured on December 27 and took about 650 prisoners. *War of the Rebellion: Official Records*, vol. 20, part 1, 154–58.

33. Soldiers and their families often numbered their correspondence, since mail delivery was undependable. The numbering helped them to know if letters had been lost or delayed.

34. Maj. Edward D. Murray from Beloit, Wisconsin, resigned on February 4, 1863.

We are camping at Danville and Monday we start back on the same road. Marched 16 miles and camped for the night. We had to sleep on our arms.[35] In the morning we marched 7½ miles when the order came to counter march. We turned around and marched to the same place we started from in the morning and camped for the night. It rained a little all day, I never saw it rain or hail harder. They woke us up in the night and said we were going to Lebanon. At least we started toward Danville which we reached about one o'clock, tired and sore I assure you. I was on guard that day and night, so you see I saw the old year out and the new year in, all alone. Today I feel pretty tired and sleepy. We have now marched over 80 miles and have shot no rebels either . . .

Your soldier son, Lute

NOTE

35. "We slept on our arms." This expression, appearing several times in Lute's letters, meant sleeping in the open without protection from the weather, often necessary for long marches or quick movement of the troops.

Camp Baird, Danville, Ky, Mon., Jan 5, 1863

Dear Family,

It does not look to me that we are as well off as we were a year ago. On our last march we found a man in a house, that said he fought the d— Yankees and he would fight them again. They took him prisoner and he kept for about two miles and then the Colonel said to let him go. He has such good grit. When we will whip them at that rate!

Mr. Smith is in the hospital. He has what they call jaundice. He is yellow as a gold dollar. Frank has got detail as a nurse in the hospital so he can stay with his father.

Yesterday I was on picket about two miles from here. It rained dreadfully but we all have rubber blankets. We have not marched as we expected when I last wrote. Can't tell how long until we shall.

The paymaster is here and has paid us what is coming to us till the 1st of November. I allotted $10 a month to father. There will be $15 paid to you there if they do as they agreed. They paid me $5.86. They tell us they will soon pay us up til the first of January. I will be careful of what money I have, for I know just how hard it comes. Last night Andy Bibbons died. He owed me a dollar he borrowed in Racine. Bibbons is the one who used to work in the mill. He lived in the Austin house near the Hannifords. He had his discharge and would have come home in a few days. He was dreadfully homesick.

I suppose you know about Rosecrans victory. We heard that Mr. Bragg was killed.[36] I tell you that news comes at a good time for all we have heard in a long time has been very discouraging. It was lucky for us that we turned around the other day, for if we had'nt we would have seen action. They have been fighting down there where we were going. We seem to be lucky. We have been issued new clothes, new pants and a new blanket. We are well clothed.

Frank Goddard, an old school mate of mine, was sick and came home to Beloit. He was a 1st Lt. in an Iowa regiment. He was here the other day, came down to take care of his brother who would certainly have died if he hadn't come to take care of him. I think he was well paid for his trouble. He said it cost him $16 to come to Nicholasville.

This afternoon I am going downtown, they allow two to go at a time. We are still at Danville.

It was very lucky for us that we were thrown out of Gen. Swains [Swaine's] brigade, for that one was in the late battle at Murfresboro [Murfreesboro] and we of course would have been there if we hadn't been thrown out. The reason he threw us out was because we let the negros come into our lines and would not give them up.[37]

Give my love to grandmother, write often and give me all the news.

From your boy, Lute

NOTES

36. The Battle of Stones River (also called the Battle of Murfreesboro) was a victory that boosted the morale of Union troops despite high casualties. It was also strategically important, allowing the Union continuing control of railroads and productive farms in the region. Maj. Gen. William S. Rosecrans had replaced Maj. Gen. Don Carlos Buell in commanding the U.S. forces in Kentucky (later known as the Army of the Cumberland). The Confederate Maj. Gen. Braxton Bragg was not killed but retreated to Tullahoma, Tennessee, following the battle. Ridley Willis II, *Old Enough to Die* (Franklin, TN: Providence House Publishers, 1996), 88; Klement, *Wisconsin in the Civil War*, 82, 83.

37. Col. Peter T. Swaine commanded the Second Brigade, Third Division, of the Army of Kentucky. Wisconsin's 22nd Regiment was assigned to the First Brigade, under Col. John Coburn, during the reorganization in November 1862. Colonel Swaine, along with many commanders, disagreed with the practice of harboring contraband black people. By this time, the 22nd Wisconsin had several "Negroes" in camp and had gained a reputation as "the Abolition Regiment." William M. Fliss, "Wisconsin's Abolition Regiment," *Wisconsin Magazine of History* 86, no. 2 (Winter 2002–2003): 5–19.

∽

Camp Baird, Jan 9, 1863

Dear parents and brother,

I have answered cousin Fanny's letter so I thought I would send it to you.[38] I want to know if I sent some letters home that I want to save, one at a time in my letters, if you will save them for me. They are all opened but I don't want you to read them; if I should not come back, burn them.[39]

It may be news to you that the 22nd are at Danville Ky. And they are not in the rear of Rosecrans. I don't see how such news gets to Beloit about us. I heard that Capt. N. [Northrop] went to a ball with one of the Moore girls, is that so? You said that Mrs. Perry came to see you often. I like her first rate, but Pole is one of the meanest fellows I ever saw. All the boys hate him. He owes me money but I never will ask for it or lend him any more.

You speak of crying—do not cry any for us. I don't for you. I want to see you as bad as you do me. You also spoke of my getting weaned from home. NEVER! Our Lt. Brown received a letter from our honorable Capt. N. [Northrop] stating that he did not intend to come back to the company. Lt. Brown does not think much of him. Capt. N. took away some company funds that we have saved in our rations and that belongs to us all. There is over $300 due this company from the Capt. A man that will steal from a whole company, in my humble opinion, needs not the sympathy of any.

My health is pretty good. Was on guard last night and Pole [Napoleon Perry] and Aus [Austin Smith] are on picket today. We come on twice a week.

We have a white negro in our regiment. He is a curiosity. He has sandy curly hair and is as white as I am, the worst of all he has red eyes. Did you ever see one? His brother-in-law is with him and they keep lugging water all the time. A negro was killed the other day. He found a bomb shell that one of the batteries had shot into a bank while on drill. He carried it to camp and held it on an anvil and while the blacksmith was pecking at the fuse with a hammer and cold chisel it went off, blowing the negro to pieces. What is strange it only shocked two or three others that stood near. There were strings and pieces of flesh lodged in trees.

Write me often and long. Give my respects to all my friends. Direct as before to Danville.

From your affectionate brother and son, Lute

38. "Cousin Fanny" has not been identified in the Moseley family's ancestral records. Apparently she was one of Lute's faithful correspondents throughout his Civil War service.

39. In order to reduce the weight of their packs, soldiers often discarded letters they received or mailed them home for safekeeping.

Camp Baird, Danville, Jan. 15, 1863

Dear parents and brother,

I understand by your letter that you intend to celebrate your wedding anniversary. I thot as I could not be there in person I would write a few lines to let you know that I join in your celebration. Let me wish you a pleasant time on that day. Think only good thots of me and I have to thank you for the kind and parental care you have always used over me. You have trained me in the most tender way and I hope my life can be spared to return to you and that I might make your old age easy and pleasant. This is my wish.

We have been in the United States service five months today and I am not sorry. We have not been called into active service yet, not very hard times. I suppose I would think it hard to march all day with the rain pouring down hard and at night to make one's bed on the wet ground with nothing but a blanket to put over wet clothes. We have all gone thru such without much murmuring.

The country thru this part of the states is, to a northern boy at least, anything but inviting. Nothing but hills and rocks. Until he thinks it is not the country but the union we are fighting for, he feels like complaining and wonders why so much blood is shed over so poor a country, while there are so many hundreds of nice prairie unoccupied in the west.[40] The people are different from our northern ones. There have been young men from the ages of 15 to 30 come to our camp selling such articles as we want, that cannot either read or write, and some cannot even count. To these the boys trade old postage stamps they have taken off old letters. They will believe they are worth 10 cents a piece, if they are told so. Here we can march all day and see only one school house, but oftener not to see any.

When we first enlisted we all thot that by the first of Jan. we would hear of movements that would at least be encouraging. We even dared to think that by that time we would be allowed to return home and peace would be restored. Now it looks like we will be here our entire enlistment. If our officers were as desirous as the enlisted men to bring this terrible conflict to an end, we would be home sooner.

It has stormed for three days and is now snowing like it does in Wisconsin. Winter is commensing. So far the weather has been like our northern springs.

We stand guard every third day, the rest of the time we have pretty much at our disposal. The evenings are spent writing letters or talking over old times. In our tent we get along pretty well. We also have washing and cooking to do. We are now 24 miles from the R.R., which makes it bad for us, for we have to wait for the stage to bring us our mail. I don't feel much like writing, it is cold and uncomfortable in our tent.

All for now, Love, Lute

NOTE

40. "It is the Union we are fighting for." Lute did not mention President Lincoln's Emancipation Proclamation, announced on January 1, 1863, which marked a turning point, refocusing Lincoln's objective to abolish slavery as well as preserve the Union. The Proclamation stated that "all persons held as slaves within the rebellious states henceforward shall be free." It did not, however, apply to slaves in the border states (Delaware, Maryland, Kentucky, and Missouri) remaining loyal to the Union. Alex Wong, "Emancipation Proclamation," History Channel, January 26, 2022, https://www.history.com/topics/american-civil-war/emancipation-proclamation/.

Headquarters of the 22nd Reg, Wis., Camp Baird, Jan. 20, 1863

Dear parents and brother,

Again I find myself seated flat on the ground writing to you. The weather is anything but pleasant. We have had as hard a snow storm as I ever saw, altho not as cold. The ice and sleet were so heavy on the trees that it broke off limbs as much as six inches thru and now is raining very hard. The last two days it has been good sleighing. Sunday I was on picket on Lexington Pike rd. It was a very pleasant day. George Dates has got his discharge. He was examined yesterday. Nothing in the world ails him but being homesick. I think Mr. John Dates gave old Dr. Bricknell a hundred or so to get him out.[41]

They say now that we will go tomorrow, but I will be out on picket. Will keep you posted of my where abouts as often as I can.

I can't tell what we are coming to, labor so low and the price of everything so high. I think poor folks will see harder times in the north within the next year, I hope not.

I think they are now about to make another attempt to take Vicksburg, but there will be a great many lives lost in the attempt. I think we will be held back as a reserve. Anyway I don't think we will have to go into the thickest of the fight . . .

George Harwood died last Sunday. He was buried yesterday and I acted as a bearer. There are now 55 of the regiment died, five from our company. They bury the soldiers in one end of the city cemetery. Silas Wright was sick but got well. He came back to camp but the wet weather was too much for him and he is back in the hospital with a relapse. His father is coming to take care of him. We have a man in our company that has deserted, his name is James Dwyer from Iowa. We would all like to come home because we think the head men of the army have not tried to bring the war to a close and I do not think we will conquer the south by fighting. We will undoubtedly have to stay our three years. After we have been one year we are entitled to a furlough of 20 days. The boys say if they don't give it to us they will go without asking leave. They can't hurt us for it either.

We are still in Danville and under marching orders. Our destination is not known to us, some think it Vicksburg. We will probably march out to the railroad and then take the cars to the river and then down the river in transports. This may not be true but I will write when we know. If we go we will probably have a hand in the great battle of the war. We are all ready and most want to go. Don't be concerned, it will be a good thing for all of us.[42]

Love to all, believe me I do love each of you. Lute

NOTES

41. George Dates was discharged on disability on January 18, 1863.

42. The winter camp in Danville, Kentucky, had been a long, cold, and dreary time for the troops. Most were glad to leave when they began their march to Louisville on the morning of January 26. "[Dr.] Blanchard remained behind, in charge of the regiment's sick and the nurses who cared for them . . . Covering between fifteen and twenty miles each day, the troops marched in the foulest weather imaginable . . . There were a few for whom the ordeal was too much, who stole away from the ranks to enter the murky underworld of deserters and draft dodgers." Groves, *Blooding the Regiment*, 65.

Nashville, Tenn., Sunday, Feb. 8, 1863, on boat Champion[43]

Dear parents and brother,

If you feel as anxious to hear from me as I am from you, I will pen you a short note. We arrived here in Nashville last night. They are now unloading the boat. We do not know where we are going. This is a short note to let you know where I am and how I am. My health is good. It has done me good to take this trip. I have not had a letter from you since we left Louisville. Then I wrote a line to send you by Sid Wright. I hope he came up to see you. He said he would. Pole is well. Yesterday one of our men by the name of Wacther went to the edge of the boat early in the morning to dip up some water and fell overboard and we hav'nt seen him since. How many ways there are to take off the boys.[44]

The day before we reached Ft. Donelson, there were 7,000 rebels tried to take and less than 700 to defend it. They fought like tigers. A colonel of the sesesh rode up to within 20 feet of a large siege gun and hollered out, "I demand the surrender of this gun!" The Capt. of the gun replied, "Well, after this shot" and then touched it off, blowing the Colonel into a thousand pieces. His regiment all wheeled and run. The men hadn't another fuse to shoot the gun with, and this shot was taken off with a coal. It is the biggest victory gained since the war began. Our men were from the 83rd Illinois Regiment. I went all over the battle field and saw lots of bodies of horses and bodies of soldiers; some shot in the body and some in the head. They were burying them when we were there. It snowed the night after the battle so we could not find anything. Some found money and some matches etc. There is a report here that the rebels made another attempt at it yesterday and were again defeated. I guess it is true. I saw one large two story house that the rebels took refuge in, that was just like a sieve, so full of bullet holes. You can stand on one side and see thru in a million places.[45]

I am writing this on my knee, and in a hurry, so excuse. I will write when we get to camp.

L.S. Moseley, a soldier. Love to all.

NOTES

43. After an exhausting march of about seventy-five miles, Coburn's brigade arrived in Louisville on January 30. Here, following conflicts and delays over the contraband "Negroes" they had taken on board, they were transported down the Ohio River to the mouth of the Cumberland River and up to Nashville, with instructions

to rendezvous at Fort Donelson. The fleet consisted of fifty-four transports, six gunboats, and a number of barges. Welcher and Ligget, *Coburn's Brigade*, 45–47.

44. Pvt. Jacob Wacther, Company B, from Geneva, Wisconsin, drowned in the Cumberland River on February 2, 1863.

45. On February 3, 1863, Joseph Wheeler, the Confederate Brigadier General, arrived near Fort Donelson with his cavalry command, Brig. Gen. John A. Wharton's brigade, and part of Nathan B. Forrest's brigade in attacking Col. Abner Harding's 83rd Illinois Infantry. The Union transports and gunboats arrived at Fort Donelson the following morning, causing Wheeler to withdraw to the south. Welcher and Ligget, *Coburn's Brigade*, 47.

∽

Camp near Nashville, Mon., Feb. 9, 1863[46]

Dear parents and brother,

Just two weeks ago this morning we left Danville, Ky. Then we did not know which way or where we were going. We marched 14 miles on the pike toward Louisville. Then I was anything but well and had the blues a little. It rained almost constant. I rode in a government mule team most of the way. Had the diarrhea pretty hard. The boys found some straw to make a bed of, about 1½ miles from camp. The next morning we started pretty early and marched 17 miles. The rain turned to snow, which thawed about as fast as it fell, which made it not pleasant marching and not very pleasant sleep at night, altho we got a good lot of straw. The three days we marched 20 miles—thru the village of Shelbyville, spoken so often in "Uncle Tom's Cabin." It snowed and froze this day. At night we had hay to make our beds. Uncle Sam never furnishes straw while on march but we run off and confiscate it ourselves. The fourth day we marched 16 miles. The ground was frozen in the morning and it was good marching but about noon it thawed out and if it wasn't slippery and nasty. The fifth day we marched 16 miles and camped within two miles of Louisville, making good 85 miles we marched in 5 days. We were then camped in an awfully muddy place and it was so near the city we couldn't get straw so I stole an armful of hay from the mules to tell you the truth I felt as mean and sick as I ever did. Sid Wright was there that night and got his son Silas Wright discharged from the United States service. Silas was not as sick as I was. So you see what a little money and Masonism will do for a man.[47] Sid told George Perkins, the young man that is engaged to his daughter, that he would get him discharged after a while, if he wanted him to. That is the way the machine runs.

We were ordered to pack up Saturday and did so but for some reason or other did not go. There were more peddlers around camp than one could count, with bread, cookies, pies, tobacco, butter and anything you could think of. The prices were full as high as the peddlers were thick. Butter was 35 cents. I offered one boy 5 cents for a potatoe but he would not let me have it . . .

The lieutenant let me put my knapsack on the wagon. I was very weak and felt miserable. We first went on the transport Commercial. On the lower deck, a perfect hog-pen, two companies crowded into the room behind the engine. We all began to think our time had come, but fortune favors the brave, and they took us off to make room for the mules and put us on another boat, Champion No. 4. There were but three companies on the boat and we had plenty of room and everything was very convenient. Two companies had one little stove with three griddles, so we got along first rate. There were 64 transports and 9 gunboats in the fleet. Sunday we went upriver about two miles and loaded on a good quantity of coal, then dropped down to our old place and remained there until this morning. The other boats were all busy puffing up and down the river, loading and putting on coal, so as to be ready the next morning to start for someplace entirely unknown to us. I asked the Captain of the boat where we were going and he said he didn't know anything about it.

In the morning the boats all started down the Ohio River and ran until about noon. Then we stopped a few minutes at a small village, then started on and ran until about ten in the evening, when we took a barge loaded with hay. We were ordered to hitch on to it but it was so heavy we could not tow it, and contrary to orders we left it. About eleven we had to tie up on account of the wind. Early in the morning we started on. It was very cold on the river but it agreed with me and I felt first rate. I spent most of the time on the hurricane deck or in the pilot house. I got on the right side of the pilots and enjoyed myself first rate. We had a good supply of beans and bacon and hard bread to eat and I bot a loaf of bread and a few biscuits and cheese before we left Louisville. We ran until about 10 p.m. Then we tied up about two miles below the mouth of the Cumberland River and took on some coal. Then we were just across from Illinois and it seemed as if we were almost home. To know that Illinois was not one mile distance seemed old-fashioned. They had a strong guard on to be sure that none of the boys took advantage and went home. We all thought we were going to Vicsburg [Vicksburg] sure. But in the morning the ol boat turned around and started up river again and turned up the Cumberland. We ran until about twelve in the evening and tied up at Dover—one mile from Ft. Donelson. We had to stay there until the boats came up. We were all very glad of it, for it gave us a chance to see the Fort and the battleground of one year ago and also of two days before we got there. It gave us a good opportunity to see the realities of war.

As far as Ft. Donelson is concerned, it is not much of a sight. There are heavy earthworks on all sides. It takes in about 10 or 15 acres. There are now no guns or soldiers there. There is a little piece of cane that grew in the Fort, I sent you in this letter. The last battle was one mile above the Fort at Dover. The rebels probably intended to take that place, and they would have fired into us as we came along, but fortunately we had a regiment there that was true grit. This will be seen by their bravery. There was less than 700 of them and 7000 of the rebels. They were expecting an attack and telegraphed to Ft. Henry for help. The 13th Wisc. started off to help them but were too late. The rebels came up on all three sides. Our men fired the first shot. We had one 32 pounder and four field pieces. The battery opened on them. Our men said the first thing they heard was the rebel order to forward march and then they could hear "closeup, closeup"! That was the space our shots were making. Our men occupied the livery stables—two of them and they were in some houses that stood back a little from the river. We shot two of the rebels that had been peddling pies to our boys for over a week. One boy about fifteen was shot in the right eye while he was taking aim around the corner of the house. I wrote in my last letter about the rebel Col. demanding surrender of the gun and getting blown to pieces.

The boys that were there that day before found revolvers, money, guns and other things. They hadn't buried all their dead and I saw them. They were laid out in an old tavern. They had the same clothes on that they fell in. Some were all covered with blood and in holes and weren't found right away. The rats had gnawed on them and made them look dreadful bad. This is enough of terrible happenings of war. I will close.

Your loving son and brother, Lute

NOTES

46. On February 9, 1863, Lute found time to describe events of the past three weeks, including the difficult march from Danville, the river transport, and the carnage at Dover, near Fort Donelson.

47. Apparently, Silas Wright's father, Sid Wright, was a Freemason, with membership in a local Masonic Lodge. As members of this philanthropic and social organization, Freemasons developed strong bonds and helped each other whenever possible.

CHAPTER 2

Surrender, Prison, Parole

March 8, 1863–June 11, 1863

We have passed thru very much.

—LUCIUS S. MOSELEY, April 21, 1863

Wisconsin 22nd Volunteer Infantry Regiment assigned to Coburn's Brigade, Baird's Division, Army of Kentucky, Department of the Cumberland.

Service: To Brentwood Station, Tennessee, February 21; thence to Franklin. Reconnaissance toward Thompson's Station, Spring Hill, March 3–5. Action at Thompson's Station, March 4–5. Nearly 200 of Regiment captured by Bragg's cavalry forces under Van Dorn (nearly 18,000 strong). Ordered to Brentwood Station March 8. Action at Little Harpeth, Brentwood, March 25. Regiment surrounded and surrendered to Forrest. Exchanged May 5. Regiment reorganizing at St. Louis till June 12. Ordered to Nashville, Tennessee, June 12, 1863.

—DYER, *Compendium*, vol. 3, 1682, 1683

The following narrative by Esther Moseley is based on Lute Moseley's letters, newspaper clippings, and oral history passed down through the family. Many details are consistent with Richard Grove's well-researched account of conditions at Libby Prison.[1]

NOTE

1. A letter dated August 16, 1862, smuggled out of Libby Prison by a Wisconsin soldier named T. J. Widvey, described the prison as "dark and filthy beyond description. We sleep on the damp, dirty floor, without blankets or bedding of any kind. Our food is bread and fresh beef, without salt. We get only half rations, and are excluded from buying anything outside. We are deprived of water, except what is drawn from the filthy James River . . . You have no idea how shamefully we are

treated." Edward. B. Quiner, *Military History of Wisconsin: A Record of the Civil and Military Patriotism of the State, in the War for the Union* (Chicago: Clarke & Company, 1886), vol. 3, 56.

Lute's letter, dated February 9, 1863, was the last time he was able to write his family for several weeks. During battle at Thompson's Station he was captured and sent to Libby Prison in Richmond, Virginia.

Lute was later promoted to corporal as a result of his courageous action in the field. He could see the Confederates in heavy force in front of them, through the trees which partially screened them, and asked permission to fire. Permission was given and he fired the first shot. During the progression of the fighting he was struck above the right knee by a partially spent ball, making a painful bruise but not seriously disabling him. In the desperate fight against overwhelming numbers, Lute was taken prisoner with most of the infantry of the brigade that were not killed.

Libby Prison was an old brick warehouse on Tobacco Row, located on the waterfront of the James River in Richmond, Virginia. The enlisted men were housed in a room 40 feet wide and 100 feet long. The prison had barred windows of which many were broken, causing it to be drafty and cold. It offered little chance of escape. It was densely crowded and was teeming with vermin. The bare floors were filthy. That is where the men slept, jammed so tightly together that there was just enough space to lie down. Each prisoner ferociously guarded his territory. At night the prisoners all slept in a row, curled up together not only to keep warm but also due to lack of space. Sick bay had no doctor, only a former undertaker who would try to aid and comfort the ill. The Confederate army had taken all available doctors for their own wounded. There were few supplies such as medicines, clean sheets and bandages. Sick soldiers were on their own.

The prisoners were gaunt with eyes set in sunken hollows, their flesh pale and ashen. Many men sickened or suffered mental derangement under the strain of prison life. Lute made up his mind that he would survive and someday leave the nightmare. The nauseating odors of decaying flesh, unwashed bodies, and human wastes were hard to bear.

Lute was confined in Libby Prison for 29 days, after which he was exchanged for a Confederate prisoner. Both sides agreed, under the cartel of prison exchange of July 1862, to trade and parole all prisoners within 10 days of capture. Unfortunately, the agreements were not always observed. Both sides violated the rules, and in 1863 General Grant suspended further exchange, mainly because the Confederates had more to gain through exchange than the Union.

~

The following letter was written by Ira P. Nye, 2nd Lt. in Company I, 22nd Wisconsin, from the Beloit area, while he was held in Libby Prison. Somehow he managed to have the letter smuggled out and mailed home, which was a difficult task since letters were carefully scrutinized by Confederate officers, and few found their way north. Ira Nye describes the battle of Thompson's Station at Spring Hill, Tennessee, and the journey to Libby Prison in Richmond, Virginia. Many letters from Civil War soldiers were published in local newspapers. A descendent of Lute Moseley transcribed Nye's letter, possibly based on its publication in the *Daily Gazette*, Janesville, Wisconsin, April 11, 1863, or a later printing.

~

March 8, 1863

Dear Father,

I will write you a few lines, whether it ever gets to you or not. I wrote the other day but had to do so under the supervision of a Sesesh officer. I have seen more of the stern realities of war. On the fourth of March we left Franklin and felt the enemy. We went about four miles when we encountered a rebel battery which opened on us. Our battery was brought up and the fight lasted one hour. Then the rebs retreated, leaving 14 dead. We had two wounded.

We camped on the field and the next morning advanced four miles farther, when we met them again. We fought for 5 hours when our ammunition was spent, and when our battery and cavalry fled we were surrounded and surrendered. It was a bloody fight and one man in four was hit, I think. Thirteen were hit in Company B. All the dead and wounded fell into the hands of the Rebels. John Pomeroy was shot through the thigh. I can't name them all. I had several narrow escapes but was not touched, although I was in the midst of the hottest fire.

We marched 75 or 80 miles fording streams and lying on the ground at night. It rained most of the time. We were robbed of our overcoats and sent to Chattanooga. From there we were sent here to Libby Prison. My health is good and I think I can stand the confinement pretty well till cold weather. I tell you we made our marks among the butternuts.[2]

They had 14 thousand men while we had less than 3,000.[3]

I go in for fighting them to death. I can't write much as I will have to smuggle this out. I will tell you the rest when I get home.

Your son, Ira P. Nye

NOTES

2. "Butternuts" was a nickname for Confederate soldiers, whose homespun woolens were dyed with the grayish-brown husks of butternuts or walnuts after supplies of gray British woolens were no longer available.

3. "The result of the unequal contest was 150 of the Confederates killed and 400 wounded; of the Union troops, 100 were killed, 300 wounded, and 1,306 captured, including most of companies B and I of the Wisconsin Twenty-second. That part of the regiment which escaped fought again at Brentwood, Tennessee on March 25, and about 300 (about all the rest of them) were captured and taken to Libby Prison." William Fiske Brown, *History of Rock County, Wisconsin*, vol. 1, 352.

Another letter, written to Lute's mother by Rollin L. Adams, 1st Lt. and Assistant Adjutant General to Col. John Coburn, was saved along with Lute's letters to his family.

Camp—10 miles south of Nashville, Tenn., March 10, 1863

Mrs. Moseley, Dear friend;

Thinking you would be glad to know concerning the condition of your son Lucius, and knowing that he is in all probability cut off from communication with his friends, I have thot best on the receipt of your letter dated Feb. 26th, which was broken open in order to know your address, and according to the judgment of our highest remaining officer, and also considering it a privilege to give you all the information within my reach concerning him. He is probably now a prisoner of war. I will give you in brief the details of our late misfortune.

On Monday the 2nd of March our brigade left this camp and started for Franklin. We remained there Tuesday, but on Wednesday morning to be ready to march immediately as lightly equipped as possible. Soon our brigade, composed only of four regiments of infantry a battery of artillery, a battalion of cavalry, started out on the road to Spring Hill, farther south. We had gone but 6 miles when we met the advance guard of the enemy, consisting of one or two regiments of cavalry and some artillery, where we had a cavalry and artillery skirmish, killing about a dozen rebels, with no loss on our side, except one man wounded in the 13th Mich. We then marched a little farther and turned into camp for the night. The next morning we marched on rather reluctantly, expecting or fearing that we were coming on a force much superior to our own, and a very imprudent step we found it for our General to take, but for some reason on we went. Yet we had advanced scarcely four miles before we came upon the enemy in full force, and were saluted by a few rebel shells which were thrown among us. Then the artillery fight began and continued about half an hour, when the infantry, having advanced close enough, the musketry began their music, but we paid dear for it, altho we have lost only about half as many killed as the rebels. But their number being four or five times as great as ours, and their position much superior, we could but expect to be overpowered at last.

Our company was the most exposed in the regiment and quite a large number were wounded but I have not heard that any were killed. Only six of us who were wounded escaped.[4] Mine was only a slight wound being only a shot in the left hand. Twenty-eight in our company, including our commissioned officers, are missing and are probably all prisoners. I will give you a list of them and enclosed in this. We expect they will be paroled soon, if not exchanged. About 150 of our regiment are missing and Colonel Utley is with them. We were all on a hill firing as fast as possible into the rebs, who were considerably screened by fences and the underbrush. I remained there until I was wounded, and we were in danger of being flanked, and then I tried to find my way to the body of the regiment but could find none but our Lieut. Colonel, retreating with a part of several companies. The six of us then who were wounded made our way toward him and succeeded in escaping the clutches of the rebels. I forgot my own wound in a feeling of aggravation to think we were drawn into such a trap. This is the discouraging part of a soldier's life, but still I trust the hand of providence is in it.

We are now encamped again 10 miles south of Nashville. We will preserve your letter unread, subject to your order. We thought your letter perhaps contained money and it would be best to return it to you.

Lucius, we find, has left his knapsack with us and some other things, all of which we will take as good care of as we can.

Sincerely yours, R.L. Adams

NOTE

4. The final report of casualties among the officers and men of the 22nd Wisconsin listed 2 dead, 29 wounded, and 129 captured or missing, for a total of 160. Casualties for the whole expedition totaled 1,446, most of these becoming prisoners. *War of the Rebellion: Official Records*, Series 1, vol. 23, 75.

～

Libby Prison, Richmond, Virginia, 1863 (courtesy of Wisconsin Historical Society)

Drinking gourd carved by Lucius S. Moseley (courtesy of the Moseley family)

Lucius Moseley was interviewed in the summer of 1921 regarding his Civil War services and confinement in Libby Prison. He was 77 years old when the following item was published in the *Janesville Gazette*, July 1921, along with a copy of the letter from Ira Nye, dated March 8, 1863.

"Lute" S. Moseley, 907 Portland avenue, who is still living and has a remarkably accurate memory of the old days of the rebellion, was a prisoner at Libby Prison at the time Nye wrote his letter. Colonel Moseley[5] still has a little cross that he carved with a pen knife from a bone left from one of the few pieces of meat they got.

"We didn't know where our officers were for a long time at the prison," Moseley said. "Then one day I followed a nigger upstairs who smoked out the prison rooms. He went thru a big massive door and I looked thru to see all our officers in a big room. The second day he left the door open and I went in to visit with them. I made three visits in this way, and discovered one of them, that all the enlisted men were to be exchanged, but that the officers were to be retained.

"I was sitting down in a little antechamber when an officer came and sat by me.

"'You belong downstairs, don't you?' he said.

"But I wouldn't talk to him, for I thot he was a reb spying on us, and he realized it.

"'Look here,' he said. 'I'm no spy. I'm the colonel of the Eighth Ohio Cavalry, and I've been here seven months. Now you're going to be sent out of here tomorrow. You won't come up here again. Now I'll give you an order for $3,000 in gold if you will change uniforms with me right now and let me go out in your place. And I'll bring half a dozen officers in here to identify me and indorse my agreement.'

"'Colonel,' I told him, 'I wouldn't trade places with you if you give me ten times as much!'

"Just before I left, a lieutenant came up to me and said, 'Moseley, you're from Beloit, Wisconsin, aren't you?'

"'Yes.'

"'So am I. My name's Tamberg [Tanberg], and I'm a first lieutenant in the 15th Wisconsin.[6] I want you to take a letter out with you when you go and mail it when you get into our lines.'

"Well, Sir, they'd have killed me in my tracks if they caught me with such as letter as that; so I said to him:

"'Tamberg, don't put me in that peril. Tell me what you want to say, and as soon as I'm in the northern lines, I'll write it.'

"The man cried with anguish and made this plea:

"'My mother is very old and ill and she can't possibly live till I get out, and this probably will be the last chance I ever have to get a written message to her. For God's sake take it with you for me!'

"And I took it—written on blue crisp paper that would rattle. I sewed it on the inside of an old shirt and put an extra shirt I had managed to keep hidden from the Johnnies on over it. Then I kneaded it down till it didn't crackle and took my chances."

Years afterward, this incident was being recounted from the platform at a G. A. R. [Grand Army of the Republic] reunion at Janesville.

A man leaped up in the audience.

"It's the truth!" he cried, tears streaming down his face. "I'm the man who gave him the letter, and I haven't seen Lute Moseley since that day in Libby Prison!"[7]

NOTES

5. At the time this newspaper article was written, Lucius Moseley, age 77, was a colonel in the L.H.D. Crain Post, Grand Army of the Republic, Beloit, WI.

6. Christian E. Tanberg of the 15th Regiment, Company D, was the officer for whom Lute smuggled the letter from Libby Prison. He was promoted to 1st Lt. on May 27, 1863, was wounded at Chickamauga, and resigned on October 31, 1863. Vesterheim Museum, Civil War Portfolios, https://collections.vesterheim.org/civil_war_database/tanberg-christian-e/.

7. "Reunion of Old Badger Battery Recalls Incidents of Famous Libby Prison," *Janesville Daily Gazette*, Janesville, WI, July 1921, Wisconsin Historical Society, Local History & Biography Articles, https://wisconsinhistory.org/Records/Newspaper/BA 14523.

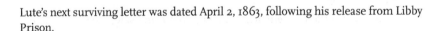

Lute's next surviving letter was dated April 2, 1863, following his release from Libby Prison.

College Green Barracks, Annapolis, April 2, 1863[8]

Dear parents and brother,

We are now at Annapolis, Maryland. We came here on the flag of truce boat, Metamora, this morning. You have of course heard all about our fight, capture, etc. We have been 29 days in Dixie and seen some rough times.

I was in the foremost of the fight; in fact I fired the first shot from our regiment and was there until it was all over and did not receive a scratch. One spent ball hit me on the knee. That lamed me for a few days pretty badly. I have not been very sick. I can tell you I feel dreadfully thankful.

Pole and I will send our letters together because we haven't either stamps, paper or anything else. The cursed Godforsaken rebels took everything, even our clothes away from us.

We expect to leave here tomorrow, or next day, for some western camp, probably Madison, and then we will have furloughs home. We are now drawing an entire new suit of clothes. I guess there is over 1000 body lice on me and I am no worse than the rest. We have been nearly starved to death, getting at the best only ½ loaf of bread and some stinking meat per day, but thank God I am back in our lines, well and sound, and will spend my life if need be to kill off the miserable, unprincipled wretches.[9]

You don't know how anxious I am to hear from you but I cannot until we get someplace else.

It is very strange that we four boys—Pole [Napoleon Perry], Aus [Austin Smith], Al [Albert Getten] and I who enlisted and came together, were in the hottest of the fight, and never even got scratched.

There is enough to write but I am going to write but little now. I wish I had some money. I have never wanted any so much in all my life. Oysters are only 15 cents a quart, and make your own measure, but can't get it now until we get where the oysters are.

I guess I write no more this time as it is an awfully bad place to write, and I am afraid you cannot read what I have written. We get good victuals here, it is a splendid place. Please hand this other note to Mr. Perry and we will write again soon.

I remain as ever your affectionate son and brother, Lute

NOTES

8. Following twenty-nine days of confinement in Libby Prison, Lute and his comrades were sent to College Green Barracks at St. John's College in Annapolis, which served as a hospital and interim camp for released prisoners before they moved on to parole camps in other locations. Welcher and Ligget, *Coburn's Brigade*, 96, 97.

9. Infestations of body lice were persistent problems for soldiers, due to crowded conditions, inability to maintain personal hygiene, and inadequate sanitation.

☙

Cincinnatti, Ohio, Friday, April 10, 1863

Ever dear home,

Again I have an opportunity to drop you a few lines. We are now at the depot waiting for the cars to take us to St. Louis. We arrived here just before dinner and went up to the soldiers home where we had an awfully good dinner which did me good. The cars start at seven. My health is good and I am most thankful for it. Pole and Al Getten are still at Annapolis in the hospital. Neither are very sick. Pole is able to be around. They get good care, have a warm room, nice beds, access to a large library, plenty of oyster soup, green tea and everything as nice and comfortable as they would at home.

We have got a brand new suit of clothes thruout. I tell you, you have no idea how I want to hear from you. I want you to write just as soon as you get this. Direct to L.S.M., Co. B, 22nd Regiment, Wis. Vol, Benton Barracks, St. Louis, Mo., put in a few postage stamps. We are expecting to get some pay within a few days.

We are all going to make a desperate effort to get furloughs and I think we will be successful. The boys all say they will never take their guns again, until they go home. I have a longer story to tell you than I can write in all day.

There are 120 of our regiment here. A great many have died and been left along the road at hospitals. I have thot a number of times I was going to be sick, but with good care have avoided it so far. We are all pretty well worn and beat out.

I must hurry up and close or I won't get this off here. Write me a long letter and tell me all you can. I would write more if I had time, but I am going out in town to beg an envelope and stamp and haven't much time to spare. Tell me if Joseph Hackett has been heard from or not.[10] We don't know what became of him. I will write again as soon as I get to a stopping place. We started from Annapolis Monday morning and have been on the cars about ever since.

Love to all. Write as above stated and you will oblige your son and brother, Lute.

NOTE

10. Joseph Hackett of Beloit died of disease on April 23, 1863, in Annapolis, MD.

Benton Barracks, April 12, 1863

Ever dear and respected home,

It is now Sunday afternoon and I find myself at Benton Barracks, located on the Fair Grounds.[11] I don't like the place very much. When we were at Cincinnatti I wrote a letter and begged a stamp and sent it. This one I will have to send without a stamp.[12]

My health is pretty good but I have a cold. We have pretty good quarters. They are going to fix them up tomorrow. About our future prospects we know but little yet. There is not much prospect of our getting any pay for a long time. Boys that have been here six months have received none. I therefore would like to have you send me $10 by express, that is if you can spare it. I am in need of every thing I once had, such as a knife, comb, handkerchief etc. They were all taken from us south and I borrow a little from the boys. Besides I have not eaten but one meal of victuals in two or three months and I do want a piece of pie and some other things of like sort. Can you blame me?

There is not much prospects of getting furloughs but there is not a boy here that has been here any length of time but what has been home on a FRENCH one—some of them twice, and they don't say a word to them. Every one of us boys in the 22nd are going to wait a little while and then come on a French one too. There is no danger of being troubled. What do you think of it? I want to come home dreadful bad but *I don't want to do anything disgraceful.* I think there is no danger of being noticed. All the boys say they will never take their guns again until they come home. We may have to stay here six months before we are exchanged, and in this time we can't do any duty at all, and I can't see any use of staying here. Tell me what you think.[13]

If Eddie sees friend Dave, tell him I want him to write to me and tell him my direction. I can't write to anyone until I get some money to get stamps, paper, etc. But I do want them to write to me. I have written twice since I got back to America. Tell me if you received them ... Give my love to Grandmother, love to each of you. Write immediately, for I do want to hear from you dreadfully. Direct to L.S. Moseley, 4th Battalion, 7th Co., Benton Barracks, St. Louis.

P.S. Also direct the money in the same manner.

NOTES

11. Benton Barracks (Camp Gamble), located on the north side of St. Louis, MO, served as a parole camp where Union soldiers could be kept in a noncombat role, usually involving guard duty or other routine work. Paroled prisoners were required to remain out of action until properly exchanged through a central clearinghouse administered by representatives of the U.S. and Confederate governments. Both North and South maintained parole camps for soldiers who had been captured and according to exchange agreements. Roger Pickenpaugh, "Prisoner Exchange and Parole," Virginia Tech Center for Civil War Studies, 2010–22, https://www.essential civilwarcurriculum.com/prisoner-exchange-and-parole.html/.

12. Beginning in 1861, Union soldiers could mail letters without a stamp by simply writing "Soldier's Letter" on the envelope. Postage would be collected from the recipient.

13. During this period of inaction and lapsed leadership, many soldiers headed home without official leave. "French leave" was a term derived from an eighteenth-century French custom of leaving a social gathering without a formal goodbye.

❧

Sunday, 19 of April, 1863

Dear parents and brother,

This morning I found a letter advertised for me at the General Post Office. I found two letters and I was so pleased to find them I could hardly wait to get back to read them. I was afraid I would drop them and pinched them all up in my hand, and if you believe me I even cried, I was so glad. I have read them over and over and shall do nothing else but read them and write all day. God bless you, my dear parents. I fear you have suffered more in anxiety than I have suffered in reality, altho the reality has been bad enough.

I will give you a short detail of our trip south, altho it will be brief. We had a skirmish with a small number of rebels on Wed. the 4th of March, but they soon skidaddled, we having killed 14 of them and only one man wounded on our side. We went on for near one mile and camped for the night, sleeping on our arms. At three in the morning we were called out and got our breakfast and as soon as light marched on. At about 8 sharp skirmishing commenced in advance, which continued until the first we knew, a shell came over our right but did not burst near us. We filed off to the left and then marched about ¼ of a mile and took position under a hill behind a stone wall. All the time our battery and theirs were firing. The 9th Michigan was at our left and the 33rd and 85th Indiana were the other side of the road. Soon the rebels opened up with a battery to our left, and ours and theirs fired back and forward directly over our heads, then the balls cut off limbs of trees not more than 15 feet over our heads. Our battery soon left; their ammunition having given out, and we went up the hill they had just left, and we were ordered to lie down. They were fighting hard down on the right. Soon I saw some of the butternuts behind a fence and I told the Colonel and asked him if I might shoot. He said, "Yes, if I was certain," and I took aim and fired, but I shot too low. There was now war in earnest, there was such a volley come back. Here noble Alex Anderson received his wound. He has since died. Noble Fred Goddard fell close by my side.[14]

Lots of our boys were wounded here. We soon had to retreat down the hill, behind the railroad. Here we made another stand but could not hold it, so we fought them from one place to another until they had us completely surrounded. Then about 20 of us tried to make our escape. We hid in a canebrake, but soon were discovered and they opened fire on us lying flat on the ground. The ol Colonel ran out and held up a white handkerchief. We then all went out and delivered ourselves up to the most ragged, God forsaken saucy lot of men that ever lived. We hid most of our guns in the mud. The ol Colonel had thrown his sword away. They took everything we had that they wanted. We then started for parts unknown to us. We had to pass over the field and saw the wounded and dead lying. Some, most of ours, stripped of all their clothes but drawers and shirts. The weather cold enough to wear overcoats.

I saw three of their officers—Van Dorn, Forrest, and Wheeler.[15] They had five Generals and we had nothing but a Colonel. They had full 5000 men and we over 3000. Theirs were all oldest and best troops. Not withstanding this odds, we fought them over six hours and they acknowledged that we killed more of them than they did of us. I will not give any number of killed as correct, but as near as we can tell theirs was 150 and ours 60.

They marched us to what they call 10 miles that night. Every house for the first five miles was a hospital, and full of wounded. We had to wade one creek that was cold and deep and wide and had muddy banks. They were all on horseback. We went to Columbia for the night. It was about 2 in the morning when we reached quarters, making a long day of it. I tell you, we were then started on the longest and hardest march we ever made. They started us by a back road to Shelbyville. After going about two miles we stopped for something to eat. They furnished us with very little raw bacon and nothing else—being the first since our capture. It rained all that day and all that night.

At night they gave us a little corn cake. We had to spend the night in the woods and in the rain too. We marched on in this way until we reached Tullahoma, Alabama, wading creeks and swimming rivers. They for some reason took us by a back road, leaving the pike. The night we reached Tullahoma we had marched 10 of the muddiest miles that every layed out doors, and waded three large creeks. There was one that I got into that was over my head and I had to swim. It rained most of the day. This night it rained all night, but they put us into an enclosure with a strong guard around. As true as I live there was not a spot of dry ground as big as my hat in the whole enclosure. They furnished us with a few brush to burn, and as true as I live all we had to eat was a little bacon and some raw injun meal and a little salt, with no possible way under heaven to cook the meal.

We were to take the cars in the morning for Richmond. We were ordered to fall in and then as we marched out they took every overcoat. I thought then we would die, for we were wet to the skin, hungry and tired. In the town I went into a tavern and the negro cook gave me some fried bacon and corn cake but he did it slyly, I can tell you. Thanks to the negro. I went into a candy shop near by and stole, for I had no money, ten sticks of candy. The value, at their price, was $2.50. They put us in a box car as thick as ever hogs were loaded. No seats and so thick we could not sit down and the car so low we could not stand up. Their R.R. are all used up. A man could travel as fast with a horse and buggy as they took us. We were over 24 hours going the last ten miles on account of a snow storm. The snow was about a foot deep. They took us into Richmond in the night and brot us out in the night so we could not see their fortifications. It was about 3 in the morning when the put us in the noted Libby jail. Here every window was broken out and as we had no fire, the wind drawing thru made it very cold. We were so weak we could not walk to get warm, so we would, as we called it, "stack down," that is, sit as close as we could to keep warm.

We had two meals a day. In the morning a ¼ of a small loaf of bread and a cup of soup made from beef we had for breakfast, thickened a little, sometimes with beans but generally rice. Thus passed 29 days of our lives but at length the day of deliverance came, and we were allowed to start for City Point. [This location was in Prince George County, VA, behind Union lines.] Only he that has been in like circumstances knows our joy when we saw our flag, and greater still, when we were on our own boat and received a whole loaf of bread, all for ourselves, and a piece of meat, with a promise of a cup of coffee. I used to steal everything I could get my hands on from the rebels.

At length we reached Annapolis where plenty of cleanliness prevailed. We washed ourselves and put on entire new suit. I sold my old one for 10 cents and bought a dish of oysters with the money. We have indeed seen hard times. I have seen the time, as mother use to tell me I would, that I would have been glad to get to our swill-pail. But a few of us are left. I am now in the hospital, have been since we came here, but I am going back tomorrow. Came here near being sick. All of us were worn out. Some have the scurvy.[16] There are but 18 of our company here. I am as poor as a snake, but I have gained since I got back to America. I feel like fighting them as long as I live. We all got as lousy as we could be and our hips are all worn from lying and sitting on the floor so much.

Was it old letters or the ones written that has not been opened, George Baily sent home? I have my diary and pictures but I lost a great many valuables.

Our officers are all left in old Libby. They fare better than we tho. I was offered $2000 to take a Captain's place and let him come out in mine, but it was too much like suicide.[17]

I will write again soon. Do write often. How is George Dates?[18] Give my love to grandmother and all. My respects to Mr. Miller and Mr. Fisk, if you see them. I wrote to Dave, but poor boy, he is gone. Write often and direct as below.

From your affectionate son and brother, L.S. Moseley

NOTES

14. Sgt. Alex Anderson from Beloit, who was wounded in the battle at Thompson's Station, died on March 28, 1863. Fred Goddard, also from Beloit, died at the Thompson's Station battlefield, March 5, 1863.

15. Lute referred to three Confederate generals at the battle of Thompson's Station: Maj. Gen. Earl Van Dorn, Lt. Gen. Nathan Bedford Forrest, and Maj. Gen. Joseph Wheeler.

16. Scurvy was a dreaded disease afflicting many soldiers who were deficient in vitamin C, due to the lack of fruits and vegetables in their diets. Effects on the body often included bleeding and ulcerated gums, leading to loss of teeth; sometimes the body was covered with scaly yellow spots, which could ulcerate and lead to gangrene.

17. Officers were released from Libby Prison on May 5, 1863, after several weeks of negotiations. Welcher and Ligget, *Coburn's Brigade*, 106.

18. George Dates of Beloit was discharged on January 18, 1863, due to disability. Welcher and Ligget, *Coburn's Brigade*, 106.

Benton Barracks, Friday, April 21, 1863

Dear Mother and brother,

I have just received your kind and welcome letter and will answer it immediately, as I have nothing else to occupy my time. It is a very pleasant day, the air being fresh from a very heavy shower last night. I have returned to the regiment in good health. It would be an ungrateful person indeed that wouldn't in like circumstances feel thankful for it.

We have passed thru very much. I cannot, and at this time will not, try to describe. We fancy we have seen as rough times as any of the boys. We are now fast fattening up and look entirely different than on our arrival. The worst of it is we, most of us, are quite corporal. But I think that appearance will soon leave us, for we are getting so filled up we do not tax our stomachs as hard as at first. I have not yet received the money. Am sorry to send for it, as my allotment has not yet reached home, but I suppose it has been sent to you as they promised us they would. Father I know has ways enough for all he has, without my drawing on him. The greatest reason I sent for it was because when we were south a number of times I got so hungry it seemed to me I could not stand it and borrowed money from the boys to buy a loaf of bread or something to eat. The boys who had watches, or anything of the like, sold and lent a part of the money to those who had none. One little loaf of bread cost 50 cents, sometimes only 25 cents, but very seldom—and they of course want their pay as was promised. Besides I thought I would indulge a little in the luxuries, but that will not do. I will try to get along as prudently as possible. We have been mustered for the pay due us for rations we did not use south amounting to nearly $9.00, but I can't see much show of getting it very soon our pay due us. They don't even make promises of paying. They owe us now nearly 7 months, but it will be good when it comes.

Aus Smith and I thought of asking you and his parents to send us a box. I don't know as if it will pay. We can get everything here, but always where there are many soldiers prices are up. Butter here costs 40 cents, eggs, which are brot around every day by an old woman, at 12½ cents. I have not been down to the city yet. It is nearly 5 miles to the river. We are in the fairgrounds. If there was to be a box sent, butter and some sauce and the like. Besides I want a towel. You spoke of handkerchiefs, I have one, a calico one, given me by the Ladies Aid Society of Boston, which will have to do. I received the comb all right and very glad of it. I also had the honor to receive the first Beloit paper. It was asked for by all the Beloit boys, as soon as I had read it. Every word that comes from Beloit is caught at by all very anxiously.

As far as news is concerned, I have none. I hope you will get a copy of the Madison Daily Journal with that petition we sent to have published in it. If you do, send it to me.[19]

I was disappointed in not having a word from Eddie. He generally gives me a lot of news. I hope, brother, you are going to school and making good improvements. If you will take my advice you will put in your best licks and learn all you can. Write me, Ed, about the school. I like to hear about every little thing about the school and home and friends there . . .

Love to Mother, Father and Grandmother. Lute

NOTE

19. No published petition from Lute's Company B has been located in the Madison *Daily Journal*. It is likely that the soldiers were petitioning for furloughs during their long period of parole. As Lute reported in his letter dated April 10, 1863: "We are all going to make a desperate attempt at getting furloughs."

❧

Benton Barracks, Tues, April 21, 1863

Dear parents and brother,

I have just received another welcome letter and altho there is little to write, I will employ a few minutes in conversing with you by means of a pen. I am as usual well. I am usually favored in this respect.

Barracks life is monotonous and more so because we have no chance of communicating with the outside world, only by letter. Occasionally we are allowed to pass to the city. Yesterday I went down. It is called five miles from here to the courthouse. I walked I recon over 20 miles; visited a great many of the curiosities of the great city, and at nite, if I wasn't a tired boy. I am not a good judge. I climbed to the top of the court house where a splendid view of the city can be had. I had no idea this was so great a city. At noon I went to the soldier's home and had as good a dinner as I wish to set down to, which of course cost me nothing. After dinner I went to the great horse sale and saw them dispose of Uncle Sam's castaways.[20] I got something of an idea as to the profitability of one's coming from Wisconsin to purchase. In the first place there are no horses offered for sale I should want to take my girl out riding with—and second, the prices. Horses we bought for $10 are $35 to $40 dollars. The greatest fault with them is they were so poor and small. They have got some up here that suit me. They are not fancy but of good size and with good treatment will do good service yet. I will keep watch and if I think it will pay will let you know. So much for horses.

As to general news, I have none. Dawson [William A. Dawson of Beloit] started from here last night. He said he would call you. I owe him 35 cents. Money he lent me to pay Ira Nye, who had to stay in Libby Prison when we came away. It was sesesh money. If you have any garden sauce you can trade him, I don't care if you pay it . . .[21]

You speak about poor Joseph Hackett. Jo is, without exception, one of the best fellows I have met. He fought as brave as any man could. I don't know how he escaped, for he did not run with the rest before the fight had just begun. When I was sick in Louisville he brought me a large piece of cheese and some crackers. I hope he will get well.[22]

Father speaks of my getting home before next winter. I know too much of the way we are carrying on this war to think of coming home before my three years are up. I don't think you know how this war is carried on. You certainly haven't had a chance to see what I have. Don't believe the war will close soon.

They now begin to talk a little about paying us two months wages, but it is an old story to us and we do not credit it, nor will we wait until we see it. I hope they will, for we could all make good use of it. Prices are high, butter is 40 cents and $2 for a shirt. We are like a young couple starting in life, everything to buy, and a soldier's wants are more than a citizen thinks. I am going to try to save as much of my wages that I can.

It is now evening, about 200 paroled men have been tearing down the fence. They have broken holes thru all along on one side. The officers rode down there and the boys gathered around them. They told the boys they didn't care how much of the fence they tore down but not to be so noisy about it. One of the commanding officers told the boys we would never get furloughs . . . I don't blame them either for we are in a perfect prison. They can't keep 2,000 once free men of the northwest, who are battling for freedom and country, in such a prison as this. We are not uncomfortable but it is like prison. We have earned better than this. There are whole companies here that say as soon as they get paid they will go home en masse. Our company (each company consists of 100 men) are getting the fever and some—yes most—declare they will too. I take no part in the brawls, for I don't believe in them, but I am a silent sympathizer.[23]

I trust you will excuse the blot on this envelope. If I don't send it to you I don't know who to send it to and it would be a dead loss on my hands.

For fear you won't know who this important epistle is from, I will subscribe myself,

Yours, Lute

NOTES

20. Approximately three million horses and mules were put to use in the Civil War; half of them died, mostly from overwork, injury, or disease. Horses, mules, and donkeys that were no longer fit to serve in the army (as mounts for cavalry, couriers, officers, and scouts, or used to pull wagons and artillery pieces) could be sold at auction. National Park Service, August 25, 2020, https://www.nps.gov/stri/cw-horses-and-mule.htm#-text/.

21. "Garden sauce" was a household term for stewed and preserved tomatoes or other vegetables produced from the home garden.

22. Joseph Hackett of Beloit died of disease in Annapolis on April 23, 1863.

23. With no regimental officers directing the reorganization of the regiment or imposing discipline, many men began drifting home. Others became discontented, depressed, or disorderly. Groves, Blooding the Regiment, 161–64.

Benton Barracks, St. Louis, Friday, April 24, 1863[24]

Dear parents and brother,

Having just fitted up a writing desk, I will christen it in writing to you, altho there is but little news to write.

I received father's letter last night. In regards to coming home, I would say the probability is that most of us will get a furlough of 10 days, and that will be all. You forget when you speak of Abe's proclamation that that would have nothing to do with us, for we are paroled prisoners of war and will not be counted as deserters, if back when exchanged.[25] But I have no idea of coming that way at present. I shall want to come, even if I find I am not going to be able to come honestly.

In regard to Gov. Salomon's efforts to get us to Madison—I have no faith in it.[26] Most of the boys say they will go as soon as we are mustered for pay, which will happen the first of next month. I shall take your advice and wait for a short furlough of ten days. Dawson, I believe, starts today or tomorrow on one. But I will leave, not over six short days to spend at home, the four being occupied by travelling.

I received the express package day before yesterday and think there must have been a mistake somewhere, for it was marked $10 and contained only nine. There was $1.00 in stamps; four 50 cent pieces; one dollar bill and a five dollar bill—making in all $9.00. I speak of this so you can find out what the mistake is. In father's letter there was a five, which I think I can make good use of when we leave here. There is nothing current here but greenbacks, but it is no trick for a soldier to pass off anything that has the least appearance of money. I should have asked you to send me uncurrent money, if you had any, before but was afraid you would think I could be in better business than passing poor money . . .[27]

We are expecting a fight to come off near here. I can't think of the name of the place. So they have taken all the troops from here, all those exchanged men, and now they make the paroled men stand guard, which is very wrong in my opinion; for we have taken the oath not to take up arms or in any way aid or give comfort or do guard or garrison duty until exchanged. So they make us break our oath. I wish you could step in and see us. How we are fitted up, we think it is very comfortable but you would think it no more fit than a cow stable. The rats are thicker than ever. We have a great fun in the evening killing them. We take a pine board and get one end all on fire. Then one will take it and run up and down between the barracks, which are fully ½ mile long, and a crowd of about 20 or 50 of us after him, all armed with sticks or clubs. Then woe to the unfortunate rat that is out reconnoitering. For we soon surround him and if he doesn't surrender he gets pelted with clubs and other weapons until life is extinct; great bravery being displayed on both sides. At nite the rascals make great havoc with anything that is not put out of their reach. They take that time to drill, going thru their motions on the double-quick. The clatter of their hoofs making quite a clatter on the floor, which often keeps one awake for hours at a time, and makes him heap curses on their heads. Sometimes the boys give orders to them, such as "rally by fours," "deploy as skirmishers," "charge bayonetes" and the like. I don't know if they obey the commands, for it is generally so dark it is impossible to see. Well I presume this will not interest you.

Yesterday I volunteered to do a little fatigue duty. We went up to the Benton Barracks warehouse and handled over 2000 bushels of oats. So you see I am stout and healthy. I now weigh 150 A.V.D. and am gaining every day.[28] There are more old women peddlers here every day than—rats I was going to say. I have bot a few eggs every day off them. That seems to go to the right spot. There are also, in our enclosure, a number of stores. We call it soldier town. There is a high board fence all around the barracks so we can't see anything of the outside world, only as we get a pass to town. It seems to me as tho they treated us more like criminals than men who were fighting for freedom and their country. There are over 200 acres in the enclosure tho, so we can have a pretty good chance to travel around. I make it a point (of duty) to take exercise every day. I think it is very necessary to retain ones health . . .

I guess I have written enough, I only write because I have nothing else to do, so I sit down and write what I happen to think.

Love to all, your affectionate son, Lute

NOTES

24. On April 24, 1863, the *Wisconsin State Journal* in Madison printed this notice: "A large number of the members of the 22d Wisconsin paroled prisoners are now at Benton Barracks in St. Louis, waiting to be exchanged. They published a letter to Governor Salomon, giving some account of their capture and captivity, closing by an appeal to him to use his influence to have them brought to this state and maintained here where they could see family and friends until they are exchanged."

25. President Lincoln's proclamation, dated March 10, 1863: "All soldiers enlisted or drafted in the service of the United States, now absent from their regiments without leave, shall forthwith return to their respective regiments by the 1st of April, 1863, without punishment except for forfeiture of pay and allowances during their absence. All who do not return within the time above specified shall be arrested as deserters and punished as the law provides." John Woolley and Gerhard Peters, "Proclamation—Recalling Soldiers to Their Regiments," The American Presidency Project, University of California-Santa Barbara, accessed 4/20/22, https://www.pres idency.ucsb.edu/documents/proclamation-recalling-soldiers-their-regiments/.

26. Edward Salomon, the governor of Wisconsin from 1862 to 1864, visited the paroled troops in St. Louis and attempted to allay the fears of those who had been absent without leave. However, he lacked the authority to grant furloughs. On May 16, 1863, The *Wisconsin State Journal* published a notice declaring that "By advices of the Executive Office from St. Louis, it appears that a considerable number of the paroled men of the 22nd regiment (Col. Utley's) have become restive under the confinement to barracks, and thoughtlessly, or recklessly taken 'French leave.' . . . All are now exchanged and all absent without leave will be rated as deserters, forfeit all pay and be subject to other punishment, if they do not return at once to duty." Major Charles W. Smith was temporarily in charge of the 22nd Wisconsin.

27. "Uncurrent money" referred to the privately issued notes, coins, or tokens that circulated in Union as well as Confederate states. Paper notes that became

worthless were called "shinplasters"—useful only for stuffing in soldiers' boots to prevent chafing.

28. Lute used the avoirdupois weight system of pounds and ounces as units of measurement (16 oz = 1 lb). He reported weighting 175 pounds at the time of his enlistment so he had lost some weight. Many Civil War soldiers wrote about their weight as an important indicator of health and diet.

Benton Barracks, St. Louis, Thursday, April 30, 1863

Respected parents and brother,

You may be somewhat surprised at my writing so often when there is so little to write, but the reason is this—we have nothing to do but eat and sleep and after sitting around as long as one can stand it, and reading all we can get, I get thinking of home and sit down to converse with you via paper and pen. . . .

It is very warm today—no air astir at all. This afternoon we were mustered for two months pay. The commissioners promised us at Racine that if we were taken prisoners we would still get paid our allotment. If any money comes, just mention it in your letters . . .

The three boys from the 6th company that were court-martialed, and this afternoon when we were mustered their sentence was read to them before us all. The first was for taking French leave. He had to forfit one months pay for the time he was gone, perform one months labor of tending horses or driving teams and also he was reduced in rank. So you see he was not shot. This is the only case we know of there inflicting any penalty what so ever, and every day there are from 5 to 20 coming back . . .[29]

Benton Barracks, St. Louis, Tues., May 5, 1863

Dear parents and brother,

As you will probably be expecting a letter from me, I will write a short one. My health is good. On the 23rd of last month I weighed 150. Yesterday I weighed 152½ so you see I am gaining. I think if I were home for a few weeks I would come up to my old weight of 175.

As there is nothing to write, I will tell you how we live. Our barracks consists of two buildings. The one a large bedroom that accommodates 100 of us. The other is a kitchen and a pantry. We hire two out of the company for 25 cents per months for each of us, to cook for us. Dawson was one of our cooks. In the morning we have coffee with a little sugar in it, bread and some fried bacon. At noon we have bread, meat or hominy, and sometimes beans. At night bread and coffee. Those who have money buy a cup of milk or some eggs. There are old women without number peddling milk, eggs and some dutch pies or cake. They are all german.

There is one little item that may be new to you since we have been here. There have been a company of the 23rd Mo., with no cavalry guarding us. They are a regiment that run at the battle of Shiloh—more sesesh among them than union men. They have put men in the guardhouse for no offence at all, until they got the guardhouse full. In some cases they shot at the boys for looking over the fence. It went on in this way until Sunday afternoon, they heard a man say that "Browns men ran at Shiloh." They gathered around him with their revolvers drawn and pointed right in his face and put him in the guardhouse. They put 5 or 6 men in this way without orders, until the boys got pretty mad and gathered around (about 3000 of them) with stones and clubs, told them to let those boys out, or down would come their shanty. It has turned out just as I supposed it would. The officers telegraphed down to the arsenal for a regiment. Our boys hollored and yelled around the barracks until around 10 o'clock in the evening, and then one by one went back to their quarters. The most brave and daring waited until the last. The cavalry were drawn up in line of battle all the time with their guns loaded. I went up to the guardhouse to hear what they had to say. They are a pack of cowards—called us paroled men all traitors and copperheads.[30] They say if we were not we would not be here. I have taken no part and do not intend to but I think we are used anything but right. The consequence of it is they have brought more men here to guard us, refuse to give us anymore furloughs, and what makes us all mad—they say they won't pay us yet. They say they were going to pay us every cent they owe us this week, but now they will wait to see how we behave. This I am afraid will raise a bigger fuss than the other, for they have no right to stop our pay. It is only another excuse to get rid of paying us as they ought. It puts money in their pockets. I am afraid we will not get home on our 15 day furlough. The news in the paper is encouraging this morning, looks a little like we are cleaning them out . . .

I have played ball until my arm is lame. The weather is cold and disagreeable today. Some of the boys are asleep, it seems very lonesome. There is no place to loaf. I have received only three of the papers you have sent me.

The boys are most all of them making rings and trinkets out of bone, playing cards to pass the time away.

You said grandmother would write to me if she could use the words she wanted to. Her grandson is not particular, tell her I cannot use words to suit me. Give her my love . . .[31]

Ever yours until death, Lute

NOTES

29. Discipline was maintained by a combination of shame and pain. Common offenses were straggling, drunkenness, fighting, dereliction of duty, theft, cowardice, bounty jumping, and insubordination. Punishments ranged from extra duty, fines, time in the guardhouse, reduction in rank, and physical penalties. Desertion could result in execution by firing squad or hanging, but during long periods of parole and inactivity, unofficial absence was sometimes excused or lightly punished by commanding officers. Patricia L. Faust, ed., *Historical Times Illustrated Encyclopedia of the Civil War* (New York: Harper & Row, 1986), 220, 221.

30. "Copperheads" was a term commonly applied to Northern antiwar Democrats who did not accept emancipation of the slaves as a legitimate object of the war, or who advocated for a negotiated settlement with the Confederacy. These "Peace Democrats" were compared to venomous copperhead snakes. An anonymous opinion published in the *Wisconsin State Journal*, April 24, 1863, declared: "The class of men styled Copperheads in the North are our most deadly enemies. Were they in the Southern army with arms in their hands, they could do us but little harm, comparatively."

31. Lute mentioned his maternal grandmother, Dolly Chase Gage of Beloit, in several letters. They clearly enjoyed a close relationship.

Benton Barracks, St. Louis, Friday, May 8th, 1863

Ever Dear Beloved Parents and Brother,

. . . I wrote in the last letter about a muss we had here. It has raised a great row with all of us here, for they say on account of this they will grant us no more passes to the city and refuse to give another furlough at all. What is still worse, they will not pay us a cent. I think it is mean in the extreme. Now all hope of coming home is gone. They have issued an order prohibiting all railroad, stage lines, boats, hotels and even private home, from carrying or harboring in any shape, any soldier. So you see we cannot come home in any way. It has given us all the blues, and why shouldn't it? All our fond hopes of visiting home and friends are gone. Our regiment are all that are here but what have been home, and we have faired the hardest of them all . . .

The report is current with us this evening that we are all exchanged. I think it may be true. At least I hope so, that we may move from here.

The war news for the last few days has been very encouraging. We thought if Gen. Hooker was successful we would once more, ere long, be citizens instead of soldiers, but I will write no more of this for fear you will think I am entirely discouraged.[32]

I don't see but I will be under the necessity of asking for a little money. Our rations now are such that my weak stomach will not bear them. For instance, our principle things are bread and bacon. I can't eat bacon grease. Tonight we had nothing but coffee with no sugar and bread. This is not enough and it is more and more so . . .

You very often speak of my being promoted but do not think of this, for it is not the brave or the ones that deserve promotion that get it. Since I left home I have tried as well as I could to do my duty faithfully and if possible to merit a position. I shall continue to do so, but expect to come home as I went away—a high private in the rear rank . . .

It is very lonesome here, I hope they will put us in the field soon, only I am afraid they will send us way down to Vicksburg, and that will be very bad thru the hot weather.

Mother said she was unwell. Oh how I do wish you were well, Mother. I hope you will be so before long.

Your affectionate son and brother, Lute

NOTE

32. Maj. Gen. Joseph Hooker's forces were defeated by Robert E. Lee's smaller army in the bloody Battle of Chancellorsville, April 30–May 6, 1863.

ᕦᕤ

Tuesday, May 12, 1863

Dear Home,

Don't feel much like writing to anyone but will. Saturday I went down to the city and had a pretty good time. Sarg. Fairservice [Marshall L. Fairservice of Summit, WI] went with me. We went up to the museum. It is worth a great deal to see the curiosities there. They have the skeleton of what they called Zugladon, found in Alabama.[33] It is 96 feet in length, there is but one other in the world, and that is in England. They have the best lot of birds I have ever seen. It beats Cincinnatti all to pieces. We spent most of the day there. We went up to the soldiers home and got our dinner there, for it is strictly against the law for a soldier even to go into a hotel or saloon in this city. If he goes he will be arrested and confined to jail. I think I know what it is worth to be an American citizen instead of a soldier, if I ever get to be one. I wouldn't enlist again after being used as we are. I will do my three years and that is all.

A few days ago we went to the park, six citizens came up and started talking to us. They started to sneer at us for being soldiers. They hit Greg from behind and knocked him down. Then they kicked him. This would not do for soldiers so we went after them and caught them. The police would not give us full sway with them, but we pounded them up dreadfully. As it was we tore the broadcloth coats all off of them and chased them about a mile.

Gov. Salomon and Adj. Gen. Gaillard [Augustus Gaylord] were here and spoke to us yesterday. They have settled the question of coming home. They told us it was beyond their reach, and they have done all in their power to get us there but to no avail. This has turned out just as I supposed it would. The boys have all left, but about 30 from our company. There were over 60 in our old company B when we first came. Now there are 12 and one of them is Dawson, who has been home . . .

My mouth is so sore I can't tell the truth (but I can write it). I received the money sent by Dawson, it was very acceptable. In a few days I think I shall box up my overcoat and a few things I don't need anymore and some letters I want to save and send them home . . .

Love from your soldier brother and loving son.

Eddie please write to me. Send me some pictures and tell me about the sheep.

NOTE

33. The "zugladon" (*Basilosaurus*) was a prehistoric whale, believed to have gone extinct 35 million years ago.

The gap of more than three weeks between Lute's letters to his family is due to his "French leave"—a trip home that several paroled soldiers made during the long period of inactivity while waiting for official exchange and return to active duty.

꙰

Camp Jackson, St. Louis, Sunday, June 7th, 1863[34]

Ever dear home,

I am once more in camp. I arrived here a few minutes ago, all right. I got to Chicago about 6 in the evening and had to stay there until the next morning to get transportation, and then intended to start at eight in the evening Friday. We got the transportation and found we could go then or stay, just as were a mind to. So ten of us stayed until Saturday morning. Thursday evening we all went to the opera and when it was out Fred Butler came up and was right glad to see us. I went home with him and spent the night. They urged me to stay until we came away but it was so far from the depot I thought not best. This evening we went to the Varieties, so you see I spent my money free.

We stayed on the other side of the river last night . . . We are all right, came back just in time. The payrolls are all made out and we are in time to sign them so we will get our pay. They are not going to do anything at all to us for going home.

I am going up to Alton this afternoon with some rebel prisoners, so I haven't but a few minutes to write . . .[35] I guess we will be kept here some time yet.

Now my dear parents and brother, don't feel sad on my account. Never was there a boy who felt more love and respect for parents than I, but I must close, so good bye. Write soon and direct to: L.S. Moseley, Co. B, 22nd regiment, Wis. Vol, St. Louis, Mo. Camp Jackson.

Lute

NOTES

34. Lute and a fellow soldier, Osa Freeman, traveled by train and stayed a week before heading back to camp in St. Louis. In this letter, Lute gave his address as Camp Jackson, an alternate name for Camp Gamble, located near Benton Barracks.

35. The prison at Alton, MO, was located about 30 miles north of Camp Jackson. Most prisoners were captured Confederate soldiers, but civilians accused of aiding escaped Confederates or committing acts of treason or vandalism were also held there. American Battlefield Trust, accessed 4/20/22, https://www.battlefields.org/visit/heritage-sites/alton-military-prison-site/.

꙰

June 8, 1863, Camp Jackson, Mo.

Dear dear folks at home,

It is now 8 o'clock on Monday evening. I am again in a position to write and will endeavor to pen you a few lines. Allow me to tell you in the first place, my dear good parents and brother, that I never did anything against my will in my life—not even when I gave myself over into the hands of the rebels—as when I left you at our dear good home. But that is what I enlisted for, and I must not complain. Now do not worry too much about me. I did not say one half I wanted to while at home. When I came to part with you, altho I might not have shown it, I felt as if I could have bawled even. O, I hope I may be permitted to come home again and not to part for the purpose of shedding my fellow beings blood. Yes, my dear good parents and brother, I know you love me and have always done for me the very best you could, and now I beg of you to believe me when I tell you that I love each of you. For this very reason I am here, to protect my home, and I pray God that freedom may once more prevail, and that ere long this cruel war will end. But if it does not, I am bound to do my part as well as I am able. If I may be permitted to live, and if it shall be the other way ordered, pray for me that I may be prepared. I do not write this because I am more serious now than before, but I have always believed in Christian religion and I believe in a hereafter, and hope I may be so happy as to die the death of a Christian, that I may join my dear sisters in a better world.

Well I will tell you about our journey here. After leaving you, I met a great many who had a goodbye and a good wish for me. It was with a sad heart that I took my seat in the cars and moved away from home. We paid half fare to Clinton, then we paid $1.65 to Chicago. In Chicago, I told you I went home with Fred Butler . . . We had a good dinner at the city Hotel and a fine time. In the morning we started for St. Louis. We got there at 9:15, it was dark and we didn't know where to go, so we went to a hotel and stayed until morning. We crossed the river and made our way back to camp. That afternoon I volunteered to guard some reb prisoners going to Alton. We took 17 Rebel Bushwackers to jail in Alton.[36] Three of them are to be shot— one to stay in prison for 15 years. The rest were not so bad, but believe me I felt very different guarding them than having them guard me. It was more agreeable to me at least. We had to stay at Alton all night, and as it was Sunday, I went to the Presbyterian church to meeting. A gentleman and wife saw me standing in the hall. He came up to me and asked me to sit with them. When church was out a man paid our lodging and breakfast at a first class hotel—three of us. In the morning we took 5 prisoners back with us that were to be released. We went down on a boat.

They will do nothing to us for leaving, we got back just right. I am afraid it will go hard with Pole and those that stayed at home. They didn't get back to sign their payroll . . .

Camp Jackson is about 1½ miles from Benton Barracks. I guess I shall go over in the morning. We are under marching orders, they say for Tennessee—Franklin, the boys all say. They will not go one inch until we are paid. I guess we will have our pay in a few days. Most of the boys hate dreadfully to go, but I don't know as I do. Some of the boys have not been home yet. Most all that went are back. If we go there we will have what is called shelter tents—one tent for two men. Most of the boys have got the blues dreadfully, but that is of no use, for we would have been contented enough if we had not been taken prisoners at all. We are all sick of the war, but who ain't?

Now they want us to buy our own guns in our company. They will cost $3 a piece. They are 16 shooters. I don't think much of it, but if the rest do, I shall of course . . .

Love, Lute

NOTE

36. "Bushwhackers" was a Union soldiers' term for civilian fighters who fled to the rugged backcountry where they resisted the occupation of Union troops, engaging in small skirmishes and hit-and-run attacks.

❧

Thursday, June 11, 1863

To the dear ones at home,

. . . It is a lovely morning and everything looks cheerful and pleasant. Our regiment were all paid off yesterday—$78 for six months.[37] It was all paid to us here, and the last night I assure you, a great many of the boys were full as drunk as when we were at home. They were noisy and boisterous . . .

Today the camp is full of peddlers of every description. I guess over a hundred watches have been sold. We have bought our brand new set of instruments. I gave a dollar toward them. I expressed $70 home. The

receipt is in this letter. I have expressed my overcoat, cap, shirt and satchel
... The express charges are all paid—on the money and all ... We have
been expecting to start for Nashville every day but have not gone as yet, but
probably in a few days. I do not dread it much. I would just as leave be there
as here.[38]

Last night I ate the last of my tongue and bread and apples. It rather
made me feel sad, for I couldn't help wondering when I should be able to
get some more of my mothers own cooking. I thot the bread was the last I
would get in a long time . . .

NOTES

37. Although Union soldiers were supposed to be paid every two months, it was
often impossible, due to sudden troop movements, long distances, and difficult terrain. Families back home who depended on allotments from the soldiers' pay were
affected by the delays.

38. The official prisoner exchange came on June 9, 1863. On June 12, the 22nd
Wisconsin Infantry Volunteers were ordered to proceed to Nashville and report for
duty to Maj. Gen. William S. Rosecrans, commanding the Army of the Cumberland.
Groves, *Blooding the Regiment*, 173.

CHAPTER 3

The News from Tennessee

June 14, 1863–April 29, 1864

How thankful I am to have my pen to communicate with you.

—Lucius S. Moseley, September 5, 1863

Wisconsin 22nd Volunteer Infantry Regiment attached to 3rd Brigade, 1st Division, Reserve Corps, Army of the Cumberland to October 1863. Coburn's Unattached Brigade, Department of the Cumberland to December 1863. Post of Murfreesboro, District of Nashville, Department of the Cumberland to January, 1864. 2nd Brigade, 1st Division, 11th Army Corps, Army of the Cumberland to April, 1864.

Service: From Nashville, Tennessee, to Franklin, June 22; to Murfreesboro, Tennessee July 3, and garrison duty there till February, 1864. Moved to Nashville, Tennessee, February 24, and duty there till April. March to Lookout Valley, Tennessee, April 19–28, 1864.

—Dyer, *Compendium*, vol. 3, 1682, 1683

New Albany, [IN], Sunday, June 14, 1863

Dear Parents and brother,

It is now just ten months since I put my name on the enlistment roll. I have been spared so long and I hope I will be spared to return to you again . . .

We left St. Louis Friday afternoon; came out on the Ohio and Mississippi Rd to Mitchell. There we changed cars and came to New Albany arriving here last evening at nine. We slept in the R.R. depot last night and slept well too. We are now just across the river from Louisville. There is a report that we are going to stay here until morning but we may go this evening. We are going to take the cars for Nashville. Day before yesterday the rebels burned up two trains on that road, but they had no soldiers on. There is no danger of them attacking us, for they dare not when there are soldiers on board . . .

I don't think our government uses us as well as they might, for they put us in old box cars, and it seems to me that might furnish us better in this hot weather. They gave us nothing but bread and water since we started, but I get along first rate as long as I have money.

There are a great many sick and wounded soldiers here, but they are well cared for . . .

There is considerable dissatisfaction, both among the boys and the officers, in regard to the officers. Most all the line officers are down on the ol Colonel [Utley], and most of the boys like him and are down on the Lt. Col. [Bloodgood]. The two never can agree together again. I think the ol Colonel has not come back yet, but we are expecting him every day.[1]

I don't know of any more to write . . . if you are a mind to write you can direct to me—22nd Wisc. Vol. Co. B, Nashville.

As ever, your affectionate son and brother, Lute

Written with that pencil you was so thoughtful to put in for me.

NOTE

1. Defeat and surrender at Thompson's Station exacerbated the rift between Utley and Bloodgood. Utley returned to the regiment on June 18 and began imposing stricter discipline, adding to ill feelings among the troops. Welcher and Ligget, *Coburn's Brigade*, 109.

❧

Nashville, Tues., June 16, 1863

To the dear ones at home,

A few minutes ago I was very happily surprised with a letter from you. I was not expecting one quite so quick.

I arrived in Nashville last evening (Monday, June 15). Last night we stayed in a building called the Zollicoller [Zollicoffer] Barracks. It is a building built by that rebel General. It is not finished, but it is the largest hotel in the U.S., for it was built for that purpose. We were quite comfortable only the feed that was poor.[2]

I wrote you a letter when we were in New Albany. This is the fifth since I left the quiet home circle to try again the fortunes of war.

We are now just on the edge of the city, in camp, but will stay here only a day or two. It is likely we are going to a place called Triune, about 20 miles from here. It is not at Franklin, but near the center of the right wing of Rosecrans army. I would rather be there than on the right, as we were before, for the rebs won't pitch on to the center. There is fighting all the time, along the line, but this is the least of my troubles, for I am not afraid of being taken prisoner again, nor of getting shot either, for I have felt all the time that I wouldn't be. There were two trains captured and burnt on the Louisville-Nashville R.R. before we came. So they took half our regiment through the day we got there and the rest of us waited in Louisville until the next day. There were five large trains came with us. We were guard for the whole and the major called for volunteers to go up on top of the cars to keep lookout. No one wanted to go hardly. I went up and came out all right. I don't believe they can call me a coward yet and I don't believe they ever will.

At Nashville I saw two of our boys. One was Frank Smith, he is with us now, well and hardy. The other is James King. He was wounded in our first fight, and is a cripple. Old man Smith is there but sick. He is trying to get a discharge and I guess he will. They say Hank Hodge is at home. He met Bill Minot. He is alright again and is with us.

The weather is awfully warm, I never saw it so hot in my life, but hot weather does not affect me as I thot it would. I am well, eat little, but feel well. All I ask is my health!

Ed Fairbanks has now gone to see his father. The old man will make his usual $500 this season, for you have no idea how high everything is. They ask more than twice as much here for everything as they do in Louisville. There is a big chance for speculation here I think.[3]

I have mother's photograph. It looks pretty well I think . . . you don't know how much I think of my pictures. I look at them very often.[4]

You said the weather was dry up there. It is raining here. The crops are rather poor here. All for now.

All my love, Lute

NOTES

2. The Zollicoffer building (built by the Confederate Brig. Gen. Felix Zollicoffer (1812–62) later became widely known as the Maxwell House Hotel, which was demolished in 1961.

3. Inflation was rising rapidly throughout the South as confidence of victory and faith in the value of currency continued to decline.

4. Photography was a relatively new technology, one that became very popular among military families. Many soldiers and loved ones at home who could afford to have their portraits taken, later exchanged them in the mail.

❧

Wednesday, June 17, 1863

I thought I would write a little more this morning. Yesterday afternoon I went over to the corral and helped Silas Wright get our company team. Our regiment drew 13 six mule teams. We had the privilege of picking two of the mules and the other four they gave us just as they came. We got two good steady ones. The other four were ones that were never handled a bit. We hitched them on to the wagon and Silas and I took them. You had better believe we had some fun before we got to camp. But there were no lives lost, we got them to camp all right.

In the morning we went down to the river bathing. We had a nice time. The Cumberland is low, but it is deep. I have no news to write . . .

The war news is not very encouraging today, but let us hope for the best. Do not get discouraged. I will come back yet again I think. Yes mother there is something that says to me "cheer up." I have no doubt that you love me and miss me and would rather I would be there than here, but I am sure it is harder for me to be deprived of you all, than for you to be deprived of just me.

I have no more to write about. Just that I am on guard. I left my old diary at home. If either of you have time, I should like to have you get me another book and copy it off, so I could save it. You can see by it what I was doing when out before.

Must close, so goodbye for now, Love Lute

Direct as before to Nashville.

❧

Camp near Nashville, Sunday, June 21, 1863

Dear ones at home,

It is now near dark and I thought I would pen a few lines to you. We have orders to march, and will start by four o'clock in the morning for Franklin—twenty miles from here.

I have received only two letters since I left you and have written six or seven. I want to hear from you very bad and hope I shall before long. Mother asks if I don't feel more attached to home after my short but pleasant visit to you. I can answer infallibly "yes," and more too, for I can't get over it . . . I long for the end of this war to come.

They say there is a fight now going on near Franklin, if so we will probably have another chance in, before long. But the report is not believed here, for if it were so they would not wait until morning to start, and we could easily hear the cannoning. If I get a promotion soon, as I most know I will, I will feel better. Do not say anything about it yet.

I was talking to the Colonel today about the guns we have got and he said he believed I was the young man that fired the first shot. I told him I was. He asked me some other questions besides. If I did not do my part that day, brave and good, I never will be able to . . . I hope my military career will be one I am proud of.

Love, Lute

༺

Camp at Franklin, Tenn., Wed., June 23, 1863

Dear ones at home,

Again I find myself way down at Franklin, pursuing the monotonous duties of a soldier's life. We started from Nashville Monday morning, June 22, at four o'clock. Our company was sent on in advance of the regiment as skirmishers. When we had got to Brentwood we found that the night before there had been some rebs there. We stopped for a short time, and quite a number of the boys found their revolvers and knives they had hid the day they were taken, for this is the place the rest of our regiment was taken. We expected to have trouble before we got to Franklin, for we had to pass through between two hills—a very bad place. But we met with no resistance. If we had come when we expected, we would certainly be gobbled, for there was a whole brigade of rebels waiting on the road for us. We reached here a little before noon.

Yesterday we moved our camp over near a large fort that has been built since we were here. They took all the forces away from here but our regiment and the 85th Indiana. You will soon hear of a move here and at Murfresboro [Murfreesboro]. I think we are all the time expecting the rebs will make an attack on us, but they will rue it if they do for we are fortified with plenty of ammunition and cannons. We say "let them come." We all turn out at 3 o'clock every morning and form in line of battle and wait there until morning or sunrise. When we reached here we found 5 of our company that were not taken. They saw those rebel spies hung, and I never heard of men dieing so bold in my life. They did not say anything, only that it was right and just. They placed them on a cart and tied the ropes around their necks. They ask our men not to tie their hands, so they were not tied when they drew the cart out. One of them jumped up so as to come down hard. He never put his hands up at all. The other was a Colonel—acting general. His rope was not tied right. He put his hand up and motioned them to fix it. He then took hold of the rope and raised himself up until it was fixed and then let go.[5]

The rebel pickets are not two miles from here. Almost every day our pickets exchange shots with them. Yesterday I was on guard. All the rest of my tentmates were out on picket. One of our boys brought in three prisoners last night, but I believe they were citizens here.

Don't have much to write . . . We have had the nicest kind of weather. Give my love to grandmother, write soon.

I desire to be worthy of your love, an affectionate son and true brother, Lute

Direct to L. Selden Moseley, Franklin, Tenn., to follow the regiment.

NOTE

5. The hanging of these men was a troubling affair that haunted Colonel Baird throughout his life. A detailed account is found in Welcher and Ligget, *Coburn's Brigade*, 111–19.

Camp at Franklin, Thursday, June 25, 1863

Dear Brother Eddie,

As I have a few minutes to spare, I thot I would write a few lines to you. I haven't anything new to write, only to let you know we are still alive and have not been attacked yet. I don't know but we will be soon.

It has been raining very hard for two days now, but it is clearing off. Tomorrow I am on picket guard. I shall write pretty often until there is not so much show for a fight. You must not be concerned about us, for we shall fight—if at all, in a very strong fort. There are six large cannons or siege guns in it, and plenty of ammunition. I am in hopes we will come off best this time.

I have not heard from you but twice since I left, and feel pretty anxious to get a letter. I am writing this with Silas Wright's gold pen, he says to tell you how he and I went after a big pig this afternoon. He and I went out to kill a sesesh pig, but we could not find one without going outside the pickets. We did not dare do this so we had to come back without the pig. One of the other boys killed one, and they are now eating it. It looks first rate. They baked it. We have a nice brick oven. I have some bread in baking for my supper, but I guess I can't write anymore. Excuse this note, as it is written in great haste . . .

Love to all. In haste from Lute

There is good news tonite. Our men have driven the rebs back and Bragg is on the retreat.[6]

NOTE

6. Confederate Gen. Braxton Bragg began a general retreat from Middle Tennessee toward Chattanooga due to steadily increased Union forces in the region.

∽

Monday, June 29, 1863

Dear friends at home,

I suppose at this hour in Beloit there are some sad hearts, for I suppose the boys are about to start for the seat of war. I very well know how they feel, for it is the hardest battle we have to fight when we leave our friends and relatives at home. People may think that it does not look well for a soldier to shed tears, but although I tried as hard as I could to keep them back, I could not. I can look at the corpses of our poor boys shot to pieces on the battlefield and not shed tears, but I could not leave you with dry eyes.

We have had considerable excitement here for a few days, for we have been momentarily expecting an attack. Negros come in daily and tell us that the rebs are coming. Today the rebs—a few of them—came up near our pickets and fired on them. They soon schaddled for tall timber. Our scouts have been all over reconnoitering and find no rebs. We feel pretty safe and expect them to pitch in as soon as they are a mind to. We will give them all they want this time, for we are dreadful well fortified. We all were ordered out in line today when the pickets fired. We are very cautious, and I felt as safe as I would if I were home. Let them come.

. . . I have at last the pleasure of telling you that your son Lute has been promoted and is now a corporal. I am very glad and will now try for better yet . . .

You would laugh if you could see me now, for I have had my hair cut off tight to my head. I have been cutting hair for the boys all day—have cut ten fleeces. . . .

We have our tent fixed up nice. They took our nice little tents away from us and gave us shelter tents, which are a piece of cloth about 4½ ft. sq., for each man.[7] We take four of them and fasten them together and fix it over a frame. We have some boards here and we built up a wall and cover it over with the tents. We have a place fixed to sleep on some boards in one end; in the other we have a table and some stools to eat on. We have built a kitchen out of boards and cook on a little stove I found. We get plenty of good rations here now. We have perfect liberty to take anything we find we want. I have my eye on a splendid three year old steer . . .

Since I wrote the above the pickets have been firing, and we have been out in line. But it was only some fellow that scared up some cow or mule, but it is well enough to be in readiness. I don't fear it one bit . . .

News tonite is that our men have driven the rebs out of Shelbyville, and that they, the rebs, have gone further south. I don't think there is any force near here. There are two good forts here, and reinforcements near that could get herein three or four hours, and I know we can keep any force they can bring at bay that long. I write you the facts of the case so you can know just how we are situated. You must not feel the least bit worried about us, for we are all right. I will write often as long as the danger is as much as at present. I go to sleep as soundly every nite as I would at home . . . Please send me in a letter a few steel pens—Gillette pens. I can't get them here. The one I have is very poor . . .

Yours as ever, in love, Lute.

NOTE

7. Shelter tents were easier to transport and quicker to disassemble when troops were ordered to move on. Harvey Reid of Company A and brigade commissary clerk for the 22nd Wisconsin, wrote about the change of tents in his letter of June 20, 1863: "All of Rosecrans' army in the field must have shelter tents . . . generally hated in the army. . . . The shelter tent, or dog tent as the boys call them, is simply two

pieces of linen cloth buttoned together and stretched over a ridge pole, leaving the tent open at both ends and scarcely high enough to sit up in." Reid, *Uncommon Soldiers*, 73.

∾

Tuesday morn and all is well, breakfast and dishes all cleaned up. We are going to cook beans for dinner and buy a ham. Cheapest thing we can buy. I am on picket today and tomorrow. Last night some bushwackers pitched into our pickets and they had a pretty good fight. There were 25 of them and only one of ours. They shot our man twice—one in the thigh and one in the arm. He shot one of them and ran his bayonet thru another. They got his gun and ran. Now there is one of the boys going by with a "butternut," so you see we have some fun here. I wish now that I had bought me a revolver, for it would be a good thing here now . . .

Write soon and often. From your old son and soldier, Corp. Lute

Direct to L.S. Moseley, Franklin, Tenn., Co. B, 22nd Reg. Vol. to follow the regiment.

Love to grandmother.

∾

Camp at Franklin, Thursday, July 2nd, 1863

To the dear ones at home,

It is now Thursday, just before sundown and dark. I have been to bathe in the big Harpeth and just got back. It has been a very warm day. We have our tent all fixed up and comfortable and now we have orders to march, and will start sometime tomorrow for Murfresboro. It is about twenty five miles from here. We will probably take two days for it, for it is so hot . . .

I have a little news to tell you, and I wish I did not have to do it, for it is an awful disgrace on both our regiment and our state. Ever since our fight there has been hard feelings between our officers—the ol Col [Utley] and Lt. Col. [Bloodgood] have been at swords points and each watching for an opportunity to prefer charges against the other. Some of the commishioned officers were on one side and some on the other. About a week ago the Lt. Col. was brigade officer of the day. It was his duty to mount his horse and visit every picket post on the line, or make what is called the grand rounds, to see if each man is doing his duty. This has been omitted a great many times before now, but the Lt. Col. omitted it and immediately the ol Col. preferred charges against him and had him arrested and his sword taken from him. At this all the Lt. Colonel's friends signed a petition asking the ol Col. to resign, stating as reason the ol Col. was not competent to handle the regiment and that he was not liked by the other officers or men—which is not so. The ol Col. is too good grit to be turned out in this way, so he went and had all the signers arrested on the charges of mutiny. Now how this will terminate, no one knows, but certainly it is the biggest kind of disgrace. All the officers except three or four are under arrest. This is all I will say about this. Ira Nye is one of the unlucky ones.[8]

I find a corporals duties are considerably lighter than a private's ... I should like to have you tell me what is going on in Beloit on the fourth. I can tell you we will be all that forenoon marching. In the afternoon we will be pitching our (as we call them) doghouses, and fixing them up ... We have been mustered again for pay, but I don't think at the present state of affairs we will get it and I hope we won't for I had rather wait until it is more. I have a little money left and am getting along first rate.

Write soon, Lute

NOTE

8. Harvey Reid's letter of July 2, 1863, states that the petition was signed by twenty-three out of twenty-seven line officers and by the quartermaster, the officer in charge of accommodations. "How the matter will end I cannot guess. Some think that all the officers will be dismissed ... An order has been received this evening for us to march tomorrow for Murfreesboro. I presume Rosecrans cannot trust a regiment without officers in so responsible a position as this." Reid, *Uncommon Soldiers*, 76, 77.

July 6, 1863

Dear ones at home,

... I wrote to you on the 3rd and told you we were going to Murfresboro. Here we are where one of the largest battles that have been fought. It is only 28 miles from Franklin here, and we expected to march it with ease in two days, but we found the roads almost impassable, so we only got here last night. You will see by this that we stop not for Sunday, but on the contrary, the hardest work we have done since we came into the service has been on that day . . . It was very hot and the roads dreadful rough. Two or three times our advanced scouts saw rebs ahead, and we had to hault and form a line across the road, but there was no fight. At nite we lay right down on the ground without anything . . . Yesterday I put my coat and blanket on the wagon and about 3 o'clock there came up a shower and I never saw it rain harder. I got as wet as a rat but I didn't care . . . I wouldn't have believed I could have slept so. The nite of the 4th I was on picket, and you can believe I cast a good many thots toward ol Beloit . . .

❧

Murfresboro, Tues., July 7, 1863

To the dear ones at home,

. . . As you probably know by my last letter, we are at Murfresboro. We came here July 5th, last Sunday, and expect to go on to Tullahoma every day. You don't seem to have heard the news in these parts Ol "Rosy" is giving them fits.[9] We have driven them out of Tullahoma, the place they tell us we never could get. They left some large cannons there. That is the place they shut us up in a hog-pen and fed us on ground cobs and smoked sowbelly, with no wood to cook it by. There is nothing I would like to do better than camp there a few days. On the way we will have to pass through Shelbyville, the place I sold my knife to keep from starving. There is a minister there that was very insulting to us. I would like to meet up with him.

All the war news is good and we begin to have hopes that we will all celebrate the next 4th at home.

It rains almost every day. The weather is as warm as a dutch oven and the flies are as thick as mules in a government coral. I feel great.

This forenoon I helped Lt. Nye put up his tent and built a shade over the front of it. We are in the first division, third brigade, of Rosecrans army of the Cumberland—under Gen. Granger.[10] We have no Brigadier-General yet. All our regimental officers, except the Major, are under arrest and we expect he soon will be. There are 10 Captains and 20 Lieutenants in the regiment. All but 6 of these are under arrest, so you see we are in a pretty mess. We can't tell how it will end, but we feel pretty sure we will have a new Colonel, Lt. Col. and Major. I as well as most of the regiment have been great friends of the Colonel [Utley], but now we have all changed our opinion, for he is using both officers and men very mean since we came back. For it is he that has caused all this fuss. His charges are mutiny and insubordination. I think it will result in sending some of them home. I wish I had gone in some other regiment, for I know I could have done better than I have . . .[11]

Lute

NOTES

9. "Old Rosy" was the soldiers' nickname for Maj. Gen. William Rosecrans, who commanded the Army of the Cumberland.

10. Maj. Gen. Gordon Granger, Reserve Corps, Army of the Cumberland.

11. Richard Groves wrote in *Blooding the Regiment*, 203: "By this time the regiment had pretty much fallen apart; all semblance of discipline was gone . . . The absence of officers was being felt at every level of the command, aggravated by the blustering threats of Colonel Utley, who lacked the ability to carry them out, as the boys well knew."

∿

Sat., July 11, 1863

Dear parents and brother,

. . . It looks now as we will stay here a good while. They say now we are thrown out of the brigade we were in.[12] So now we have no brigade, all our officers are in a big mess. Capt. Brown preferred charges again the Colonel for not drilling the regiment, for he never drills us himself—but twice. Then the Col. preferred charges against the Capt. for cowardice on the battlefield. Someone has preferred charges against the Major. So now I believe all our officers are either under arrest or have handed in their resignation. No telling how it will end. Some think the officers will either be put in the ranks or dishonorably discharged and sent home. Others think the whole affair will be dropped. It is a big disgrace on our state and regiment. We are now in a very safe place, as far as fighting is concerned, for the rebs have all left, or most of them. Murfresboro has been a splendid place but it has seen the effects of the war. There is hardly a store, except military stores.

I have thot not to write another letter until I received one. I know it is not your fault, the railroad has been impassable for about a week, being torn up by John Morgan [Confederate General John H. Morgan] who is now in Indiana. There is now 5 days mail in Nashville for our regiment. We should get it tomorrow. We drew rations today, first rate ones. We got some nice soft bread, salt pork and corned beef. We have to get along with just what we draw, prices are so high we can't afford to buy much.

I think father should not come down here. It would cost him more than he could make, there is no one to sell to and he could not buy anything. The R.R. only brings government supplys.

No more to write. This is as long as I hav'nt heard from you except when I was a prisoner.

A few days ago a boy who acts as a marker in our regiment found a springfield rifle.[13] Probably thrown away in some engagement. I gave him $1 for it and got me a bayonet for it. It is said to be the best rifle in the service. Ours were the worst. Now I can tumble a reb within 500 yards. If I come back and still have it, I shall fetch it with me as a relic.

Love to all, Corp. Lute

Please send me some postage stamps.

NOTES

12. The 22nd Wisconsin was now attached to the Third Brigade, First Division of the Reserve Corps, Army of the Cumberland.

13. The Model 1863 Springfield rifle was a muzzleloading .58 caliber weapon, favored for its range, accuracy, and reliability. The Confederacy was unable to obtain large quantities of these rifles, which increased the Union advantage as most of the raw materials and arms-making equipment was located in the industrialized North. National Park Service, "The Arms of the Confederacy," updated July 20, 2021, nps .gov/spar/learn/historyculture/arm-confederacy.htm/.

Camp at Murfresboro, Wed., July 15, 1863

Dear Parents and brother,

Again after a lapse of ten or twelve days we received mail. I was so happy as to be a recipient of a letter from you. The one I received today was written first of July . . .

Major General [Rosecrans] passed thru this place last night. He sent up an order to the old Colonel [Utley] to release the officers of this regiment, and give them back their swords; but this is only temporary. So the officers can go on duty. The mess is not settled yet. I hope it will be dropped, but am afraid it will not.

You of course know more of the war news than I do, so I won't write any. I am glad that Morgan has gone into Indiana. It will cause the people up north to wake up, and they will see some of the evils of war and be willing to try to put it down. It is now 11 months since I enlisted. During that time I have indeed seen some very hard times, as well as some pleasant ones. Have seen considerable of the ways and manners of the world. I would not take considerable for my trip thru the south. Altho I have no scar to show, I am certain I will recollect the part I have acted. So far there have been some reduced to the ranks for cowardice on the battlefield but I was promoted for bravery, and I trust you will excuse me if I do feel proud of it. Supper is ready and I must adjourn for a few minutes.

Well I am refreshed by a sumptuous meal of hard tack (we call it sowbelly) (bacon). So I will continue.

You say father and Eddie are cutting hay. Just one year ago I was helping cut hay. I think before another 4th we will be home. I think we will stay here but can't tell. We are quite safe as far as the fighting is concerned.

Write more often, give my respects to all, your loving son and brother, Lute

∽

Camp Murfresboro, July 16th, 1863

Dear parents and brother,

I have this day received a very welcome letter. So will answer it. We are still in the land of the living and well. I received the packages and money. I wish it were in my power to return some of your many kindnesses, if I live maybe I can do more for you in the future.

There is a report that "Rosy" [Rosecrans] is repulsed and retreating at double quick this way. Oh how I hope it isn't so, but I fear it is.[14] You will hear by the papers, so don't put any reliance on this. There were reb deserters came in this morning. I did not see them. You spoke about the war closing. I honestly don't think it will inside the next year.

I don't feel much like writing this evening, besides my eyes are sore and I can't see very well. We have had fine weather, only we want rain. It is not very hot, but we had one week that was hot, I tell you. We have a nice tent now. We built up the sides about three feet, then put up a ridge pole and covered it over our tents. My bed is built on this rise. I drove four stakes in the ground, leaving them up about one foot, then nailed two stripes from one to the other and covered it with some old corn sacks. So it is nice, better than feathers. I dug a hole in the ground and put down a box for a cellar where we put our bread and canteens of water to keep cool and fresh.

The revele has sounded, and Sel [Lute has begun using his middle name] must draw to a close. Mother, your plan for the future suits me very well, all but the wife. Now, good evening, write soon, I will do better next time.

Love to all, Selden[15]

NOTES

14. Rosecrans was preparing his army for a further advance on Chattanooga and Bragg's army, a slow and laborious operation.

15. Lute began using his middle name occasionally in his closures, possibly to honor Selden, his father. He may also have considered it a more dignified name, fitting for an experienced soldier who had been promoted to the rank of corporal.

∽

Camp at Murfresboro, Tues., July 22, 1863

Dear ones at home,

. . . The reason you didn't hear from me was as you supposed, Morgan's raid. But they now say he is caught.[16] We were expecting to go to Louisville, and there be mounted and sent after him. But now they won't want us there. I don't believe the dishonored 22nd will every fire on rebs again, for we are in the reserve corps and way in the rear. But no way knowing, we may be in a fight before this reaches you. It is just so hard for a soldier to tell one day where and what he will be doing the next. I think we will stay here a long time. We get all the war news. I guess, before you do and more reliable for it is telegraphed to head quarters officially . . .

NOTE

16. Brig. Gen. John H. Morgan, C.S.A., and his "Morganites" had cut rail lines and communications from Louisville. Their raid into the border states of Indiana, Kentucky, Ohio, and West Virginia ended in failure, with capture and incarceration in the Ohio State Penitentiary. Morgan and several officers managed to tunnel out and escape. Geoffrey C. Ward, *The Civil War: An Illustrated History* (New York: Alfred A. Knopf, 1990), 255.

∽

Murfreesboro, Thurs., July 24, 1863

Dear beloved parents and brother,

It is now Thursday evening, about 10 o'clock. I have not written to you today for I did not get your letter. We just received orders for Co. A, E and B to leave here in the morning to guard a bridge across Duck river.[17] Oh, my God, the battle that is now raging, decidedly the largest of the war. I may not be able to write you in a long time, but don't feel the least concerned about me, for I am glad to go. We think we will whip them sure, if we can only keep the communications open to "Rosy." There is a good stockade there, and we can hold the bridge sure, we think.

There are two trains of our wounded gone thru here today and there is a train of fifteen cars loaded with more of them now in the depot. We boys have been cooking our last mouthful of everything for them. They are going to stop when they come up here, and we are going to feed them. Would to God I had my last dollar here. I would buy the poor fellows some bread. But they will get plenty as soon as they get to Nashville. If I had time I would tell you lots, but please excuse me this time. You don't know anything about war, I tell you. The rebs say that if we whip them there, they are done. So you see I will be home to tell you before long.

Now I beg you don't feel the least uneasy about me, for I am glad to go. I think I can do some good. I sha'nt carry my knapsack down there, so won't have my portfolio. This is the reason I can't write. There is nothing but gurellas molesting the R.R., and we can clean them. There will be six companies of us, and we will be in a stockade, so I know we can whip them. It is not clear down in the front either. Must close.

Love, your son and brother, Lute

NOTE

17. The Duck River railroad bridge was located a few miles south of the village of Wartrace. Lute's writing of the battles that were "currently raging" may be a reference to Union victories at Gettysburg and Vicksburg.

∽

Murfreesboro, Tenn. Tuesday, August 18, 1863

Dear ones at home,

I am going to write you a few lines just to let you know I still exist, and not because I have any news to write. It is nearly as dull here as it was in

St. Louis. I hardly know what to do to while away the long, long days and weeks, but time will keep on, and it may be the time may yet come when peace, having been restored, will allow us to come home to enjoy ourselves only the more for the absence and hardships we have endured. I don't know but our separation causes you to kind of feel less my absence, but it is not so with me, for every day makes me feel more anxious to get back to my quiet home. I felt this last Sunday, for it was a very quiet still day, and I employed my time in thinking of loved ones far away. I believe I would have given a months wages if I could have just gone to church that evening in Beloit—even without speaking to anyone. I could get homesick very easily if I would give up to it.

I am well, altho I do not feel as well as I would like to. The health of the regiment is better than it was, I think. There has been but one man died since we came back, and I think that is very well. Pole is better.

There is a report in camp that we are going to start for Bridgeport, nearly 60 miles I believe. How true it is I don't know. I do hate to march this hot weather, but I just as well leave here as not . . .

Well I aint going to try to write anymore. There is one thing I would like you to get. The boys all say that I am getting round shoulders, and I guess I am, and I want a pair of shoulder braces. If you can get them there, and they don't cost too much. Send me a pair by mail. I don't like to ask for something every time I write, for you will get so you won't want to hear from me for fear I want something, but every one has his failings.

I will close, your loving son, L.S. Moseley

I forgot to tell you that I received the letter with $5. Thanks.

Headquarters 22nd Reg., Murfresboro, Thursday, Aug. 21, 1863

Dear ones at home,

As I received a very welcome letter from you, I will write a few lines in answer, but there is no news . . . I am well and rugged as ever. The boys are all better. Since payday every one of us have lived at our own expense and I feel that it is necessary that we do because one meal of bacon will give me the double-quick.[18] It certainly would kill me. I live on potatoes and bread. The potatoes have come down to $1.20 per bushel . . . Fairservice got a box from home last nite, and as he thinks considerably of me, I had the pleasure of tasting some Wisconsin cake, wine and butter. I shall use all my wages I can't get along without rather than live on our rations, until hot weather is over. There isn't anything we eat here that hurts us as quick as blackberries. It starts any of us in a short time. There was another man died, he like the others, had the bloody flux. There is no other sickness with us that I know of.

You may not get a letter from me again for a long time, for there is a report current here that there are 13,000 rebs within 40 miles of here, and coming this way. They will probably tear up the R.R. so as to cut off our supplies, and again they may come here and attack us. We are going to move over nearer the fortifications. They say they can never never take us here for there are too many big guns here for them, and altho there is only one brigade of us—the ones that have been prisoners once—here they can't whip us this time . . .

[Next morning]

I am on camp guard today. Tomorrow the whole regiment are on picket. Pole has come on duty again. J. Ross is on duty. He is the same as I use to be—his blood is out of order, and he has large sores all over his feet, so he can't wear his boots. Sime Sage is sick with the Tennessee quickstep . . . I wrote you a letter telling you about my money affairs. Did you get it? I didn't get any pay as my allotment was sent home. I tried to get some money from Pole, but he wouldn't give me any. I was sick then and needed some badly. I borrowed some from Miller and need to pay him back.

Must close. Lute

I do hate dreadfully to hear you are going to move, for I can't think of you but only in the brick house.

NOTE

18. The "double-quick" or "Tennessee quickstep" were slang terms for diarrhea or dysentery, common ailments suffered by soldiers due to poor sanitation, polluted drinking water, and inadequate diet.

∽

Murfresboro, Tenn., Sat., Sept. 5th, 1863[19]

Dear parents and brother,

It is now Sat. nite and I am on camp guard, and have to stay up nearly all nite . . . All I have to do is go around every two hours and wake up the men, and see that they are at their posts and doing their duty . . . How thankful I am to have my pen to communicate with you and my absent and far off friends. I often think of those poor negros leaving their families to go and help in this great struggle, for few can either read or write. There was the other day, over 1000 of these poor human beings here. They were captured from the rebs, who were running them down south. They were mostly men but some women and children. I don't know what they will do with the women and children. The men they have put into a regiment and taken the rest to Nashville. I pitied those poor negros, so down hearted and discouraged. Most every day the cars are loaded with reb prisoners being sent north. I like to see them going, but there are also a great many of our poor boys with wounds to show the price of the rebel prisoners. A person can get some idea of war, even if he goes no farther south than here. It is a great wonder to me that those prisoners that go thru here and see us well clothed and holloring and running and feeling so well, and also our large warehouses filled with plenty of hard tack and sow-bely, can ever want to go back and support a government that allows its soldiers to go about half clad and half fed as they are. I am thankful I was brought up in the north. A great many are going north each day. There are wagons drawn by old mules or a broken down horse, some old cavalry horses. They say they want to go where they won't have to pay $12 per pound for salt.

You will see that we are still in Murfresboro. We may be here until summer or leave tomorrow. We are now in the 11th corps instead of the reserves.[20] The boys are all well.

I want to tell you a little about Pole. He is down at the corral, and of course there are some horses in it that are not branded. So he got one of these out and sold it to a negro for $25. He may run clear this time, but if he does he will only feel more free to try it again, and the first thing he knows he will be sentenced to six months of hard labor with a ball and chain. I would rather be honest if I need money, and send for it rather than run such a risk . . .

All for now, Lute

NOTES

19. Although Lute did not mention it in his letter of September 5, 1863, this was the week of Lieutenant Colonel Bloodgood's trial by court-martial, for charges including misbehavior before the enemy at Thompson's Station, cowardice in surrendering at Brentwood, gross neglect of duty with regard to military discipline,

and insubordination. Colonel Utley was one of the witnesses for the prosecution. The court found Bloodgood guilty of all charges and sentenced him to dismissal, but the bitter conflict between the officers of the 22nd Wisconsin was not over. Groves, *Blooding the Regiment*, 225; Reid, *Uncommon Soldiers*, 87–89.

20. The 22nd Wisconsin was now part of Coburn's Unattached Brigade, Department of the Cumberland.

◦◡

Camp at Murfresboro, Sept. 12, 1863

Dear ones as home,

. . . This morning when we came to camp, Orderly Bullock handed me a package from you containing a pair of shoulder braces, some pens and some camphor. Father said he would send me two dollars per week. I think one will be a great plenty. This is the way a great many of the boys do, have money sent to them every week. I have sent the $2 to town for apples which I am going to sell and I think I can make something on them and thus try to lessen the expense of living. All we get now is sour bread—worse than hardtack—coffee, dried peas—worse than caster-oil—and bacon, which we are allowed to cook in no other way than boiling. I don't tell you this to complain . . . I am now as well as I ever was.

We have moved our camp about two miles. Now we are inside the redouts, near the fortifications.[21] I wish you could see these works. You would think it out of the power of man to take them with a small force inside to protect them. We are in a much safer place than before, but not near as pleasant. We were in a splended grove with a nice well in our camp. Now we are without shade of any kind, the air shut off by high earth works, and have to go a long way for water. All the soldiers have left here except one section of battery 19th Mich., and our regiment. Not as many men as in our regiment a year ago. There are enough of us I think. Every few nites we have to sleep on our arms, for there is quite a large force of rebs scouting about here, and threatening an attack on the depot and government storehouse which is filled with provisions. Let them come. I want them to come. We have organized a scouting party to scour the country for guerilltas. Sile Wright is one of them. I tried my best to go, but volunteered too late, for I didn't know it soon enough. They have been gone three or four days.

I heard this morning that four rebs are to be hung down town. I want to see it . . .[22]

No one lives near the city outside the lines, every house and fence having been destroyed.

I am very glad to hear that you are so comfortable in your new home. I wish I was to be at home this winter to have a good time. But the longer this time the better I will like it when I come.

"Rosy" is giving the rebs fits in front. They have got Chattanooga, Cumberland Gap, etc.[23]

I wish you could see some of our negro regiments. There is one near us and we have to laugh to see the negro sargent drilling squads of them. They just got their guns and acutrements, they wear them all the time and carry their guns. They will get tired of that, you bet . . .[24]

NOTES

21. Redoubts were satellite fortifications associated with a larger fort.

22. Executions of soldiers for desertion or other crimes were rare but were sometimes carried out for their deterrent effect.

23. By this date the Army of the Cumberland had crossed the Tennessee River and was preparing to fight Bragg's forces at Chattanooga, a small but important industrial center and railroad gateway to the South.

24. Harvey Reid wrote from Murfreesboro on September 11, 1863: "A number of negro regiments are being organized in this Department . . . all negroes coming here must be set at work for the Government or enlist in the regiment and therefore they are recruiting fast. Few have any objections to becoming soldiers for they feel very proud of the honor." Reid, *Uncommon Soldiers*, 90. Although they constituted less than 1 percent of the North's population, black men would make up nearly one-tenth of the Northern army by the end of the war. Ward, *Civil War*, 252.

Camp 30 miles from Murfresboro, Sunday, Sept. 27, 1863

Dear Parents and Brother,

As I have a leisure hour, I will employ in trying to tell you of my whereabouts. As I wrote you the other evening we had orders about ten in the evening, while we were cooking rations for the wounded, to start in the morning for someplace farther south, at seven in the morning. So we routed out at 3:30 and hurried down to the depot, and like all Military movements, had to wait until twelve. About six in the afternoon we reached this place, 2 ½ miles from Wartrace—guarding a high and long bridge across Duck river. There are three of our companies here, and two of the 19th Michigan, and one of the 85th Indiana. There is considerable excitement here on account of the guerillas. They appear to be very anxious to cut the R.R. and thus having cut off Rosecrans communications, compelling him to retreat for want of rations. But I think we are well provided for them. A few days ago some of our cavalry caught some of them tearing up the tracks. They hung three of them to the nearest tree, and put this notice on a board over them. "A warning to all who tear up the R.R." The rest they kept prisoners. This is the way to use them. I have not heard the news from the front today, but the last I heard it was all going very well. We are gaining ground and constantly receiving reinforcements, but you never heard of such slaughter. Some regiments . . . now have but 60 men left for duty. There is one company in the 6th Wis. that has only one man and a Lt. left. This is fighting I should say. The Battery that belonged to our Brigade—the 18th Ohio Battery—they are all killed or wounded, and every horse was shot down.[25]

Love, Lute

NOTE

25. Lute described the news from the front, which he believed was going very well. The Battle of Chickamauga (Sept. 18–20, 1863) was actually a tactical defeat for Rosecrans and his Union forces, with a cost of 4,000 lives and more than 35,000 casualties in all. Ward, *Civil War*, 225, 226.

Camp Duck River, Oct. 3rd, 1863

. . . We are at the river but now I think we will stay a right smart while. We have seen but few rebs, for they make themselves scarce where-ever the invincible sharpshooters of the 22nd appear. I allow they are afraid of our new notoriety—if nothing else, and well they may be. This is a lonesome place I assure you.

Sunday, Oct. 11, cont.

As you will see I was obliged to leave off writing, and will now finish it. We have had a right smart of a time since, as you probably have heard, the R.R. between here and Murfresboro was all cut by the rebels, and there has been no communication for about a week. We have laid on our arms for this time, and the rebels have been very thick. They camp up within 4 miles of us and burned the R.R. bridge right in our faces, and they would not let us go out to stop them. We could have done it if they had let us go. We have been fortifying all the time—day time and some at nite. We built a nice fort, built a stockade too, and dug a lot of rifle pits, for we were expecting every minute that they would pitch into us. Our scouts were fighting them all the time. But now we have whipped them to our hearts content. There was at first only one company at the bridge, but it was reinforced until there were over 5 regiments and 8 cannons. We all expected there would be a big fight, but old Wilder [Colonel John T. Wilder] got after them and has whipped them nicely—so they were glad to get out. It did not take ½ day to fix the R.R., build the two bridges and have the cars running again.

Yesterday was the first mail we have had in two weeks. I got two from you and a dollar in each. There are any quantity of soldiers going down to help ol Rosy. There will be a big fight, I tell you. You said you heard we were dreadfully whipped the last fight. It is not so. We were overpowered in numbers, and driven back, but not whipped, and what is more we aint going to be whipped. We have been sent 2 ½ miles further to guard a little bridge. There are three companies of us and we are up on a mountain, over the track. IF the rebs come here, we will stone them away. There is a large cave in the mountain about half way up, that is 30 rods long. The mouth is straight before the bridge and well fortified, one company can go in there and the whole southern army can't get us out, only by siege. Cannon can't hurt us, and they can't get up to us. Besides we are building a block house and fortifying that. We have felled trees all along the edge of the mountain, and filled in behind with stone and dirt. It is awful steep. A man can't come up without stopping to rest. So you see we are safe. We belong to the reserve corp, and will not have to fight, unless we are needed dreadfully. So I don't care what Fairbanks told you—don't worry about us—we are safe. The most that worries us is that we are put on ½ rations. But we won't go very hungry. There are lots of fat cattle and pigs running around. We killed a hog yesterday that weighed about 175. When that is gone we will kill another. I shot a nice three-year old steer, and another fellow shot another a few days ago. We dressed them off, and then made the old reb that owned them yoke up his oxen and take them to camp. His name is Troxler, and owns a large farm and lots of cattle and negros, but can't read or write—a fair sample of all the inhabitants of Tennessee. Our boys captured a reb Major a few days ago.

All for now, Love, Lute

Sunday, Oct. 17, 1863

Dear Parents and Brother,

Camped again at Murfresboro, we have been for the last three weeks off on the R.R., 32 miles from here, guarding a bridge, at a place called Normandy. We expect to stay there, but yesterday morning, just as we finished our breakfast, we had orders to fall in, and then they told us to strike tents as quickly as possible, and go back to Murfresboro. So we did and went to the depot. After waiting—as is customary in all military movements—about three hours, we started and reached here about seven in the evening. So you see we are home again.

One of my tentmates was sick when we left here, and did not go. He kept the tent just as we left it, and it is a nice one. We had a big rain night before last. I was on guard, and it rained every single minute all night. I had charge of the Bridge guard. I had to sit up of course. We were within six miles of Tullahoma, where they took away our clothes.

You speak of coming down to try your luck and fortune in the sunny south, and ask my advice. I surely feel very loth to decide so great a question—one that may affect us all so much in the end. There is with this, as with all other like changes, its risks and disadvantages. There may be such a thing as that before another crop shall have matured the rebs will have possession of Nashville. It is the fortune of war you would have to contend with. Another thing, there are some union soldiers, in fact pretty near all, that consider every man south of the Cumberland a rebel, whether he is or not, and would forage on a union man as quick as a reb. So the righteous are punished as well as the wicked. But it is easy for you, if you bring vouchers from some of the principle men of Beloit, for your loyalty. Which be sure not to forget if you come, to get protection papers which will save you pretty much. For if they commense any such, you can go to the commanding officer and complain. He is bound to protect you. They did so with Fairbanks this last year.[26]

I will tell you honestly if I were in your place—and this is what I would advise—and should have advised before this if I had dared to do it. That is to come by all means—that is father, and father alone. I should never advise you to think of making a home here. Mother or Eddie would not be content here one hour. Such society and influences never would do to take any woman or child to—to ever think of enjoying themselves one bit. I haven't seen one southern person that would talk anything but negros. Over two thirds of them can't read or write and half of them can't change a dollar bill and take out 15 cents. So now the best thing, I think, would be for father to come, if he likes, have you all come. It won't cost you anything to live, for you can hire a negro to help you in the field and his woman to cook for you, for $5 a month. Please do as you think best, but the minute you decide, write to me, for I assure you I shall be very anxious to know.

Love, Lute

NOTE

26. Lute addressed the idea of his parents coming south, trying to advise them on the matter. While many in the Union states had prospered during the war, class divisions had deepened. Soldiers' families often struggled financially. Some were willing to go south to acquire cheap land, trade in captured cotton, or otherwise fill the economic vacuum. Robert G. Wells, *Wisconsin in the Civil War* (Milwaukee: The Journal Company, 1962), "Wisconsin Speculators Went South," ch. 35, 87.

Camp at Murfresboro, Sat., Oct. 23, 1863

Dear Brother Eddie,

. . . I will tell you Ed how it looks in my house. My house is 8 by 12 feet on the ground—4 ft. high on the sides, covered with cloth and sided on with pieces of board. It stands north and south. On the east side nails are driven in on which we hang our canteens, cups, coffee pot and little tin pails. In the middle of the house is a stove which is made just in the shape of a tunnel with the big side down; the pipe going down at the little end and a small hole in the side of it to put wood in. At the north is Ed Anderson's bed, over which is a box nailed to the side of the wall, which we use for cubbard. On the back side is Sam's and my bed. We sleep together. I am on the back side of our bed against the wall. At the south end we hang our coats and clothes; also the door is at this end. Sam [Miller] and I are writing at our table. Ed has gone out to spend an evening with some of our neighbors.

Yesterday I was called upon to go on camp guard and was all ready when orders came to furnish 100 men for picket and I had to go. It was raining powerful hard, but that wouldn't excuse me, so off I poked, and was sent out on the Nashville pike. It rained all day without stopping, and we hadn't the least show of shelter. We stood there just as some poor ol cows stand in a storm side of a fence. At nite it cleared off, and whew, how cold. It was so cold I could not think of sleeping. So Wm Minot sat there and told stories. This isn't hard to us but it is a fair specimen of a soldier's work. Don't you even think of going soldiering and don't let father. One fool in the family is enough. A man thinks he is enlisting to put down the rebellion, but not so, only to gratify some big Man's ambition, and at the same time to fill their pockets.

You put a wrong meaning on what I wrote you about our having only ½ rations. That was only for 10 days—until they could get the R.R. repaired again. We get our regular full rations now, excepting what the Capt [George H. Brown] steals from us, which amounts to over $10 a month. Oh, if he aint a rascal there never was one.

Mother wanted to know how we lived now. I have a bushel of potatoes, and 15 lbs. flour. We forage for potatoes, not leaving a great many for the owner, we pick apples and killed a pig before going back to camp. So we don't starve.

Eddie I am proud of you. How I would like to see you. You will beat me to pieces getting property—but go in—I love to see it. How many sheep do I own? I don't know.

Sunday morning, and it is cloudy and cold. Hope it will warm up as I go on picket tomorrow. I expect we will have some more excitement here soon, for last nite we heard 20,000 rebs have crossed the Tennessee river and probably be up this way soon, but we are well provided for and ready to give them a warm welcome.

You have heard that Gen. Rosecrans was superseded. We are well suited with the ones we have got, but hate dreadfully to give up "Old Rosy." We all had confidence in him, but I suppose he made his pile, and is willing to let someone else have a turn.[27]

I am so sorry to hear grandmother is sick. I hope she will get well soon and I will return to see her. I miss her.

Love, Lute

NOTE

27. Rosecrans, discredited by the defeat at Chickamauga, was replaced by Maj. Gen. George H. Thomas.

Sunday, Nov. 1, 1863

Dear home,

I will write a short note tonight, as I go on picket duty in the morning . . . Last Thursday Sime and I got outside of the pickets and went down to the river, about two miles and a half, after mussel shells. I got a haversack full of nice ones. We got them right where our forces and the rebs had a hard fight at the time of a large battle here. It does not look as tho a man could possibly have escaped being hit, by the holes in the trees, and the limbs that were cut off by shot and shell. Cartridge boxes, canteens, and the likes strewn all over. I found a reb pipe. I would have looked after more but we had no pass and were afraid the gurellas would pick us up. The boys are nearly all making picture cases out of these shells that are beautiful. They sell from one to five dollars a piece here. I have made one and am going to make more to send home, but I have no files. Pole got 4 in his box, but he won't even lend me one. I wish I had sent for some with my boots. They are worth 75 cents a piece here—like half round files. If you have a chance, send me one or two.

If you have any of my photographs you can spare, I wish you would send me some. For Josie and Fannie think hard of me because I don't send them my picture, after sending me theirs. I will make cases for them.

Yesterday we were mustered for pay, and will probably get it soon. There is four months due me.

Frank Kelly has gone into the band to fill the place Baker was in. He has a first Lt. commission in a negro regiment, so we are all shoved up a notch . . . Sam and I have a dog. He is a nice one too . . .

❧

Murfresboro, Fri, Nov. 13, 1863

Kind respected loved ones,

I received your welcome letter of the 8th today, and also it is after rolecall. I am going to answer this evening.

A few days ago I received a pair of boots and a box of catsup from you, and today I got the gloves, but not the tea you spoke of. Ed F. [Fairbanks] went to Nashville and brot the boots, and today the gloves came by express. The boots are good ones and suit me exactly, only they are short, but I shall wear them. But oh, that catsup—my conscience wasn't that good. I could not let it alone until it was gone.

Sam got a box weighing 98 pounds from home this week. He had 3 qt. cans filled with blackberries—three with honey—one large coffee can of tobacco—over 10 pounds of butter, six mince pies, 2 loaves of bread, 2 cabbages, some nice potatoes, etc. He told me to use it all just as if it were mine. It is just as free to me as to himself, and it is just so with all we have. He is a good boy, if he did run at the first fight. Pole and he are down at the coral guarding horses, to keep them from being stolen. They have a horse and saddle apiece to use whenever they have a mind to. So Sam brings his up to camp every day and I take it and ride, enjoy it very much.

I am perfectly content as long as they leave us here. Some of the Janesville and Racine boys have boxes from home. That will keep them nearly all winter in butter and the like. If we can get butter we can get along well enough, for we get a little baker's bread and some flour which we make pancakes of, and eat our crackers when we are on picket. Capt. [George H. Brown] bot us 10 bushels of potatoes yesterday with the company fund. They cost 12 dollars. That is just one peck per man. There is about $40 per month in this fund if we could only get it, but our noble captain keeps it. This is the first we have ever had. This evening we selected a committee—Fairservice, Rose and Adams, to see the capt. and demand our back money, and if he refuses to give it up, Ira Nye is going to carry it up and see that we get it. The capt. has no right with it at all, but a man elected out of the company as treasurer. We elected Ira. We will have a hard time getting it, but we are bound to have it, for it belongs to us. Capt. is a cutthroat, a robber, unprincipled excuse for a man, 10 times worse than Northrop, besides being as big a coward as ever lived. How can men fight and do themselves credit under such a man? How different from Ira; he is a true man and honest, one that is loved and respected. Capt. Brown is trying to get Ira into a fuss and have him discharged, but he can't do it. I don't want you to tell this from me. As far as Hank Hodges being a sargent—let me tell you that he is not even a corporal any more. I am a step higher now, 7th corp and expect soon to be fifth. You see I am coming up . . .

I have been getting into debt a little this week. I got the blacksmith to put me on some heel plates, which are necessary for marching on the pikes, for 25 cents. I got a tailor to put in some pockets in my overcoat for 30 cents. My dress coat was torn and worn out some. The lining was all out, so I got him to cut it off—making a round about with it and take the tails to mend the rest and fix it up for $1. This you see will last me all winter and save me drawing a new one, which would cost $7.50. They guessed off our last years clothing account, for the books and papers were all taken by the rebs. They put mine at $51.71—allowed $42 per year, leaving me in debt to the government nearly $10. I have to make it up this year or they will take it out of my pay. Haven't I drawn more money from home that I had there? If so don't send me any more until there is some paid in. Expect we will get paid off soon. Four months is due us . . .

I am glad, Ed, you are having some fun hunting. I have learned a lot about handling a gun. All for now, my fingers are sore from grinding shells. Write soon.

Selden, a sharp shooter from the sunny south.

Murfresboro, Fri., Nov. 20, 1863

Dear ones at home,

. . . It has been raining like fun all day and is very muddy and slippery. I have written two letters before this. Last evening I went down town to a union meeting. There were some beautiful speeches made—one by Col. Smith [Colonel Orland Smith, 73rd Ohio Infantry]. He was out in Missouri under Freemont [General John C. Fremont] and is a fine man. He says he thinks the war will last but little longer. He says all we have to do it to clean the little place between Chattanooga and Richmond. One speech was from a chaplain that enlisted as a private when the first gun was fired at Sumter. I hope they are right and the war does not last much longer. I know of one boy who would like to go home and see his Ma.

I am glad if that case I sent home suited you. I have made 5 of them. I work at them because it passes the time. If you have a piece of silver of any shape that will do to make rivits of, I wish you would send it to me in a letter. Mother speaks of getting shells to cover a frame. I could do it if I had the shells.

I don't want to frighten you but there has been for the last few weeks considerable smallpox here. There is a pest hospital outside of the pickets, where they are taken as soon as it is found out. It is mostly confined to negros, and some few citizens. There has been but one case in our regiment. I don't think you should say anything about it, for it might frighten such folks as Sime Sage's wife half to death.[28]

Father, do you know any relatives of yours in Mississippi. I saw a board at the head of a grave marked "Lt. J.F. Moseley, 10th Miss." Of course he was a reb, shot by one of our sharpshooters.

Mother speaks about her poor letters. I do wish you wouldn't Mother, for if you call yours poor, what do you think of the things I send you for letters. You don't know the value of your letters to me. I am sorry I did not improve my time better when I was at home. This war has learned me a good lesson, and as long as I can't improve by that lesson now, brother Eddie, let me with all kindness, give you a little advice. That is to go to school and learn all you can. But don't study Latin or Greek. I waisted two years at it and am no better off.

You say you all love me. I know you do. Be assured your soldier son loves you too, many an hour he sits by the picket fire and thots are on home, instead of on his business. I must close.

Your son, Selden

NOTE

28. Smallpox was one of the dreaded diseases affecting Civil War soldiers. Although vaccination had been available for three decades, many troops entered the service without that protection.

❧

Murfresboro, Sat., Nov. 28, 1863

My dear loved Mother,

I received your very welcome letter today. I would have got it yesterday if the cars had come thru from Nashville. The box came today and is down at the depot. We will have it as soon as the quartermaster will go down after it. I shall write to Grandmother this evening and thank her for what she sent me. I think everything of her. I shall write to Mrs. Miller and thank her for the splendid loaf of bread she sent me. I was on picket yesterday and ate it all myself.

Mother, I haven't words to express my thanks to you and father and Eddie for your great kindness to me, I love each of you. I cannot help shedding a tear of joy to know I have such a dear family. Ed Anderson, my tentmate, is an orphan; was brot from N.Y. City to Geneva, and a man brot him up. He don't know as he has a relative in the world. How different from me, and yet he is a good boy. How often he wishes he had a home and friends.

Last night on picket it was cold and dark and rained all nite. We did not get tired of it because we have had such good news for the last few days. Last night there were 14,000 rebel prisoners went thru here, and I expect there will be more today. They are a sorry looking set, I assure you. Our men do not run out and insult them as they did us. They (our men) had good food, and good cars to ride in and clothes to keep them warm. So you see the difference in the north and south.

Yesterday Sime Sage, Dick Radway, Wm. Minot, Sam Miller and I got some horses and saddles and went out about eight miles and got some shells. I got about ½ bushel. We had a fine time. Took dinner with an ol rebel. Wm Minot and I had some sport talking with the daughter, a young lady about 18. She is a strong rebel. Her sweetheart is in the rebel army. I spun some cotton there.

I got mother's pin done and some shirt studs for father. The shell in them is a piece the old Colonel gave me. He does the nicest work I ever saw. I was up there looking at it tonight.

There is considerable talk about us leaving here. Probably to Knoxville. News is very scarce with us.

Pole has felt very jealous towards me since I made corporal, and has taken every way he could to hurt me. So he has told I wrote home about my great and daring deeds, and how much bolder I was than the rest of the company. I wrote nothing but the truth, but you know how easy it is to get up big stories. My eyes are heavy so I will finish. Did grandmother ever get my letter? We must have permits for everything, to go into town and even to buy sugar. It is the Corporal's duty to see every pass and permit of every man that goes on picket line, and if they have goods without a permit, to confiscate it.

Love, Lute

❧

Murfresboro, Tenn., Nov. 29, 1863

Dear loved ones,

Sunday morning and it isn't quite as cold as yesterday, but it is trying to snow. I think they will give us furloughs this winter, but I may not take one. It would cost me over $60 and it would take half the time to get there and come back. What do you think?

Silas Bibbins brother-in-law was left here sick and his wife came here to see him. He died and she was reported to be very sick, so they gave Sile a furlough of ten days to take her home to N.Y. As soon as he got the furlough, she was able to walk to the depot, so instead of going to N.Y. they went to Beloit. Sile says he will get his furlough extended when he gets home. He is the biggest shirk I ever knew.

Lt. Col. Bloodgood went to Washington to the President and was reinstated. I don't know if he will come back to this regiment or not. So you see I was not alone in my opinion of him.[29]

. . . You say that you have heard Ira Nye was poisoned to death. This is the way of it. A few days after we went down to Duck River bridge, Lt. Nye and Annis of Company G, went to a union man's house to get their dinner. When they came back, Ira told me he was going to have the Ague, but he didn't have it that day.[30] So the next morning he felt so well he thot he was over it, and he and Annis went over there again. While they were waiting, Ira said he was sick and started for camp. He got about ½ of the way back and then had to stop. Lt. came running into camp and told us Ira was back there very sick, and wanted some of us to go after him. Sile Wright heard him and hollored out as loud as he could: "Ira Nye is poisoned, and is dying." Eight or more of us started after him, they all went the wrong road but me. I found him in the height of a hard fever, and dying for a drink. He was glad to see me, I tell you. I got a pail of water, a pillow and some camphor from the nearest house and did all I could for him. In about ½ hour some of the other boys came up and got a horse and buggy and got him back to camp. I took the whole care of him the next day and he had another and a worse one and I did all I could for him. He went to Murfresboro the next day. He wasn't sick any more and came back to us in a few days. Ira is the best boy I was ever acquainted with and has been very good to me. How I wish our Captain was like Ira, but he is just the other way, meanest liar I ever knew. He is trying to get a chance to reduce me in rank, and will at the first opportunity. I am ready for him. I know my duty and shall do it every time. He thot he had me one day. I said I would not work on the fortifications, and he said he would make me, so I told him to pitch in. He didn't make me after all. I know my place. They can't make a non-comissioned officer work, but I won't write any more about him, for you have trouble enough without mine.

I was on guard down at the depot a few nights ago, and there was a train came in from the front loaded with negro women and children. I never knew what want was. If they weren't a pitiful looking lot of humans, I never want to see any that are. I had a loaf of bread and some coffee, and I gave it to them. You ought to have seen their big eyes stick out. I remember the negro that gave me the corn cake at Tullahoma. They all got rations in the morning. They came from Alabama, and say there isn't ¼ enough to eat there. Some of them were real smart. I wish mother had one of them at home to help her.

I have a couple of rebel revolvers. I hope I can get a chance to send one home to Ed. They aren't worth anything, only as a relic. Our men took them from the rebs and sent them here to keep the rebs from getting them back.

I wish father would write to me what he is calculating on for business when I come home. He mus'nt place too much expectation on me, for I am not very smart, but you know that.

Give my respects to Mrs. Miller and thank you all for all your good letters.

Love to all, Selden

NOTES

29. Lt. Col. Bloodgood had made a trip to Washington in November but was not yet reinstated. Harvey Reid celebrated the news of Bloodgood's return on January 3, 1864, yet he expected Colonel Utley would be too stubborn to resign. Reid, *Uncommon Soldiers*, 111, 112. *The Semi-Weekly Wisconsin News* (Milwaukee) published an announcement on January 2, 1864: "We learn that the President has disapproved of the sentence of the court-martial which dismissed Lt. Col. Bloodgood from his command in the 22d regiment and has ordered him reinstated."

30. "Ague" was a term for the symptoms of high fever, chills, sweating, and body aches, which could be caused by a communicable disease or malaria.

Murfresboro, Sat., Dec. 7, 1863

Dear family,

. . . The reason I write today instead of tomorrow is because I have picket duty. I am sure you are tired about hearing about picket duty, but that is what we do the most. I am well now as ever except a sour stomach, which I expect to have as long as I am in the army.

You know I wrote you that Lt. Col. B [Bloodgood] was dismissed, and that I thought it was not right. Well I did think so, and still do. The boys got up a paper stating that they had the greatest confidence in him, and believed

him to be a good officer and one that loved his country, and wished his success where ever he might go. Over 100 names were already on it when I
signed it. The Col. [Utley] has already been given written orders to leave
the regiment—stating that the regiment had already been disgraced by him
long enough. This paper was to be given to B. [Bloodgood] but the Col.
found out about it, and went to the boys that had it, and demanded it from
them. They handed it to him and he looked it over and handed it back.

This morning I asked the Capt [Brown] for a pass to town, which he gave
me. Then as I was busy, Ed took it to the Col. [Utley] to get it signed The
old fellow looked at it and gave it back and said he would not sign it until
after guard mounting. I waited until then and took it up myself. He read it
and looked at me and said, "You are Mr. Moseley are you?" I told him my
name was Moseley. He signed the pass, but turned around and said, "You
signed the paper praising Lt. Col. Bloodgood and saying you had the greatest confidence in his courage and patriotism and believed him to be a
good soldier, did you?" I assumed as much of a military air as possible and
replied "Yes Sir." Then he broke out on me, you bet. He talked to me like a
dutch uncle, saying, "Moseley, I have known you to be a brave and good
soldier, and have already commenced to reward you and help you to a better
position and still intend to help you, for I believe you are a brave boy. I saw
you on the battlefield, and have noticed you all thru, and this is the reason
I blame you. For if you were a coward, I should not wonder. It is natural for
one coward to support another, but I am very much surprised that so brave
a man as you should support and indorse so great a coward and scoundrel
as Bloodgood." He said I was guilty of mutiny and treason—the penalty for
which is death. But this affair he supposed would not be looked into or that
we would be punished at all. There are about 350 men here, of which 225
signed the paper. I told him I did not intend anything such as mutiny, treason or disrespect of any of my officers, by putting my name on it, and I thot
one man could be a friend of two if the two didn't agree. I did not in the
least intend to show any disrespect by it. I always had and always would
support my superior officers. He said he knew it and knew the motives
I had in signing it, but I might take my name off yet if I felt disposed. I
talked with quite a number of the other Corporals and sergeants and they
all said they wouldn't take their name off, and as I believed what I signed,
I wouldn't be the first. I am the only one in the regiment that the Col. has
spoken to about it. He has not spoken to me in a long time. I didn't even
know he knew me. I suppose he will not take as much interest in me as he

otherwise would, but that he has a good opinion of me I have no doubt. Now father I want you to tell me if I did wrong.[31]

Hank Rosecrans came over to see me today. He has just got a letter from Flora. She sent her respects to me. I received the dollar you spoke of. The boots should come on Monday. I will be as tickled to get them as a little boy. If you send me a box, put in butter, cheese, pickles and popcorn. I should be paid on the 16th. This is all for tonight.

Write soon to you son, Selden, a soldier from the sunny south.

NOTE

31. Colonel Utley resumed command of the 22nd Wisconsin on November 4, 1863. A petition supporting Bloodgood circulated through the regiment, enraging Utley who threatened to "reduce to the ranks every noncommissioned officer who signed it." In November, Governor Salomon of Wisconsin wrote to President Lincoln, enclosing a copy of the petition, asking that the conduct of Colonel Utley be investigated. The conflict continued to affect the morale throughout the regiment. Groves, *Blooding the Regiment*, 243–46.

✺

Murfresboro, Fri, Dec. 11, 1863

Dear ones at home,

The train time has been changed here, so I did not get your letter till today, and I was glad to get it. I had a dream about you a few nites ago, and altho I don't in the least believe in dreams, I could not help but feel very anxious to hear from you. Not much has transpired this week that is very interesting. Sile Bibbins has got a detail as horse farrier at the government stable. Sime Sage, All Getten and I got us some horses and went out in the country yesterday. We had a nice time, but Al's horse gave entirely out, so he had to walk in about 5 miles.

Have you made up your mind what you will do next summer? I wish I was home, I would try something. I am not sorry I came when I did, for if I had stayed at home I would be drafted and now have the long years before me, instead of 19 months . . .[32]

I want to say a word to you father, about enlisting.[33] If I were out, no 40 dollars a month would induce me to go as a private. You may think it is easy earned. One month would convince you to the contrary. No, my dear good father, don't even think of going, for my sake if not for your own, for I never could be contented if you were in the army. Just look at it, we haven't been out only 15 months. When we left Racine we had 91 men. Now we haven't over 42 all told. Another thing, wheather you believe it or not, an old man can't stand it half as well as a young man. You won't go, will you father? I want you to promise me, and then I will feel contented.

Lennard Rose and Fairservice have preferred charges against Cap. Brown for drunkenness, dishonesty, and cowardice, which will be the means of getting rid of him. If they do succeed, we are going to give Rose 5th Sargent. That will keep me from getting up one step, but I shall be glad to have him have it. I am 6th Sargent now, so you see I have come up two notches. Sime Sage is next below me. He has charge of a lot of men building the commissary building. I expect Hank Hodge is a Sarg. now.[34]

All my love, Sel

NOTES

32. The first National Conscription Act was passed on March 3, 1863. Prior to that time, the Union army had obtained its troops from volunteers and state militia called into Federal service. Opposition was widespread, even though the need for additional troops in the prolonged war was apparent. The act declared that all able-bodied males between 20 and 45 were liable for service. It listed exemptions, permitted substitutes, and provided for enforcement. Nonetheless, drafted soldiers made up only 6 percent of Union forces. See Faust, ed., *Historical Times Illustrated Encyclopedia of the Civil War*, 225.

33. Lute's father, Selden Devotion Moseley, was 52 years old at the time this letter was written. Possibly Selden Moseley considered enlisting for financial and/or patriotic reasons. Although men 18 to 45 were considered eligible for service in both the Union and Confederate armies, many exceptions were made and it was often difficult to verify a soldier's age. Jim Sundman, "And Your Age Is . . . ?" Emerging Civil War, https://www.emergingcivilwar.com/2011/12/01/and-your-age-is/.

34. Privates had hopes of becoming corporals; corporals had hopes of becoming sergeants or even captains. A captain's earnings were almost ten times those of a private. Richard N. Current, *The History of Wisconsin, Volume II; The Civil War Era* (Madison: State Historical Society of Wisconsin, 1976), 360.

༄

Murfresboro, Dec. 25, 1863

Dear parents and brother,

It is now in the evening of Xmas day. I received your very kind letter today, and will endeavor to write a few lines. I feel greatly indebted to your promptness in writing me. You may want to know how I spent the day. In the first place I was on camp guard last night and had to sit up until one o'clock. Then I went to bunk, and did not get until Ed had the fire built. I ate a piece of bread and then got a pass to go to town. Just as I was going the mail came, and with it two letters for me. One from you containing one dollar and some stamps, and one from Oliver Smith in California. I went down town and tried to get some potatoes but couldn't, and so I came back. Ed had got a chicken, and we went to work and cooked it, and made two dried apple pies. Ed made some dumplings, and if we didn't have a good dinner I am mistaken, that's all . . .

We are having the nicest winter I ever saw. No snow has fallen and the ground has been frozen but little. We run around in our shirt sleeves most of the time. The boys never want to go back to Wisconsin.

Leonard Rose has gone home to guard conscripts. I sent my revolver to you by him. Please offer him pay for it, he is a penurious fellow, you know . . . There is a Lieutenant and ten sergeants going home from this regiment to recruit. Lt. Patton (Marshall W. Patton, Company I) is going and sarg. James Ross from our company. When they go I shall send a rebel revolver I have and some shell work. They won't go for two or three weeks.

I will tell you something now if you won't tell. Sile Wright went down town today, and is now in the lockup. The report is, he was caught stealing a pair of boots. At any rate, he was drunk and was fighting. This is a pretty mess for a soldier to have written home about him. I would rather be shot, I believe.

I guess when we get our pay, I shall buy me a watch, for a corporal needs one very much. I have to borrow one every time I am on guard to tell what time to put on the relief. What do you think of it?

Capt. Brown has been on a spree now for a number of days. I hope he will keep on until he gets court-marshaled. We boys talk to him just as we have a mind to. I don't know as I ought to write it. Give my love to Grandmother.

Love, Selden

✿

Murfreesboro, Saturday, Jan. 2, 1864

Dear Mother and brother,

This is my first letter in "64" and I have little news. The weather for the last 3 days has been dreadful cold. I never saw such a sudden and severe change of weather in my life. The wind is blowing almost like a gale. I had to run out and nail my tent to keep it from going over. Then it commenced to hail. It snowed a little and is very cold. The boys on picket suffer, they have no shelter at all at most of the posts. In camp we are very comfortable. Have plenty of cedar wood and warm clothes, we can have as much stuff as we want.

I am on camp guard again tonight, which is very lucky, for I can come in by a good fire.

. . . Today was the general inspection and muster. It is the healthiest time we have ever had. There isn't a man in the hospital now, last report there were only 15 men sick in the whole brigade. Last year they were dying from our regiment from one to five per day . . .

I went out to chop wood one day, in Ed's place. They can't detail corporals for that. The roads were so bad they couldn't draw it, so we chopped it and dragged it out and piled it up and stacked it on the side of the road. It is all clear, the trees were felled just before the fight here, for it is on the battleground, so it is dry. There were 30 of us chopping. I said I wished my folks had a pile of wood like this at home. How do you get along for wood this winter? Ed and I go to bed early and then one of us gets up about two and builds up the fire. We are warm as can be . . . Accept your son's love and excuse a poor letter.

Write soon and oblige, L.S. Moseley

Murfresboro, Jan. 22, 1864

Kind and respected parents,

I spend many a sad and lonely hour thinking of dear ones at home. But my duty is here and will be until this cruel war is over.

Our brave leader, Gen. US Grant, went thru here the day before yesterday and he told us to keep up good cheer, for we would all go home before the first of October.[35] We have some hard scenes to go thru before then, but we are not inclined to be discouraged. No, do not give up—every thing is encouraging. I will not stop soldiering now if my time was up, for I came in to see the war ended, and I will if I have to stay 2 or 3 years. I have not been as lucky as some, and have not risen as high as you have expected of me, but I have no influential friends to help me up. I do not want to hold a position until I am competent to fill it.

I was on picket last night, and slept but little, so I feel rather sleepy. Someone took my blankets yesterday. I had my woolen blanket rolled up and my rubber blanket.

We have some new recruits in the regiment—only one for our company. It makes us laugh to see how green they are. They all look so white and don't know how to eat, soldier fashion. The old Colonel says he don't want any recruits. For all that are left, that were tough enough to live thru, what we have can't be killed with clubs, and he doubts some if we can be with lead. Five of the new ones had to report to the hospital the first morning.

Father appears to feel uneasy about affairs in the front, but he need not, for our army is not weakened by furloughed men, as more than enough new ones are put in their places to fill it. I don't believe the rebs will ever be able to whip us. We all think by next Sunday we will be in Nashville. We don't feel any fear of going to the front, on the contrary—many would be glad to go. I don't think that we will be ordered front. The probabilities are that we will go to Nashville or someplace between there and Louisville or the R.R. So much for moving.

Liet. Col. Bloodgood is back here and has reported to Utley for duty; but he refuses to receive him; says his papers are not right. We all think everything of Col. Bill Utley. This affair makes both of them better to the men, as both want the men on his side. Did you see the piece in the Wis. Journal about B[Bloodgood]? It was the most abusive thing I ever saw in my life.

I sent my knife to Ed, and he lost it. I was very sorry. I got it in St. Louis for 50 cents, now can't buy one for $1.50. My fingers are cold and I can't write so had better close.

My love, Lute

NOTE

35. Following General Grant's campaign in Tennessee, President Lincoln called him to Washington (March 1864) and put him in charge of all military operations.

Still at Murfresboro, Sunday, Feb. 7th, 1864

Dear Home,

I wrote you a short letter a few days ago. In it I told you we were going to start for Nashville. I guess the letter was not half way to Nashville when the order was countermanded, so we are still here. What the reason is I don't know. We all think that before next Sunday we will be at Nashville . . .[36]

I was anxiously watching the mail for the last four days. Wondering all the time why I didn't get a letter from you, till this morning as soon as revelle was beat, I heard the boys holloring—"Mr. Perry is down at the corral." I only waited to answer my name at rollcall, and took marching orders for the corral, double quick. They were just getting up on my arrival. If I wasn't glad to see him. I never was so glad to see anyone. After talking a few minutes, he said he supposed I was hard up, and he would let me have a little. So he did. Then he said "maybe this will say something about it," handing me a letter and then another one. He said to read it and see if it tells you about it. Then he gave me the tea, apples and currents and butter. Then he gave me some gingersnaps Mrs. Perry had made. He also gave me a pie, onions, corn and paper and envelopes. Breakfast was readdy by this time and the boys ask me to eat with them, so I did. Then we went back to camp, and Ed had breakfast readdy for me, so I ate again. We spent the time talking and looking around until 4 P.M., when he took the cars for Nashville. He is to get $60 per month, and rations. He said father talked some of coming too. I am almost sorry you didn't. You couldn't get a job that would suit you. I am satisfied that if I was a citizen, I could just make money here. I would not advise you to come for fear what would happen, sickness or something. Thank you for all your kindness to me. How little I have done to merit it. Please give my kind thanks to Mrs. Perry and Mrs. Dawson.

It is so cold I can hardly write. It has been very cold all day. You ask about Capt. [Brown]. I am happy to say ere this reaches you, I think he will be disgracefully dismissed from the service, thus ridding us one of the meanest specimens of a man I ever knew. His trial comes off Thursday.[37]

. . . I have Mother's pin done and am in hopes it will suit. Shall send it, I guess. So dear ones it is late, I will close with much love and respects. Give my best respects to Mrs. M. and family. You must not get the blues, for if you could see the people here—how they get along, you wouldn't think the future so hard for us.

Love, Lute

NOTES

36. The 22nd Wisconsin had been on garrison duty at Murfreesboro since July 3, 1863; they left for Nashville on February 24, 1864.

37. Captain George Brown was tried for a long list of misbehaviors, including drunkenness, embezzlement of his company's savings, and threatening his accusers. In spite of all the evidence against him, "a very bad apple was tossed back into the barrel." He finally resigned in March 1865 for health reasons. Groves, *Blooding the Regiment*, 319, 320, 327.

∽

Camp near Nashville, Mon., Feb. 29, 1864

Dear ones at home,

It is a cold wet, disagreeable morning. We moved our camp yesterday, and fortunately for us, we got our tents up and inclosed, so we are almost dry. At the same time, it is very different from sitting in a good house by a warm, cheerful fire. We are content tho, and think ourselves much better off than the boys in the front, for they have nothing but their tents alone.

I have not received a letter from you since the 7th, excepting the ones Mr. Perry brought me. It is very strange. I think it is not your fault, I think you write and they are detained somewhere along the road. You know we agreed if there was anything the matter with either of us, we would let the other know the worst. I hope you will, for I shall. I have the blues sure this morning, and why shouldn't I have? We are in mud up to our—you know what, and it is still raining. I have a bad cold which causes my head to ache, and what is worse than all, have not heard from you in a long time. By morning I will be all right again. You must not think I mean to find fault with you, for surely I don't.

Yesterday, Messers Perry, Fairbanks, Atchley, Alexander, Rathbon, and several other Beloit men were up to see us. They are well suited, and doing well.

Our duty here is not nearly as heavy as it was in Murfresboro. We don't know for certain what we have to do. There is a detail every day for a train guard—to guard the passenger train from here to the front.[38]

I am now, as you know, twenty-one years old, and to tell you the truth, am very sorry. I wish I was but eighteen.

I wrote a short note to you, the twenty-sixth, and as we are all wrong side up, our hands full, and our pants to hold up, I shall write but little this morning.

I now tent in No. 3 tent, and have for tentmates, Serg. Murry, George Perkins, and Sam Miller. I like them first rate. Mr. Fairbanks is here now, and thinks we are pretty bad off in the mud, but we laugh at him. Please write to me.

Love to all. L.S. Moseley

38. The 22nd Wisconsin was now assigned the mission of keeping the line of communication from Nashville to Chattanooga open and serving as guards aboard the trains.

Nashville, March 4, 1864

Dear parents and brother,

I thot I would write you a few lines, for you may want to know where I am and how I am getting along. No news, we are about one mile from the city—between Fort Negley and a Fort I don't know the name of. We have had the worst storm I have seen this winter—snow and rain. I never saw the mud so bad, but it is again pleasant and the wind is blowing very hard, so the mud is disappearing. We boys all thot that when we got here every-thing would be cheaper, but we found to the contrary. The roads are so bad, it is impossible to get wood and the only thing we could get was crackers. We couldn't get wood to cook anything, so we bot our living pretty much. We got our pay a few days ago, for two months. I have been trading a little, and owe Pole $5. I also bot me a hat. The ones we drew cost $2.50. I have had two in less than seven months. Now I have $6 in my pocket, and am to pay Mrs. Perry $10. Five I owe to Pole and five to Mr. Perry. Now I know you will think I have squandered money. I am ashamed to ask you to pay this, but I haven't spent a cent foolishly, so please pay Mrs. Perry $10 when this allotment gets to you. We will get two months pay in a short time.

I am and have been for the last two days in camp all the time, for the ol Colonel has summoned me as a witness on the court-marshal of Capt. Bones.[39] I was down town all one day, but have not been called upon yet. I have to stay here so if I am wanted, they will know where to find me. The old Colonel has a leave of absence and is going home as soon as this court-marshal is over. I don't know what they will do with Capt. Brown. He stays down town and does not come near us . . .

Speaking about wood—it has sold here for $50 a cord, but now there is an order against selling it for over $15. I thot I would pick up some chips

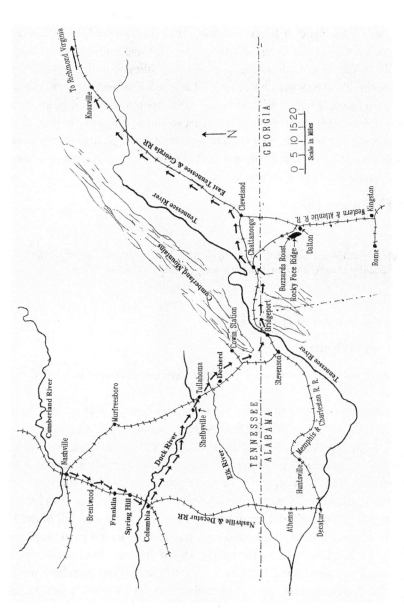

Southern Tennessee and northern Georgia (courtesy of the Moseley family)

last night, and went over a mile, and got only three little pieces of sticks, but they have furnished us enough now.

Just one year ago this very hour, I was listening to the booming of cannon, the first I had ever heard that was meant to take the lives of human beings. Then it was nothing but fun for me, for I was confident of success. We drove them, and advancing, camped two miles the other side of the encounter, but alas, what a bitter lesson I learned. The next day, one we will not soon forget. I hope I will never be called upon to take part in another such a mess. At least I tried to act my part so you would never be ashamed of your son and brother. Even if I fell, you could say I fell nobly at my post. There are some in the company that cannot say so. Supper is ready so I must close. Write soon and direct to Nashville.

Your loving son, Lute

NOTE

39. Captain William Bones, Company K, 22nd Wisconsin, was one of several officers to suffer consequences arising from disputes with Colonel Utley.

∽

Nashville, March 17, 1864

Dear ones at home,

I have not written this week yet, for I have been on duty so I could not write.

It is quite cold this morning. Yesterday the ground was covered with snow, at the same time the peach trees are in bloom. This is a queer country for sure. Mr. Perry doesn't like it here, and will start home soon. He says he can't live on government rations, and won't believe that he gets as much as we soldiers, but he does, and if he was obliged to stay he would soon get used to them. I think when he comes I shall send some things with him.

I have been down to Chattanooga, and got back yesterday. Bill Minot is detailed as train guard on the passenger trains, so he let me go in his place. I staid in the same building the 12th of March this year that I did one year ago as a prisoner of war. The place looks natural, only our men have made some improvements in the way of fortifications etc. I saw Mission Ridge and Lookout Mountain. It doesn't look possible for any force to take that place, it is so awful high and so perpendicular. The boys down there think we could take any place with U.S. Grant or old Rosy to lead. This is the same R.R. that we went through on one year ago. We passed thru the same tunnel one half mile in length and across the same high bridge that the rebs backed us over for fear it would break down.

Ira Nye has left us. He has been detailed as Civil engineer. We are awfully sorry to lose him, for a better man never lived. He told us he would not have left us, only to get out from under old Capt. Brown's command, who has come back to the company. We thot we would get rid of him but we can't yet. I guess we will after a while. He is the meanest man I ever knew. Old Col. Utley has gone home for a twenty day furlough.[40] He did not swear me in on his court-martial, for he asked me if I would swear to such and such things. I told him "no," so he didn't want me at all.

All my love, Lute

NOTE

40. Harvey Reid's letter of March 13, 1864: "Colonel Utley started for home Friday morning, having received a telegram the evening previous that his wife was much worse. He received his leave of absence the week before but wished to stay to see Captain Bones' court-martial out. Lieutenant Colonel Bloodgood is now in command of the regiment and already there is shown a difference in the attention to discipline and military efficiency." Colonel Utley's wife died before he arrived home. (Reid, *Uncommon Soldiers*, 121, 122.)

❧

Nashville, March 27, 1864

Dear Home,

. . . Colonel Utley is still at home, so now Bloodgood is in command of the regiment, and oh my! The style, inspections, battalion drills, dress parades and so forth, all the time . . .

John Pomroy [Pomeroy] is at length back with us. He was wounded and captured, and was 70 days in Dixie. He fell right by my side on the first hill— has been away from us for over one year, and he is crippled. Will probably get a discharge now. He is a good soldier and we hate to lose him. . . .

Now I want to tell you something I don't want you to tell. When we were in Murfresboro, Pole was down at the convalescent corral as guard. Every little while there would be mules or horses put in there that weren't branded so in the night when he was on guard to keep this same property secure, he would catch a mule or a horse and put it in the old log barn and then sell it to a man there, sometimes getting $45. It is pretty certain that the buyer of these mules ran them off into the rebs lines. He used to spend sights of money there for anything he wanted but didn't send any one home, so when the old man came down here he told him and gave him $175. When his father goes home he is going to buy Mrs. Perry a new piano. Now what do you think of that? Now what would you think if your son did that? He may never get caught, but if he does he will find he doesn't have civil law to deal with.

The tattoo is beating and in a few minutes we will have to turn out to roll call. Lt. Col. has issued orders against having our lights burning after taps at nine o'clock, so I will have to close. We are now doing duty in town and not standing any picket. The old 33rd Indiana in our brigade have gone into the veterans and now have gone home on furlough. One of the veterans didn't want to go home, so he sold his furlough to one of the others for $60. He said he considered that about $120 for he would spend more than $60 if he went home.

Love to all of you, remember me to grandmother.

As ever, Whitehead

❧

Nashville, Sunday, April 3, 1864

My dear mother,

I thot I would write you a few lines this evening, for Mr. Perry is going home tomorrow, and I have fixed up a few articles to send by him. Now my dear mother, I have sent you a shell pin and I am very much afraid it will not meet your expectations, but it is as good as I could make. I have seen some that I would have been glad to have sent you. There were a few sold in Murfresboro for from ten to twenty-five dollars. This one is a pretty fair one. It is made from shells I got out of stone river right where the large battle was fought. There is a pair of sleeve studs you can do just as you please with and also the other case. Tell father I have no use for his tobacco box, so I send it home with many thanks for the use of it. There is a pack of old letters done up in two packages. One is from cousin Ed and I would like to have you read them for I think they are good ones. The others are from friends of mine and I don't want anyone to ever read them. If I should not come back, burn them.

I sent an overcoat. I have worn it all winter and I think I have kept it nice and clean considering the work I have had to do in it, such as sleeping on the ground, picket duty, etc. There is a permit in the pocket such as you must have in order to get thru the lines. I took it up one day the last time I was on picket. Gen. Reausow [Lovell H. Rousseau] and staff and also the Inspector General made me a visit. I was in charge of the post.

It is raining a little now and I guess we will have a wet day tomorrow. Capt. Clarence Baker was here today. He was a private in our company, went thru Dixie with us, shared his last piece of bacon with me when mine was stolen in Bridgeport. He is now senior Capt. in a colored regiment, and is a good boy. His regiment is now in Chattanooga.

Col Holbart of the 21 Wis. was here yesterday. He was captured at the front and was one of those who dug out of Libby Prison.[41] He made us a short speech. He thinks the war will be over before many months or we will be a great deal worse off. We will probably go to someplace south of here and I wish we were there now. You must not feel the least concern. I must close now.

Yours in Love, Lucius S. Moseley

NOTE

41. Colonel Harrison Hobart of Company K, 4th Wisconsin, organized the digging of a secret tunnel at Libby Prison, through which he and 109 prisoners escaped. Hobart later led his regiment through the Atlanta Campaign and commanded a brigade during Sherman's March to the Sea. Wisconsin Historical Society, http://www.wisconsinhistory.org/Records/Article/CS8753/.

The coat is a little damp, so you had better undo it as soon as it is convenient. Mr. Perry can tell you how we get along, etc. better than I can write it. I have lost one of my blankets so I did not send any.

As ever, Selden

Nashville, Sunday, April 17, 1864

Dear brother Eddie,

I suppose I am now writing you the last letter from Nashville, for we are expected to march tomorrow and will keep moving until we reach Lookout Valley—180 miles. The worst of it is we have to carry our knapsacks on our shoulders, but you bet I can stand as much of it as any of them, the new recruits especially. I would be glad if we were there but I do hate the little walk. Guess I am lazy.

I am well and feel as strong as a bear. Lt. Parker and Booth have both had their wives here for some time. They will now have to leave them. Charley Booth has a real good looking wife and those who are acquainted with her say she is a fine woman.

I want to tell you something that happened in our tent a few days ago. Sam sent his clothes out to be washed by a negro woman. When she brought them back she came into the tent to get her money. She had on some large hoops and a clean calico dress. I was sitting close to the door on a stool. Her hoops spread her calico out so far that it reached into the fire place. The consequence was it took fire. I noticed it but it was blazing clear up her back. I grabbed her dress in my hands and by extra effort put it out. Now the joke—she looked around and saw what the matter was, but said, "Don't you get up too high thar." I blistered my hands pretty bad so the boys thot they had a big joke on me. Then she said "You will have to excuse me gem-men" and then she took off her dress and turned the burnt side in front. Charley kindly pinned it up for her. I remarked that it didn't set so good that way. She said no, she wasn't as big behind as she was before. She said she would wash my shirt for nothing as I saved her life. Well enough of this.

I have been trying to get a bag of potatoes thru, but have not succeeded, and shall have to give them up. I am so sorry for they would have tasted twice as good because my dear father and brother raised them. Thank you anyway. I did not know until I came into the army, how precious every thing from home is. We also read our letters over and over again and again. Charley is rereading his and then burning them. We have to burn them before marching, for every ounce becomes pounds on a soldiers back. My time is wearing off slowly and will soon be up and then home I come. About money, I have spent over $20 since we were paid, and now haven't a cent.

You never told me where grandmother is moving. Well Eddie, get your gun. Now shoulder arms! Load in four times! Ready, Aim, Fire! Recover arms! Order Arms! In place—rest! Break ranks—March! I must close. Write as usual and direct to Nashville to follow the regiment. I can't put a stamp on this because I am out. Hardly any of the boys have any!

Yours with a soldiers love, L.S. Moseley

∼

April 29, 1864

Dear Family,

I don't know how to date this letter—only that I am sitting facing the north on an island in the middle of the Tennessee river, at or near Bridge-port, Alabama, on the south side of the Cumberland Mountains, on the 29th of April, 1864, Friday. I suppose you would kind of like to know how I am getting along etc., so I will write you a word or two. The last time I wrote we were in Tullahoma. The 26th we marched a big 16 miles to Dechard [Decherd] station—a pretty good road but hot weather, and but little water—crossed the noted Elk river, etc. Was a pretty tired boy at night. The 27th we went to Cowin [Cowan] station and expected to stay there. But they told us we would wait until 2 o'clock and then start up the mountain. Cowin is just at the foot of the mountain. If you had been there you could have picked up more clothes than you could draw in a week. The boys threw away blankets, overcoats, shirts, pants, drawers, etc, in fact every thing but just one blanket and the clothes they had on. I put mine in my knapsack, and put my knapsack on my back and carried it. It was about 4 miles to the top and it was up, I tell you. We had to stop and rest every short ways. Then we marched about 4 miles farther, making 13 miles in all, and camped at the top of the Cumberland mountains. There was a good spring up there, but it was hot weather.

In the night it blew and rained like sixty.[42] The 28th we marched about 10 miles farther on the tops of the mountains, and then went down, so steep that your buts would drag almost. It was about 14 miles from where we started to where we camped in what is called Sweet's Cove. It seemed to me as if I were in jail sure, for on all sides there were mountains apparently 3 miles high. But it was a splendid place, I assure you, at the head of Battle Creek. That is where there was an Indian fight. The trees were all leaved out, corn up, and everything looked like June rather than April. There was the largest and clearest spring there I ever saw.

Today, the 29th we marched to where I am now sitting—fifteen miles. I never saw so beautiful a valley as we passed thru today. The creek, about two rods wide, ran beside the road. The water is as clear as it possibly can be. The river here is very wide. We came over to this island on a pontoon bridge.

We draw rations tonite and in the morning we muster for pay and then go on. I don't know how far and I don't care.[43]

All my love to each of you, Lute

NOTES

42. "It rained like sixty." This expression, used to describe high speed or vigor, appears in literature well before the invention of the automobile. Sixty miles per hour—a mile a minute—was likely associated with train travel during this era.

43. In his letter of April 29, 1864, Lute described a difficult march through mountainous terrain. Soldiers carried only the most basic supplies—shelter tent, rubber blanket, canteen, small tin coffee pot, daily rations. As was often the case, Lute and his infantry comrades had little knowledge of destination or strategies, but General Sherman was at the helm of three Union armies totaling an estimated 110,000 men, closing in on the key city of Atlanta. "The Atlanta Campaign," American Battlefield Trust, accessed July 11, 2022, https://www.battlefields.org/learn/articles/atlanta-campaign/.

CHAPTER 4

Redemption in Georgia

May 12, 1864–July 21, 1864

There is true mettle in what is left of us.

—LUCIUS S. MOSELEY, July 21, 1864

Wisconsin 22nd Volunteer Infantry Regiment attached to 2nd Brigade, 3rd Division, 20th Army Corps, to June 1865.

Service: Atlanta (Georgia) campaign May 1 to September 8. Battle of Resaca May 14–15. Cassville May 19. New Hope Church May 25. Operations on line of Pumpkin Vine Creek and battles about Dallas, New Hope Church and Allatoona Hills May 25—June 5. Operations about Marietta and against Kenesaw [Kennesaw] Mountain June 10–July 2. Pine Hill June 11–14. Lost Mountain June 15–17. Gilgal or Golgotha Church June 15. Muddy Creek June 17. Noyes Creek June 19. Kolb's Farm June 22. Assault on Kenesaw June 27. Ruff's Station July 4.

—DYER, *Compendium*, vol. 3, 1682, 1683

⌢

Snakes Pass, Georgia, Thursday, May 12, 1864

Dear loved home:

The postmaster has just told us that we can send a letter home tonight, so I am busy preparing one, for I've no doubt you feel very anxious to know of my whereabouts.

We are now in Georgia, about six miles south of Dalton. We have marched nearly every day since the 19th of last month—have marched about 230 miles. The 6th we went from where I last wrote you, out to a tannery about six miles, and threw up intrenchments and expected an attack, but were disappointed. The 7th we marched 25 miles and then came near Buzzard's

Roost. The 20th Conn. and our regiment formed in line of battle and advanced up the mountain. There were about 200 rebs on it to watch us, but
they retreated. We then threw up breastworks, and layed a few minutes—
when we got orders to go on. We moved a short distance and threw up
another intrenchment, thus making 3 miles we marched in two days, and
built three lines of intrenchments. The weather was very hot, and it was
pretty hard on us. I threw away my woolen blanket, for I could not carry it.
We have to carry 60 rounds of cartridges, and three day's rations all the
time, besides our tent and everything we have. But don't you feel the least
concerned about me. I can stand it as long as Frank Smith. I never felt better in my life. Am all right sure.

We remained here until the 11th. There was skirmishing all the time in
front of us. We were on a high hill, and the rebs were on another about four
miles from us. We could see the cannonading. The 11th we marched down
here about ten miles, and went right to work fixing the road. This morning
we came here, about four miles farther. We are now south of the enemy I
suppose. There is an awful army here, I tell you. I don't know the number,
but there are over 50,000 here, and we are all around them.[1] We expect
they will try to go out here, but we are ready for them. There are three lines
of battle in front of us, and another corp is now coming in the 14th. We belong to the 20th—3rd division. We hear of the victory on the Potomac, and
feel sure of a bigger one here, so I don't see how they can hold out any longer.

I have received one letter from you since I was in Murfresboro. I shall
not feel uneasy if I don't get another from you till this campaign is over, for
the mail is very irregular. I don't know as you will get this, but hope you
will. It isn't likely that I can write to you again for two or three weeks. But
never feel for me, I am all right. It is so dark I can't see, so I will close. If
I get time I will write more in the morning. Good evening, my dear, dear
parents and brother.

Write often and direct to, L.S.M. Via Chattanooga.

NOTE

    1. "Under General William T. Sherman, the successor to Grant as the top Union
commander in the West, about 100,000 men departed Chattanooga, Tennessee, in
May, heading south along a railroad line. In their way stood some 63,000 troops led
by Confederate General Joseph E. Johnston, who took up a series of strong defensive positions only to retreat each time after being outflanked by long, roundabout
Union marches." Jesse Greenspan, "Union Troops Capture Atlanta," History.com,

updated August 28, 2019, https://www.history.com/news/union-troops-capture
-atlanta-150-years-ago/.

◆

Friday, May 20th, 1864

My own dear home: -

I guess there is a chance to send home a letter this morning, so I will just
write a few lines. I am, as you may judge, all right. We marched to Snakes
Gap, and the skirmishing commenced. Before this we were near Buzzard's
Roost. We lay on top of a mountain which we fortified. We left there at two
in the morning of the 11th, and marched way round to the right, or Snakes
Gap. The 13th and 14th there was a good brisk fight, but we were not in it
The 15th our corps was ordered way round to the left, right in front of Mr.
Rebs, and was soon right at it. We have not lost a single man in our com-
pany, and none wounded, only Ben Kline was hit in the hip with a piece of
shell. It only made a black and blue spot. We had 17 killed and 65 wounded
in the regiment. Cap. Patton is mortalay wounded, and I guess is dead ere
now. The North never lost a better or braver man, soldier and officer.[2] Hank
Rosecrans is wounded slightly in the hand. I guess that is all that you know.

The 14th Corps tried to take the works on the 14th and failed, but the
old 20th rushed in and took them. Sile Wright is now the hero of the 22nd,
and justly so, too. The 102nd Illinois Colonel asked for a man to carry the
colors and no one came forward. Sile was separated from us and was with
them. He stepped up and said "give them to me." Then he stepped out
three paces in front of the line and boldly advanced and planted the stars
and stripes on the most formidable of the rebel works, and as heavy a fire
as ever was poured into a lot of men. I wish I had such courage, but no, I
could not do that. The Captain of the company in which he was gave him a
writing to show that the above is true.[3]

The rebs retreated in the night, and we are close in their rear, kicking them
at every jump, and taking lots of their men that fall out from fatigue and a
good many by fighting and flanking. Yesterday we marched over twenty-
five miles. The rebs are crossing a river, and so I get a chance to write while
the rest are cannonading and fight the enemies rear. Our regiment are
guard for the ammunition train—a very responsible position. I have but
ten minutes to finish this, and so can't write much. We are giving them fits,
and all feel first rate. All the Beloit boys are well . . . The boys all think we

will whip the rebs to their entire satisfaction before many months. I don't know what the news is from on the Potomac, but we hear Resaca is taken . . .[4]

Yours in all the love imaginable, L.S. Moseley

NOTES

2. Captain Marshall W. Patton, Company I of the 22nd Wisconsin, was killed at Resaca.

3. Regimental flags were symbols of the principles for which both sides fought, and it was a high honor to be able to protect one's own flag, risking life and limb. Capturing an enemy flag was also considered a great feat of gallantry. Wells, *Wisconsin in the Civil War*, "Soldiers on Both Sides Died to Protect Regimental Flags," ch. 12, p. 33.

4. In his May 20 and 21 letters, Lute described the 22nd Wisconsin's part in the Battle of Resaca, May 14–15, 1864. Harvey Reid's account of the role played by the 22nd Wisconsin is found in *Uncommon Soldiers*, 145–50. Although the battle was not decisive, the boys of the 22nd saw this battle as a glorious victory.

Camp, 22nd Wis. Reg. Co. B., Near Kingston, Ga., Sat., May 21, 1864

Dear Home,

. . . Yesterday I wrote you the particulars of our fight, but will write more today. As I wrote you, we entered Snakes Gap on Tuesday, May 10th. We camped in the Gap, and the whole Brigade went to work cutting down trees and fixing the road. The next day we went about three miles into the valley beyond and camped for the night. In the morning we packed up and moved on, and I knew there was trouble ahead. We were nearly in the advance, but we were halted and formed by divisions on the right of the road, and the rest passed by us. Just across the road were assembled the big men— General Sherman, Thomas, Hooker, Butterfield and lots of others, and Sickles with his one leg. Gen. Kilpatrick passed by at the rear of the cavalry force, and not over two hours after he went out he came back, wounded but not very badly.[5] After a while we went forward and went about four miles and formed in line of battle. There were four or five lines in front of us, and skirmishing was quite heavy. The advance soon drove the enemy off a small hill and took one gun. We were moved on about threequarters of a mile, and waited until after dark. Then we went on a mile and camped with our harness all on, right behind our guns, which were stacked in front about a quarter of a mile, we lay there and in the night we built breastworks. The fight was hard this day.

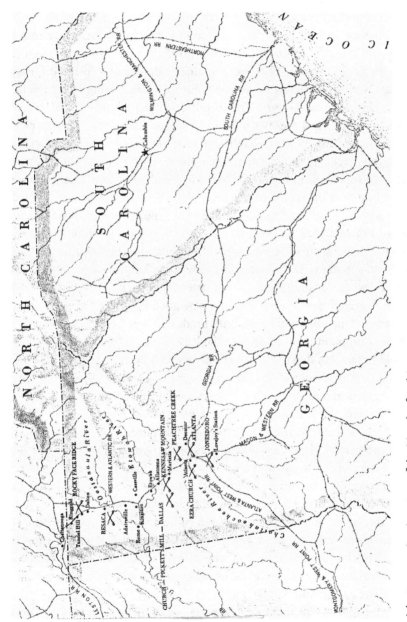

Atlanta campaign (courtesy of the Moseley family)

Sunday—I just got to where you see I stopped when the order came to pack up immediately. We moved about a mile into the woods. Now we are in an open wheat field.

Well Sunday the 15th we moved around to the right about three miles, then to the front. We formed in line with three or four lines in front of us with fixed bayonets. They were to charge the enemys fort and breast-works. We were to follow for support, but they rather hung back, and old Bill [Sherman] bawled out "Why in h-ll don't you advance." And we did advance, we charged over two or three lines, and part of the regiment clear to the works. The left wing was divided or split off, and we went across the road, the grape and canister more than howling. We drew up and formed behind a small hill, and advanced to the top, and layed down under a heavy fire. The rest of the regiment soon joined us. Soon Gen. Hooker came rid-ing along on a walk and said "You had better move some of those logs up there to protect you." So we did. Lots of the boys were hit in other compa-nies, but none in ours. Gen. Butterfield, commanding our division, ordered us farther to the right. We went and it was not long before we found out why we went, for the rebs came up determined to go thru, but we were about five lines deep, and if you ever saw good fighting in all your life, it was there. One line would fight until tired, and Brig Gen Knype [Joseph F. Knipe, commanding First Brigade, First Division of the Twentieth Corps] would order, "Lay down." The next line would pour volley after volley into them. They held out well, but at length gave way and we gave a yell. Then the shells began to come. Gen. Hooker would ride along on his horse on the very top of the hill as calmly as a man would ride across the Beloit bridge—also Gen. Butterfield. The boys would cheer them and they would stop and take off their hats, and look as pleasant as could be. Old Hooker saw a man way down behind a tree and he said to him "Doesn't that look like a coward?" One officer said to him, "Just look how the men are run-ning!" But he answered back, "Well there are plenty of brave men left here yet." You would laugh to see some men come back. One man was hit thru the haversack and the boys asked him if it hurt much. But it scart him like fury. This is where Sile Wright distinguished himself. He surely did nobly. We lay on the very ground we had occupied all day, with our accoutrements all on our guns in our hands.

About one in the night our Generals thought they (the rebels) were leaving and so sent a force to see. They found they were going and so they just threw a shell into them killing lots and lots of both horses and their disgraced riders. In the morning (the 16th) I went out a little ways to see the rebs. The most of our men were removed, but dead and dying rebs covered the grounds. I went down in one's pocket and got some pins and needles, some Confederate script, a knife, and some plug tobacco which I gave to the boys who were awful glad, for they hadn't had any for a long time. The rebs are all gone, leaving their dead and wounded on the field.[6]

We marched on thru their works, across the Conasauga River and stopped to rest. The boys found a large lot of tobacco which was confiscated and divided equally amount the whole of our division, each man getting about an old ten cent plug. We went until near morning and finally stopped on the southern bank of the Coosawauttie [Coosawatee] River. It rained like fun so we did not sleep much. At three in the afternoon (18th) we went on about 10 miles, and had a good nights sleep. Got up at three the next day and marched about twenty-five miles. The next day we were left in the rear to guard the ammunition train, and the rest were throwing cold lead and shell at the rear of old Joe Johnson [Johnston] as he was trying to cross the river. They had to burn a train. We built another line of works, making the 5th. At night we went on a mile or so and stopped. Yesterday we laid still and today moved about one mile. So now here I am, in old Georgia, a place I never expected to see.

The enemy are ten or fifteen miles from here. The reason of our halt is not to hurry the enemy so fast, for McPherson is trying them a race for Atlanta. Lots and lots of them give out, and fall in the rear, and so come into our hands—sometimes to give themselves up.

So you see everything helps to weaken them and we are bound to whip them. They tell the inhabitants or citizens that we will kill them and illtreat their women if they stay back, so everyone of them are gone and all we have to do is to go into their homes and help ourselves. Even the tables are all set in some houses and left just so, for they hadn't time to even eat.

Our men took six or seven thousand dollars worth of cotton in one place and so on. We get beef along the road etc. We expect to go off away from the rest of the army somewhere, I don't know where. Our whole corps are going, some say East Tennessee and some one place and some another. We are ready for any place.

You never saw the boys feel better. We have in thirty-two days and marched over two hundred ninety miles with everything we own on our backs and three days ration, fought one of the days and built five lines of works. We also worked one day on the road but now we have had two of the thirty-two days to rest in and all feel bully. It has taken my flesh all off but never was I better or tougher than today. More, I feel confident of success ere many months, so get things arranged for us to do something profitable when I get home. Get us a team started. I will soon have five months pay due me. This will help you to get it and I want to own part of it myself.

Major John Gordon is over to see us. His regiment is near here. He is a good man. Capt. Potter is dead; a better officer never fell. William Minot is feeling first rate. We often speak about being neighbors now. They say this can go tonight so I will close and write again as soon as I can send it. I don't know if this will go farther than Chattanooga. Next time you write put on the envelope "Twentieth Corps."

Yours, L.S. Moseley

NOTES

5. Lute mentioned the "big men"—Maj. Gen. William T. Sherman, commanding the western theater of war; Maj. Gen. George H. Thomas, commanding Army of the Cumberland; Maj. Gen. Joseph Hooker, commanding Twentieth Corps; Maj. Gen. Daniel Butterfield, commanding Third Division, Twentieth Corps; Maj. Gen. Daniel Sickles, who lost his leg at Gettysburg, commanding Third Corps; Maj. Gen. Hugh Kilpatrick, cavalry commander, wounded in the thigh at Resaca. All three of Sherman's armies were on the same field simultaneously—(Armies of the Cumberland (Thomas), Ohio (Schofield), and Tennessee (McPherson). Welcher and Ligget, *Coburn's Brigade*, 165–68.

6. Estimated casualties at the Battle of Resaca were 2,747 Union and 2,800 Confederate, possibly much higher. The battle is believed to have had the second highest casualty rate of the entire Atlanta campaign. American Battlefield Trust, accessed July 7, 2022, https://www.battlefields.org/learn/civil-war/battles/resaca/.

22nd Wis. Vol., Near Dallas, Georgia, May 27, 1864

Dear ones at home,

If you were to be placed right where I now sit and were to try to write a letter I guess you would have a hard job on your hands, for even now there is occasionally a leaden missle of death passing over our heads while to right and left cannons are booming. The 25th we found Rebels in force and advanced on them, our skirmishers driving them to their breastworks. Then our line pressed up on them and had quite a hard fight. It was about four o'clock when we came up. We advanced under a heavy fire of grape and shell. Our Captain [Brown] was wounded slightly in the arm. Sargent Rose was hit with a piece of shell on the shoulder, cutting his knapsack strap off and knocking him down. He is not marked, only bruised. Corporal Bond was wounded on the hand so that it disabled him. This is all that was hurt in our company thus far.

Yesterday we were in the front and some of our skirmishers were wounded, not from our company. Today we are in the front line and farther to the right. There is little or no firing here yet. The fight has not come off yet. We have got them to our satisfaction and pretty soon I think we shall rout them out of this. We are all feeling gay. William Minot is all right and feeling good. He is not going to write today and wants me to speak about him so let his family know.

You may let them see this letter if you want to. He says "Tell them to scull the letters down here about two per weak." So say I. We get your letters and are glad, no mistake. I don't know as you get ours or not but I hope you do. I will write as often as opportunity affords. Len Rose says his folks know how he is through the spirits, even before the telegraph could carry the news. I don't think of anything more to write now.

Love to all sure. L.S. Moseley

∼

Headquarters U.S. Forces, in the Altonia [Allatoona] Mountains, Thursday, June 2nd, 1864

Dear Father, Mother, and Brother,

Yesterday I wrote you a letter but as only a few minutes notice was given us that the mail was going out I was about two minutes late and it didn't go. So I concluded to write and then it will be ready. I will however drop you only a line to let you know my whereabouts, circumstances, etc.

Yesterday we lay in the front line and had been there for two days where we could plainly see the enemy's breast works and the Johnnies running along behind them. We had a good breastwork which protected us from the bullets of the skirmishers. We kept a skirmish or picket line out, as did the Rebs. They are all the time shooting at each other, occasionally hitting some one who is daring and steps out from behind a tree. We have been now since the eighth of May where we could hear cannonading every day and most of the time where we could hear musketry. Ten days of this time we have been under fire. Where we lay yesterday we could hear the Rebs sing, halloo, give orders, and blow their trumpets. We are on the brow of one hill and they across the hollow on the other, both strongly entrenched and within two hundred yards of each other. This seems to be a queer position for so many men to hold, each party of which would gladly kill or destroy the other. We had works about twenty rods back of where we were before moving up to this one. There was a detachment from the brigade to build this front line. Companies C & B were detailed from our regiment. We advanced and stacked our guns, and went to work under a pretty brisk fire from the reb sharp shooters. There was thick underbrush in front of us. We, that is, our company commenced and put up a little just for protection, and then threw the dirt out in front of us, and so kept under cover. But if one of us straightened up he was sure to get shot at. I tell you I had a great many close misses. We were bringing up a log, and of course were exposed. The bullets would come between us and over us, but hit no one excepting Pole. He was hit just under the right shoulder blade, cutting a gash about three or four inches long and one and a half wide, and one half or three quarters of an inch deep. The ball then struck the log and glanced, just ticking another boy on the neck. Pole is not hurt badly, is up and around. Has gone to the rear. The 33rd Indiana had two killed out there, and one wounded.[7]

Yesterday the 15th corps relieved us, and we moved around to the left about six miles. We now lay in the reserve, and have one day to reset, and take our straps off.[8]

Pole was down on the skirmish line before he was hit, and had the pleasure of shooting about seventy rounds at the rascals. He was not sure of hitting any, as they keep so close to the trees. Some of the boys have killed rebs that they know of. Sile Wright took my gun and dropped one out of a tree. They get up in the tops of pine trees and shoot at us.

One week ago last night we came in here under an awful heavy fire of shell and grape. Two or three shells exploded right in front of our company, but all the damage they did was to wound James Rose, Corp Bond and Cap Brown. James was hit on the shoulder, cutting his knapsack strap off, tearing his clothes, passing thru his rubber blanket which was rolled up and tied on top of his knapsack. It did not break any bones and he is getting along first rate. Bond was hit on the hand, jamming it but not breaking any bones. He stays with us and is a good boy sure. A solid shot struck a tree just over our company. The tree was about ten inches thru. It cut it off and the top fell over. The boys had to run to keep from under it. A splinter from it hit our old slink of a Captain [Brown] on the side and arm, and he left for the rear quick. He is a poor excuse for a soldier or man, and we have lots of fun at his expense, seeing him squat and run. Lieut Ball of Co G has been in command of our company but our old Cap has come back to us.

Ira Nye is detained in the engineer corps and is back at Fort Donalson. It is reported here now that the rebs have been strongly reinforced, and we are expecting an awful hard fight. We keep advancing our lines and drawing down on this. Our line is in the shape of a cresent. Last Sunday night the rebs attacked our lines nearly the whole length, but you bet they soon got back out of that. There are over sixty pieces of artillery on our line and all positions can be got for. And these opened on Mr. Johnnies, double shotted with canister, besides lots of musketry. I have heard of but five being killed our side, but many of the rebels fell. I never heard such a 4th of July in the night before. The rebel officers told their men that our men on the extreme right were all one hundred day men, and that the sight of them would scare them all out.[9] So they came right up at a right shoulder shift. Our men let them come till they were near enough, and then poured volley after volley into them, killing lots of them. They charged five or six times, and were handsomely repulsed each time.

Sunday—June 5th—Well, my dear ones, I will write again a few lines. Since I wrote last we have moved, first about three miles to the east or left, and advanced under another fire of shell, but none of us were hit. Major Miller, commanding the 33rd Indiana, was slightly wounded, and our brigade Surgeon was killed—being hit in the forehead.

We built a line of works there, and the next morning moved on the left. It has rained now every day for three or four days.

The 2nd we marched here near the R.R. on our left. At dark our regiment was detailed to fill a gap between Gen Hoag and a battery, and to support the latter. We got there at 10 o'clock, and had to fortify the next day. We advanced our line a little, and built our 13th line of works. Our company is close to an old meetinghouse, where I suppose many and many a sesesh lecture and war meeting have been held. The 33rd Chaplain [Alfred Averton from Avoca, WI] has just finished a discourse in it.

It is reported that the 17th Corp is now occupying Marietta, and that the rebs are leaving here. If the 17th is going in there, they will have to leave sure, and I know they are all the time drawing off. There are now two lines of works in front of us.

I don't see anyways how to send this, so I will wait a little before I write more. I have not received a letter from home now in two weeks, but there has been no mail come thru. They say there is some for us at headquarters and I have also heard that the rebs captured our mail. I guess that is not so. I received a notice from the postmaster in Chattanooga that there was a letter for me there that had no stamp on it, and I must send one to get it. I am out of stamps, so I wish you would send me two or three every time you write until this campaign is over.

L.S. Moseley

NOTES

7. In his letter of June 2, 1864, Lute described the May 25 battle at Dallas (New Hope Church).

8. The men of Coburn's Brigade were exhausted after several days of deadly trench warfare at New Hope Church. The Union army, with more than 16,000 troops, was overwhelmed by 4,000 Confederate troops; the Union lost more than 1,600 men, the Confederates lost 400, and the battle was won by the Confederates. They were finally relieved on June 1. Welcher and Ligget, *Coburn's Brigade*, 195, 196.

9. "Hundred day men" was a term applied to volunteer regiments raised in 1864, obligated for 100 days of service in the Union Army. Short-term, lightly trained troops freed veteran units from routine duties, allowing them to go into frontline combat.

∽

Tuesday morning, June 7th, 1864

. . . At two we have an inspection, and we have to be very busy to get our guns clean. For the last ten or fifteen days it has rained nearly every day, and our guns are rusty. But I will write a little more.

The morning of the 5th we found the rebs had fallen back. So on the 6th we advanced three or four miles, and found them. We advanced to position, and built breastworks, which we are now behind. I think they are crossing the river, and of course, have to make a little stand until they get their teams over. There is no fighting today as yet, and I don't think there will be much here. But I tell you, we flanked them out of some of the strongest works I ever saw. Where they just left they have rifle-pits which they expected we would charge. They calculated to fall right back, and we would of course, pitch right into them. Then they had cannon planted so as to rake the whole pit, but thank God! We did not charge them. Old Hooker wanted to, but Sherman said "no," he could drive them out with less loss, as he proved. I don't believe in charging. They charged us lots of times, but were repulsed every time.[10]

I have a Beloit Journal with a list of the company raised there. That is a big thing. Lots of mothers will shed bitter tears when the dear boys go. I suppose they will see rough times when guarding those dangerous places we have taken and driven the rebs hundreds of miles from. I wish they had to go on half rations, and march 400 miles, and be under fire over fifteen days of the time as we have and then see if they would think it so big a thing to go to Nashville, Louisville etc., and stand a little picket for three months . . .[11]

I am well and contented, Uncle Sam owes me $70, and it will be more before it is less. I am dirty and ragged, but my ragged clothes cover a healthy contented body, and this is enough. I have only one shirt to my back, because I don't want any more. I threw away the other two. I don't carry any more than I am obliged to. My old pants are ripped and patched. You would laugh to see the patch I put on the seat of them, but it is put on well if I did do it. My boots are all whole yet, and are the only pair left in the company that came to us at Murfresboro. They will last me one year, and the best thing a soldier can have is a good tight pair of boots (for those that don't have tight boots have to go around).

Charley says, Lute, come and have some coffee; for he has it ready. He is a good boy, I tell you.

I don't think of anything more to write, it is pretty warm and will rain before long. I guess all the citizens thru here have gone with the rebs. We took five yesterday that were put in the ranks. They sneaked away from them and waited in the woods until our men came up; then gave themselves up guns and all. But I guess I will drink my coffee, and then seal this up and send it. I want to tell you how Charley had a letter directed to him—

Over the hills with love and joy,
this letter goes to a soldier boy.
Overcome every obstacle; go in a hurry,
until you reach Charles P. Murry,
22nd Wisconsin Regiment, Co B.
in the city of Nashville, Tennessee.

This was all there was on it. The boys are all well. Write often, and don't forget to put in two or three stamps every time, for I want enough, and then you may send me one dollar in your next, if you please . . .

Ever the same soldier, L.S. Moseley

NOTES

10. The historian Shelby Foote wrote about the brutality and high casualties on Civil War battlefields: "It was brutal stuff, and the reason for the high casualties is really quite simple; the weapons were way ahead of the tactics. . . . Yet for most of the war they still believed that to take a position you massed your men and moved up and gave them the bayonet. In fact there were practically no bayonet wounds in the Civil War . . . but they still thought that to mass their fire they had to mass their men. So they lined up and marched up to an entrenched line and got blown away." Ward, *Civil War*, 265.

11. Soldiers in the three-year regiments had little patience with the short-term recruits ("hundred day men") who were obligated for only three months of service and not likely to see combat. Wells, *Wisconsin in the Civil War*, 65, 66.

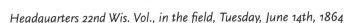

Headquarters 22nd Wis. Vol., in the field, Tuesday, June 14th, 1864

Dear home,

. . . We are still in the same position as when I last wrote you. Nothing of note has occurred since then, only it has rained all the time until this morning and now it is clear once more. The roads are very bad—almost impassable, but will soon be good again.

The cars come up within four miles of us, and it would seem that supplies might be easily furnished to us. But surely I have some—yes, a good many pretty hungry hours since this campaign commenced. I will tell you just what we drew the last time to last three days. We drew thirteen crackers, about half a pint of sugar, and same of coffee per man. We get no meat except a little poor beef. But we get along first rate, for we get a chance to buy some crackers at five cents for four. My money is all played out—I haven't a cent; if I had I could get along some better. So I wrote you in my last letter to send me one dollar. Now next time you write send me three more, if I have it at home. And another thing—I have gone to using tobacco again, and shall as long as I soldier. The boys have had it sent to them by mail from home at the cost of about ten cents per pound. It cost from two to four dollars a plug here, so you may please send me a pound or two immediately. I want good—am not particular whether it is fine cut or plug, only I want it as soon as convenient. You will, I've no doubt, get tired of sending things to me, but remember that there is but a little over one year left. Just mark it as usual, via Chattanooga, 20th corps, 2nd brigade, 3rd division. You can get it best, I think off Charlie Shott. Tell him to tie it up good, for it is for me, and he will do it.

As for news, I haven't any. The position of the armies is about the same. We keep drawing in closer and closer on them and most all the time throw shell and solid shot over at them, just to keep them stirred up. I suppose there are important movements on foot, but we are in the center, and don't know much more what is going on in the flanks than you do. But I guess it is all right, and expect to hear that they are all gone some of these mornings . . .

I wish I knew what the news is from Grant. We haven't heard for a while.[12] The last we heard came officially to Butterfield, that Grant had repulsed Lee in a heavy attack near [illegible, possibly Spotsylvania]. Lee massed and tried him. That is their game, but they don't always get thru. That is a good way to get men killed—to mass them so that grape and canister will cut regular swaths thru them.

But I will close. I am as tough as a bear. Don't weigh as much into twenty pounds as when I left Nashville, but am all right.

Yours in love, L.S. Moseley

NOTE

12. In May 1864, President Lincoln appointed Ulysses S. Grant as general-in-chief of all Union armies. That spring and summer Grant conducted his Overland Campaign in Virginia, including battles at Spotsylvania, Cold Harbor, and Petersburg.

Camp 22nd Wis. Inft, Sunday, June 19, 1864[13]

. . . It is now Sunday morning and raining like sixty. We have the worst weather all this month so far, that I ever saw. It rains nearly all the time.

It is now just two months since we left Nashville, and a hard two months it has been, I tell you. The Johnnies keep falling back all the time, but contest *every inch* of the way. On the fifteenth we had orders to move on, as the rebs had fallen back—we having turned their right, they fell back about two miles, and we advance clear, smack up to them, within eighty rods of their works, and built a line of works. It was full as near as that and I guess nearer. We worked all night at the works the sixteenth. We were rather stupid, but had nothing to do but sit and lay around. But the rebels annoyed us some from their breastworks. They have lots of sharpshooters in trees and behind places fixed on purpose, and they kill lots. They shot a Sargeant of Company H, and a man in Company A, and wounded five. Ed Webb was hit in the shoulder very slightly. Sile Wright was down on the line and went to talking to the rebels, and trying to get them to come over and talk but the rebels wouldn't, and so they went to shooting at one another. The reb hit Sile in the right arm, the ball passed through above the elbow, but did not break the bone. That is all the boys that have been wounded from Beloit since I wrote.[14]

The 17th we found the rebs had gone again, and I went over to see their works. They are without exception the strongest works I ever saw. There were two, and in some places, three lines. All that there would be exposed of a man behind them would be just his eyes, for there were only loopholes to shoot thru left.

We advanced two miles farther and found them in force again. We came up close to them and built our 18th line of works—that is the 18th since this campaign began and now the 19th find they are gone again, and I expect every minute to have orders to follow them again. Reb Gen Polk was killed on the 16th.[15] We have taken some few prisoners. The boys brot in six rebels this morning.

I don't know anything more to write this time, for I haven't time. I will send you some scraps of some old rebel letters I found. They don't amount to much . . .

I want to tell you about our old slink of a Captain. We thot the other day, when we advanced in here, that we were going to have a big fight. So he said he had the PILES so he could not go any farther, and fell out and went to the rear. He was all right you see, until he thot it wasn't safe to go any farther, and then had the piles. But the boys do give him fits. They talk about everything they see going to the rear having piles right before him. He is a cowardly slink and the Colonel says so.

I have some bad news to tell you. Yesterday, Bert Bullock was on picket. The rebs had been cross all day. Bert shot one and was watching them closely. He was talking to them. Part way between the rebs and our men there was a wounded Johnnie. Bert told them to come out and get him, and they wouldn't fire. They answered with a volley of bullets—hitting no one tho. Then Bert saw one of them off to the left sneaking down toward them, for there were eight or nine men with Bert. He allowed to the reb to go back for he said that wasn't fair. But he kept creeping up and Bert shot two or three times at him, but the reb kept so close behind a large pine tree Bert couldn't see enough of him to hit him. Then Bert told the boys in the next pit to shoot at him and they would have a cross fire on him so that one or the other would hit him. But Bert was too careless, and exposed himself too much and the reb took instant advantage of him and fired. The bullet passing thru his head—going in at the right cheek, and coming out low down at the back of the head. He was taken right back to the hospital and was conscious last night. Chas Murry, Wm Minot and Adams have gone to see him this morning, and have not returned yet. I will let you know what they say. No man has fallen in the 22nd whose loss is so keenly felt for he has always been right with us, and always ready and willing for duty besides he was so cheerful. He has never I think had a hard word with anyone in the company. Cal Bullock went with him and stayed, so I think Bert is still alive, or Cal would have been back by this time. This leaves ten men for duty in the company, three Corporals, and three Sergeants. We are all like so many brothers, and grow more and more so every day.

I was on picket the day before Bert, and had lots of fun, for we could see thru an opening in the woods, the rebs going back and forth. I had some nice shots, and rather think I hit one, but am not sure. I think every man in our company has hit his reb. Bert killed one yesterday, and made several dodge. We have lots of men back in the rear, playing sick, but they have been ordered up and will fill up the company again.

I haven't received my letter from you the last week; am very much in hopes today. I had a long one from Fannie last night. I tell you, she is the greatest hand to soft-soap and compliment a fellow I ever saw. Such nice letters as I write, she says. Now you know as well as I that I am a very poor hand to write, ain't I? She says I describe everything so *beautifully*. I believe she does it on purpose to make fun of me, and I've a good mind not to write to her again. She sends *lots* of love to you and grandmother.

. . . I wish you would, if it is convenient, send me fifty cents per week— that is, if you haven't sent me four or five dollars already. You won't blame me for this I know. There have been so many men taken the scurvy that an order has been issued forbidding the Commissary to issue any more salt meat. The fresh meat, of which we have a great plenty, is poor living in hot weather. We get plenty of hard tack, beef and dessecated vegetables—which is very poor stuff—and beans. We can buy condensed potatoes for a shilling per pound. One pound makes two of us two meals, thus costing us three cents a piece. We draw about four spoonfulls of sugar for three days. Now this is a very small allowance. We buy it for twenty cents per pound. We don't buy much, but as long as we are worked so hard, and I have funds, I think it is not only a little more agreeable, but very good policy to live better. It keeps a person's blood in better order. Now don't you agree with me?

The boys are back from the hospital, and say that Bert is alive and doing first rate. The ball came out low down on the neck, and then passed up under the skin, coming out high up, making us think it was worse than it really is. The doctor says he thinks he will get well, altho another doctor said last night that he wouldn't live an hour.[16]

There has been a report circulating for the last few days about some prisoners coming in. I did not believe it so was not going to write it, but there is a cavalry man here who says his company was there at the time and reports as follows. The rebs had a double skirmish line. During the day the front line made it up with our boys to come in at night. So they (the front line) started, and our men at the same time charged, so as to keep the rear line from charging those coming over. You see the second line didn't want to come. The rebs shelled those coming over, killing and wounding some few. But six hundred got in, and our skirmishers took the pits left, thus gaining a good position besides the prisoners. They say there were more came in farther to the right—better than a good victory. They said that one half of the rebel army wanted to get away. They are Alabamians. But I tell you, those in front of us don't want to give up yet.

It is reported that the rebs have 30,000 reinforcements coming. If so, we will have to assume the defensive. But we don't believe it. They can't drive us if they have so many more men, for if we could drive them as we have with their present number—with their 30,000 more they couldn't drive us. Our cars come right down to our lines, within (at most) two miles of Atlanta. We can plainly read the rebel's and our cars running (Their's to destruction).

... We have been cleaning up our guns for inspection today. No more this time ...

I am, as ever your affectionate son and brother, L.S. Moseley

P.S. I have just heard that our beloved companion and fellow soldier is no more. Another report still later says Bert is not dead, but about the same. So you see we can't tell what is doing by report. L.S.M.

NOTES

13. Harvey Reid reported in his letter of June 19, 1864, that the 22nd Wisconsin was camping six miles west of Marietta, GA. He was optimistic that "everything looks cheering now for a speedy termination of the war." Reid, *Uncommon Soldiers*, 160–62.

14. Here, Lute described the fighting at Lost Mountain, GA (Gilgal Church).

15. Confederate Gen. Leonidas Polk was fatally shot on June 14, 1864, at Pine Mountain, GA.

16. Albert ("Bert") Bullock of Beloit was wounded at Thompson's Station and again in the Atlanta campaign; he survived the war and was mustered out in May 1865.

∾

Three miles south of Marrieta [Marietta] Georgia, Friday June 24, 1864

Ever dear home,

. . . We have had some excitement since I last wrote, but I cannot write you all the particulars.[17] Where this army is situated at present is this— there is some cavalry first on the extreme right; the 23rd corps next, then the 20th corps, then the 4th, then the 14th, then the 15th, 16th, and 17th, and then cavalry. We are in the shape of a horseshoe—the rebs inside. Right at the toe is what is called the twin mountains, and they are all alone. The river is south of us. This is the way the thing looks to me, we are on the extreme right of our corps. Our regiment at first nearly straight with the toe of the shoe and we have gradually pressed around this end. Day before yesterday we had some pretty brisk work. We were ordered to advance our line, so Coburn ordered his brigade to forward. We advanced and soon came upon Mr. Johnnies—skirmishers—but you bet they gave back. We advanced and drove them out of their rifle-pits, or the pits dug for their skirmish lines. We built a line of works, and were just nearly ready, when the rebs advanced on us. The advance was very light tho, for we easily drove them back. The attack was carried clear down on the right (We were then on the left of our corps). On the right they came up five times in three lines. Our artillery literally mowed them. The ground was covered with dead Johnnies. They were at work all night carrying off the wounded, and yesterday our men buried lots and lots of them. I saw quite a lot. The truth is they were pretty well intoxicated.[18]

I can't write you so you will understand the way armies are maneuvering. I would like to be with the army, if I never had been, for about two weeks, and then I never would want to see a gun again. Yes, I tell you there is no fun in soldiering. But I am willing to stay my time out, and hope I will be fortunate to get thru all straight. I have been very fortunate so far.

Sile Wright is wounded thru the right arm. The rest of the boys are all right. I saw Homer Miller the other day. He looks well. Was slightly wounded in the right shoulder. He was very good-natured.

Yesterday we moved around here to the right, and you would have thot we were a pretty quiet lot of boys if you had seen how still we came around into position, and put up our 23rd line of works. We were just on the edge of a hill, and the rebs were only a few rods over putting up theirs. But now we are all right and ready for them. I don't believe but what our brigade have put up works enough since this campaign commenced to build a railroad from Chicago to Beloit—and have only used the one out of all. I hope we won't have to use but one out of the next twenty-three we build. But I tell you there is a great deal in getting used to it. I can stand fire now pretty well.

We have lost one of the bravest, best boys in the regiment. He belonged to company G. His name was Nathan Gould. He was on the skirmish line and was shot plumb thru the head. This is where the corporals have the advantage; we don't have to go on the skirmish line hardly ever, unless the whole company goes.

But I guess I will close. I have written now more than three of you write me sometimes. Mr. Adams, I tell you, makes a good soldier. There is more difference in soldiers than there is in laboring men. Some are always playing off, and some are always ready for their duty. We thot Sime Sage was cowardly, but it is not so. He is a good man. Sam Miller has proved himself a coward, and also Jim Elliot. Let others speak for me. I will write as often as I can. But goodbye for this time.

Yours in love, as ever. L.S. Moseley

NOTES

17. "The brigade did an unparalleled amount of labor, almost daily making lines of works, and this with astonishing alacrity and cheerfulness . . . In the Battle of New Hope Church, in Dallas Woods, May 25th, of Lost Mountain, of Gilgal Church, June 15th, and of Culp's Farm (or Kolb's Farm) on June 22nd, officers and men vied with each other in heroic daring." Bradley, *Star Corps*, 128.

18. In this letter Lute described the Battle of Kolb's Farm, June 22, 1864, a decisive Union victory with heavy Confederate casualties.

Still the 24th; when I wrote the first part of this letter I didn't know when I could send it, but now I have found out that I can send it at three this P.M., so for this reason I thot I would just pencil out a few lines more . . .

I have been trying to figure out where we are, and as near as I can come at it we are about fifteen miles off the Chattahoochie [Chattahoochee] river, and it is about ten miles from there to Atlanta. I am sure I cannot tell how long it will be before we will get there. But this much I can tell you, I will be glad when that day comes, for then I think this campaign will end, and we can have a rest and a chance to wash and put on some clean clothes. This is a long, hard campaign, but I am glad to see it, and hope it will be pushed on until the rebs are satisfied. I would rather do it now than to put it off and still have it to do.

Gen Sherman is acting very wisely, I think, for he flanks them out, and lets them do the charging instead of fighting them as at Stone river and Missionary ridge etc. Right on the ground where I am sitting, day before yesterday was held by the rebs. Here is where they charged so on our lines. I would give $50 if you could have gone over this place, when we advanced yesterday, and seen the dead rebs—lots of them. How far do you suppose a shell shot from a 12 pounder will go into a green oak tree? Guess before I tell you. I have seen trees that I think are more than two feet thru, with a five inch hole clear thru. How much farther it went, I don't know. Now how far would that big Lincoln gun throw a ball into wood? Some rebs had their heads taken slick off.[19] The woods are all cut up with cannon shot and musketry. One reb had five musket holes thru his breast. You bet he stopped right there. I guess that tonight the rebs will get out of this if they can, but I don't know, nor care, for the longer they stay here the worse it will be for them to stop again. Gen Johnson [Johnston] is not in command of the rebel forces here now. I don't know who it is. Some say Longstreet.[20] It don't make any difference for we are bound to whip them.

About the presidential election. I think "Old Abe" will be elected, and certainly hope he will. He will have my vote. If they let the soldiers vote he will be elected sure.[21] The only hope the rebels have is that we will elect some other man in his place. I think they will give in if we put him in again. I sincerely hope that you all at home will do your utmost for his support. You will, won't you Father?

But I will close. Bill Minot has written. He is all right; so am I, and so we all are. Frank Smith was left back sick a long while ago, and we have not heard from him since. Do you know where he is? And how he is? But I must dry up. Write often. You don't know the worth of letters in these parts.

L.S. Moseley

NOTES

19. The Lincoln gun was a fifteen-inch Rodman gun, capable of firing a 300-lb. projectile up to four miles. It was first cast in 1860; in 1862 the gun was named

after President Lincoln who did his best to equip the Union armies with up-to-date weapons. Bruce Catton, "Mr. Lincoln's Weapons," *American Heritage*, vol. 7, no. 4, (June 1956), https://www.americanheritage.com/mr-lincolns-weapons/.

20. Lt. Gen. James Longstreet served as Robert E. Lee's second-in-command for most of Lee's tenure as commander of the Army of Northern Virginia.

21. The concept of soldiers voting in the field originated in the South. From there, it spread to Missouri and Iowa. Following bitter controversy, Wisconsin was the next Union state to adopt this concept on September 28, 1862. Although Abraham Lincoln would have won the election even without the soldier vote, it did increase his margin of victory. Klement, *Wisconsin in the Civil War*, 38–40.

*Camp of the 22nd Wis., Near Marrieta [Marietta],
Monday June 27, 1864*

. . . Strange to relate, our company is all right yet. Not one has been killed and none wounded since I wrote last. I am not in a writing mood, so you won't expect much of a letter.

We have been for the last fifty days where we could hear cannon and musket firing *nearly* every day. A good portion of that time we have been under fire. We, that is our brigade, have been on the front line nearly all the time. But last night the 3rd Brigade relieved us, and now we are lying a little in the rear. We have been in only one hard fight or charge, and I guess no brigade has. We have been advanced on and have driven them back. But the principle part of our fighting has been advancing up to them and building works. We generally go up within eighty rods at least. I think there won't be much charging done on our part, but I cannot tell.

I want to speak a word about our Colonels. You remember that I was a Bloodgood man. Well, a great many of the boys were, but the majority of the regiment were in favor of Utley. Now B. is all the choice. Utley can't move a regiment its length in three times the time that B. can. He makes a good man to tell stories; is good grit enough, but lacks both ability and self esteem. He is too excitable. He makes too many mistakes. Now last night when we were relieved—it was about nine in the evening (We always wait until dark to make such moves). He said "Left face" then, "right face" for we wanted to go out by the left flank. So the four companies right faced and the six left companies left faced, and each moved right away from the other. We, the left, were right and the right ran around in the woods. Then the old Colonel just kept moving us up and down, and couldn't tell where to go, and finally stopped and we lay down until morning, and then came up here where we belonged at first. He would make a good hotelkeeper, but no soldier.

Well, have you any rain? I wish you had some of this rain that has been falling here, but now it is clear.

It is amusing to listen to the skirmishers, and hear them yell out to one another. You have heard lots about it in the papers, I suppose. I never believed it was true, but now I know it is. One of our men yelled, "Say Johnnie, how long do you calculate to fight us"? Answer—"Till hell freezes over, and then twice on the ice." Another, "Say Johnnie, here is your old sow and pigs (for there were some in the woods), come over and get them." Answer———etc. A reb begins to bark like a dog. Then one of our men crowed, which made the Johnnies mad, and they shot back. One would yell "Cease firing," and they all stop till some one says "ready." On their last retreat they left a note on a bayonet with this written on it—"You d— Yankee son of a b—, you killed our Gen Polk." And lots of such.

We are going to get some new clothes today or tomorrow and will look, if not feel, a little better. The boys feel well, are anxious to see the end of this campaign. They say the country here is twice as strongly fortified by nature than any beyond. It is open, level country beyond here. So I think when we get them out of this we can soon take Atlanta.

Old Wm. H.H. Minot is all sound; feels good, and is always full of life and fun. I don't think of anything more to write this time. I will write as often as opportunity permits, and so must you.

We have regained a good name. As you know we were rather looked on as cowardly after Thompson's Station, but now we are all right.[22]

Yours in love, from the "Whitehead," L.S. Moseley[23]

NOTES

22. The men of the 22nd Wisconsin felt "redeemed by fire at Resaca." They felt the apprenticeship was now over; they had become competent and battle-hardened soldiers. Groves, *Blooding the Regiment*, 313.

23. The origin of the term "whitehead," found in numerous Civil War letters, is not clear, but it appears to describe someone who could move at a swift pace when necessary.

◑

Camp in the field, near Marrietta [Marietta], Saturday, July 2nd, 1864

Dear parents and brother,

. . . There is evidently some move on foot, but what it is I do not know.

I received mother's letter yesterday containing the dollar and was very glad of it sure. I sent after some tobacco and more money in the next letter after the one in which I sent for the dollar . . . We have drawn new clothes, and today we are a different looking lot of boys. I have a new pair of pants and a new shirt, and am comfortable and nice. I put a pair of pockets in my pants that, I think, defy criticism . . .

Last night very unexpectedly to us, nearly half of the company were summoned to appear at court-martial today, U.S. Cap Brown. We supposed it had all blown over, and we were doomed to serve under him, but we find that justice can be done, and the suit is now being tried. I don't know how it will result but I do hope they will dismiss him, and I think they will, for he is a rascal.

Now I have something more in this line to tell you. It is in regard to our Colonel [Utley] and Lieut. Colonel [Bloodgood]. Ever since we have been here the old Colonel has appeared very childish indeed. At times not appearing to know upon receiving an order, how to execute it or what to do. At the battle of Resaca they shook hands, and said all was made up, but they kept picking at each other. Now the old Colonel has resigned, and the Lieut. said he had to be court-martialed. This morning they got to disputing about it, and at length the old Colonel called. B. a lying, sneaking, cowardly puppy, and after a little B. told him he lied. At this U. struck B. and jumped on him. B. did not touch him only to defend himself—acting the perfect gentleman— but told U. that the time would yet come when they would be on equal footing. Then U. said—"You d— pup! I will try you any time at forty paces." I never heard a man call another meaner names, nor abuse another worse than U. did B. This goes to show that I was right one year ago when I thot B. was the man.[24]

To illustrate Utley's military abilities, let me narrate a small incident. When we first came to this position we were in Brigade front. That is there are three Brigades in a division, and the Brigade front would be one Brigade in line of battle with the other two right behind it in lines. We were in front, so after we had been there two days, the 1st Brigade came to relieve us. That is, take our place and we go back where there would be less danger, and where we could take off our cartridge boxes etc. The relieving had to be done in the night so the enemy could not see us and fire on us. So when the 1st Brigade came we were to move out by the left flank, so as to give them a chance to come in, and thus keep the line full. We did not have to move over forty rods. The old Colonel came to the left and said to pass the order up the line to "*right* face." The order had to be given in this way so the enemy would not hear it. He saw he was wrong after the boys began to laugh. And then he said, "*Forward, boys, this way.*" So we had to about face without any military order. The four companies on the right moved out by the right flank as ordered, and the six left companies went with the old *women*. We were over three hours getting where we were ordered to go, which ought to have been done in less than thirty minutes. And then we did not get to the right place, but had to move again in the morning. You will very plainly see that in action such slowness of movement would prove fatal not only to the regiment, but might be to the whole army. But he is going home. Bloodgood can get us around double-quick. It was just so again last night, for we were relieved and had to come back on the last line, and it has been just so every time we have moved. One night he took us right up to the rebs breastworks where they could have shot every one of us if they had not supposed we were going to charge their works and waited. For we never could have gone near there. Near morning we were moved out. He is a good man in his place, but if he wants to soldier, a private is fully as high as he should aspire. One year ago 2/3 of his regiment were for him, but now I don't believe there are ten in the regiment. So much for officers. I don't want you *to read this letter or tell what I have written about officers* in it to *anybody*. Wait and let the other boys write about it first.

We have just received a letter from Pole. The boys are doing first rate. I wish I knew what was going to be done, but as I don't, I can't write. I hope I shall be spared, but lots of young men as anxious to live as I have to fall. Let us hope for the best. I feel as tho I was going thru all right. I will write as often as convenient, but if you don't get letters from me you must not worry. This is the greatest of my fears—that you will all the time be worrying about me. We are seeing hard times to be sure, but they can't always last. I am feeling as good as I ever did in my life; have good clothes, food enough—such as it is, and it is good enough for the times. It tastes as good to us now as a boiled dinner used to at home. The boys are all well, and *lousey*. Frank Smith is in Nashville sick.

It is raining again. I hear you have had a good rain at home, for which I am *very thankful*. The papers report a severe drought in Texas.

If old Fisher is not to severe in price, please send me a little paper, for I am out. This is some Cap gave me. I can buy sugar for 15 cents per pound. We buy it of the commissary with the officers, for they have to buy their provisions. We have no suttler with us, and can't get a single thing only in this way. We see where we drive the Johnnies, that they have peas, potatoes, and everything of the sort. They, of course, can get such things. We can't, for we are on a ridge of the Altoona mountains where there is nothing— just woods . . .

NOTE

24. This confrontation with Bloodgood led to Utley's resignation, citing ill health as the documented reason. Utley gave a farewell speech to the troops on July 2, 1864. He left the 22nd Wisconsin and never returned. Groves, *Blooding the Regiment*, 323.

꩜

Tuesday, July 5th, 1864

Ever dear home,

When I last wrote we expected it was the last chance we would have in ten days, but we find that we can write again. I received your very kind letter last night, dated June 26th, and containing $3 greenbacks. I received the $1 sent before. The tobacco has not reached me yet, but I guess it will next mail. I am very sorry I sent for the last money, or the tobacco, for I could easily get along without either. We get a great plenty to eat. Don't for one minute think we are going hungry. At the time I wrote for the money we were having an awful wet time. The roads were so bad the supply trains could not keep up very well, so we were a little short then. Now we have an abundance . . .

When the order was issued about the mail, we were going to abandon the R.R. back to Dallas, and move the whole force forward round in the rebel's rear, but the Johnnies were too smart for us. The morning of the 23rd we found the rebels had evacuated and fallen back, leaving Marrietta and the Kennesaw mountains in our possession. They had five lines of works in our front. I heard our Gen Hooker say that he never saw such strong works.

We marched on the 3rd about ten miles, nearly all the way in line of battle, thru woods and thick underbrush, and if it wasn't hot and hard work! I never saw it. Our company were on the skirmish line most of the time. Our regiment were reserved for the skirmishers all the way.

Gen Butterfield has gone to Washington and Gen Ward is in command of our division, and as usual, he was very drunk this day, so he just kept us going until he ran us right spang up to the rebel breastworks. We were in about threequarters of a mile of them. It was all open field and we were on one hill and they on another. We had no support on either flank. Part of the time we were a head or even with the rebel columns who were retreating on each side of us. When we came up on the hill, the rebs opened with shell on us. They threw too high or low all the time, and only two or three were hit in the brigade—none in our regiment, but it was very uncomfortable for us to lie there. If the rebs had known our position they would have taken the old 2nd brigade all prisoners. But they soon dried up. Gen Hooker rode up to Ward, and told him not to move a man, but to remain there and make as good a show as possible, and he would have support up as soon as he could. He gave Ward an awful blowing for running us up so fast. Ward was going right on to charge the rebs. The truth is, the rebs are so afraid of us that they just get out of our way as fast as they can.

We were relieved at night and moved about three miles to the right and rested. The 4th, we lay still until four P.M., then moved on to the right about four miles. Then old Ward saw a line of men in front of us and taking them for Johnnies, ordered us to build breastworks as fast as possible. Just as we had finished, or nearly so, a man came up from the supposed rebs and proved to be a Union officer. It was the 16th corps. We lay there until the morning of the 5th and then found the rebs had fallen back again. So we advanced again, and are near the Chattahoochie river, probably will be reserve for quite a while as we have always been in the front.

Every day we see lots of rebs who come in and join the union. They are awful sick of fighting us, and come over to us just as fast as they can get away. They guard their ranks to keep them in, but they keep coming in squads of one to eight or ten.[25] It surely looks encouraging, but it gives me the blues. Oh! What are you going to do. I feel very much afraid of the future. No one can tell what it has in store for us. I don't feel concerned about myself, but for you. You are getting old and it pains me to know that you have to work so hard for even a good living. If we can't, what will thousands of other do who are in worse circumstances than we? I am getting $18 a month now. I shall spend but little, and I know we can get along *first rate*. I don't want you to give yourselves the least uneasiness about our rations, for since our muddy time we have all of us had *all we wanted*. The cattle you spoke of, or some others are here, and in fact, have beef all the time. We get all the fresh beef we want. It is hard to keep in this hot weather, but we boil it and it is good. We have plenty of hardtack, a little good salt pork, plenty of good coffee, and a little sugar. We can guy good brown sugar off the commissary for 15 cents per pound. So this is good enough, isn't it, on a campaign? . . .

NOTE

25. Both Union and Confederate armies had problems with desertion through-out the war. Confederate desertions and defections to the Union lines increased in the final months as Southerners recognized that the war would likely end in their defeat. An estimated 103,000 men left Confederate ranks over the course of the war; more than 280,000 Union soldiers deserted. Actual numbers may have been much higher as many felt compelled to return home to their suffering families. See Mark A. Weitz, *More Damning than Slaughter: Desertion in the Confederate Army* (Lincoln, NE: University of Nebraska Press, 2006), 208–10, 290.

ᐁᐁ

Thursday, July 7th, 1864

. . . Yesterday we moved about eight miles round to left, to get about two miles . . . The boys say they can see the city of Atlanta from the tops of the trees, so it can't be many miles off.[26]

It is very quiet this morning. We will lie here until there is a force thrown around the enemies' flanks, and then will probably leave again. It will take some four or five days so you see we have a *good rest*, which we need the worst way. The boys are all very tired. I feel very much worn out, but a little rest will put me to rights again.

I wish father would ask Fisher if he knows the laws passed for sending things to soldiers, and see if he won't make it right. I don't care so much for the amount as I do about being swindled by such a man. He must have lots of patriotism to swindle a poor boy who is off fighting for his sake in that way. If so, why all we can do is stand it I suppose for the present—but not so always. The Janesville boys get it for twelve cents per pound. It must not be sealed up, only tied. This is the law, and I know it.

We have just drawn rations. We have some vinegar and some dessicated vegetables extra this time . . .

I tell you, I just believe that company of 100 day men are going to see a hard time. They are not used to the living or climate, and don't know how to take care of themselves, and I believe lots of them will die. They don't see half such times as we do, but they will be sick of soldiering before they are out.

Well, I don't think of anything more . . . Cap. Schoening of Company B is losing his sight, and went to the hospital this morning. It is strange about it. But I must close,

Yours in love and respect, L.S. Moseley

NOTE

26. "On July 5 Sherman and Johnston fought the minor Battle of Chattahoochee River; another five days and Johnston had retired to the defenses of Atlanta, Sherman on his heels. Now at last Atlanta was in sight." Henry Steele Commager, *The Blue and the Gray: The Story of the Civil War* (New York: Fairfax Press, Bobbs-Merrill Co., 1950), 935.

Camp of 22nd Wis. Reg., Tuesday July 12, 1864

Loved and respected parents –

. . . I have not received the high-priced tobacco, and I guess I never will, for we had ten trains captured by the enemy—at least it is so reported here. As it has not come yet, it must have been on one of them. Some of my good luck.

The rebels are now across the Chattahoochie river. It seems to me that every time they leave stronger and more impregnable works than the lst. The ones they left here in front of us have trees about eight inches thru, put into the top of their works, very solidly, about ten inches apart. They are about fourteen feet high, and sharpened on the top. So if there was nothing to oppose, it would be almost impossible for a man to get over.

We now go on picket within two rods of the river, and the rebs are as near on the other side. The river is not over fifteen rods across. Night before last was the first time we were down so near. We went out in the night and built pits to get in, and in the morning the "Johnnies" found the "Yanks" right under their noses. They yelled out to our boys and said "Oh Yanks! If you won't fire, we won't." "Well, Johnnie, agreed." So there the two enemies were. Both went right out in plain sight, and built fires—our boys went to cooking coffee and they to making johnnie-cake. It was not long before there was some of them over on our side of the river, drinking coffee with our boys, and our boys went over with them and they gave us tobacco. Every time they crossed they had to swim. Last night some of them came over and joined the union.[27]

Will Minot is on picket now, and I go on tonight. They all say in front of us that they are sick of fighting. They say that if the officers were to put Tennessee troops on picket, they would come over to us. But they keep them in the rear to build works.

I saw an Atlanta paper of the eighth. It says we do not fight them fair, for we won't come right up in front of them and charge their works, but go around and shoot into their ends. It says Lee has provision enough in Virginia to last them twenty months, and the Yanks never can take it. It certainly is a hard job, but I guess Grant will take it if we will only be patient and give him time. I can see now that it takes time to do such things. It is natural for people way off at home to become impatient and want the armies to rush right in, and clean them out and have it done with. But a soldier in the front would rather wait ten days, and flank the enemy out of strong position, than to rush right on to them and charge their heavy works. Gen Sherman seems to be taking it very easy at present. All he wants is to keep them busy, so they can't go to Virginia. He is letting our Corps which has seen the hardest time, lie here and rest, and has sent the 23rd and 16th with some cavalry across the river. I don't know what they are doing, but I expect the first thing we know we will hear of them on old Johnson's [Gen. Joseph E. Johnston's] flank, or perhaps rear, and they getting out of this. If we did not have a superior force we could not drive the rebs at all.

. . . Father says he is falling away in flesh. I should suppose he would some. I guess I have fallen off more than that, for I used to weigh 175 pounds, and now I don't believe I weigh 145. When we were in Nashville I weighed 155, and I have lost lots since. You never saw me so poor as I am now, but I feel well, only am lazy. The hot weather makes us all feel stupid. I always thot I would be a large heavy man, but guess I never will weigh 180. How much does Ed weigh? I'll bet he is as heavy, if not as large as I am, but he can't take me down. The boys are all well and feeling good.

I wrote a letter yesterday to Bill Latta in the 40th. I'll bet lots of those boys will be sick down there. They are beginning to talk about our regiment reinlisting. They say they will give us sixty days furlough, and I've no doubt but lots of the boys will go in again. But you may rest assured that Corp. L.S. Moseley is not going in again—at any rate until he has been a citizen a while first, and then if he goes it will be in some other branch of service than Infantry. For Infantry does all the fighting and carrying knapsacks etc. I will forgo the pleasure of sixty days at home for the greater pleasure of knowing that if I ever do come home I can stay.

You have no idea how dreadful thick the flies are—in fact every description of insect imagineable. They just torture a poor fellow to death nearly. But I must close. The reason I have written so fine is because this is the last sheet of paper I have, and I must save half of it until next time. It costs 75 cents per quire here, and I have to go three miles to get it then.

Yours in love, L.S. Moseley

NOTE

27. "Johnny Reb" and "Billy Yank" were frequently in close contact. "Civil War narratives are filled with examples of fraternization across picket lines, the exchange of tobacco and food, acts of courtesy and friendliness." Commager, *Blue and the Gray*, 325.

❧

Camp 22nd Wis. Vol. in the field near the Chattahoochie [Chattahoochee], Sat., July 16, 1864

Dear Parents:

I received a letter from you dated July 3rd and on coming in from picket duty before yesterday I found another dated the 5th. I was a little afraid at first to open it, as I had received a letter so lately. But it did not take me long to find out that it was all right. I never had a letter do me more good, for I was thinking all day how I would like to hear from home. Besides, I was on duty with some of the 33rd Indiana boys and their time is up now in a few days. They were talking all the time about what nice times they were going to have soon. And when we were eating our hardtack they would say, "Well, boys, in a week or two I will have some of mother's hardtack with butter on them." I must confess it made me a little homesick. You can't blame me for it, can you?

We are in the same place as when I wrote you last. We have great times talking with the Johnnies. Our skirmish line is right on the edge of the river, and theirs is as close on the other side. The river is not as wide as the Rock River is, but is deep, swift and muddy. We go in swimming on our side, and they on theirs, at the same time. The day I was down there, there were 100 of each on the banks, talking and trading. We would swim over to them and trade anything we had for tobacco. One of them gave me a piece. They are very generous and talkative. Not a shot is fired from either side the whole length of our corps. Up in the 17th corps they pop away all the time. Our line is right under their forts but they sit and run around all over it and each is true to his word, as maintains the silence. There are orders on both sides now, not to talk. Both go in swimming but neither cross or speak.

We have the camp all cleaned up nicely and shades built over our tent so we manage to keep as cool as possible. But it is hot here, I can tell you.

It doesn't seem to me that there would be any further move made until cooler weather, but I don't know of course.

I don't know of anything new to write this time. I have had the same luck with my tobacco as with my potatoes. It has not come yet and I am pretty sure it never will. I am so sorry but it can't be helped now. Sime Sage had a nice pair of checked shirts come by mail the other day for sixteen cents postage and Serg. Dennison of Co G had one for eight cents. If old Fisher didn't act so mean I would have a pair sent to me, but as it is I will wear the government goods entirely. Woolen pants, woolen shirts and woolen coat is pretty hot suit for Georgia in July. Some of the boys have the checked shirts and overalls which they are allowed to wear as the overalls are about the same color as the pants. But as long as we lie still they are not so bad.

Will M. has gone after blackberries. They are not so thick as they were at Murfresboro. We have to go some three or four miles to get any but Will's traveling propensities are so great that he would go, I guess, twice that distance for them. He brot into camp a tin full of nice ripe huckleberries.

We expect to get our pay now in a short time. I hope we will for we all want it and some poor men that have families to support are actually in need of it.

I always supposed that this state was thickly inhabited but I actually should think that we have marched over a great many hundred miles that never were seen by white men before. Where we are not camped it is all forest, not a fence or house near.

There has a Corps suttler come up. He paid forty cents a quire, and forty cents a bunch for envelopes. It was not two hours before he sold all out, so now it is as bad as before.

I don't think of anything more this time. You last letter was mailed the 6th and I got it on the 13th—seven days coming. Some of the boys haven't heard from home in nearly a month and they say they know their folks write every week. So you see the mail doesn't run very regularly. I must dry up.

With love, I am, L.S. Moseley

Camp in the field, July 21st, 1864

More dear than ever parents and brother –

If you knew what the 22nd had been thru since I wrote last, this letter would be the most acceptable one you ever received from me.[28]

Sunday the 17th we moved eight miles up the river and crossed on pontoons made of canvas. The 18th we moved some five miles and went into camp where we lay all day the 19th. At two in the morning of the 20th we had orders to pack up and moved on to the southward about eight miles and the 22nd Wisconsin was detailed as skirmishers for the Division. Then after being deployed, we advanced, Co B being reserved for the left of the skirmishers and Co D on the right. We just everlastingly drove the "Johnnies" for some half or three quarters of a mile. Then we were just on top of a ridge. In front it descended irregularly. The boys just threw up some rails in front of them. You see, skirmishers are five steps apart—of course, could not make much of a line of works.

About 3 o'clock the boys saw the rebs advancing, and reported the same to the officers. But for some reason or other—no man knows why—our line of battle was not advancing, they being back over two ridges. Co B was ordered up in line with the skirmishers and in about five minutes we could see the Rebels just swarming out of the woods. You see they had come up thru an open field about eighty rods. Just as they began to come out of the woods we began to throw the lead pills at them. Gen. Geary threw shells at them.[29] I never saw such good shots in my life. We just put the lead to them in good shape, and let me add, there is no discount on the old 22nd and none on Beloit companies either.

We received lots of praise from big men for our acts of yesterday. We stood our ground and stuck to it, in hopes that our line of battle would get up to our support. But alas! They were too slow, or were too far off to reach us. We heard them coming and we yelled as hard as we could to hurry them up, but on came the rebs and we at length had to leave—they having forced our right back, and were getting in our rear, and to within five or six rods in front. So we fell back with the "Johnnies" close on our heels. About fifteen rods down the hill there was a ravine. Along both sides of it were very thick bushes. Our line of battle had just got into these bushes so the rebs did not see them. They thot they were driving us at a great rate, and on they came till they were so near we could almost shake hands with them. Then our men poured a deadly volley into them, just mowing the rascals, and you bet they began to get back over the hill again, covering the ground with their dead and wounded.

You will plainly see what an advantage they had over us. They had four lines, we only two, and one of them back. Here were on higher ground and if we had to fall back we would just have about forty rods of gauntlet to run, as we would have been exposed to their fire all the way. But thank God we did not have to run this gauntlet. On the contrary, they had to run a like one in gaining the top of the hill behind them. We did not lose the opportunity either, but poured volleys after them. That quickened the pace of some, and some—yes, a great many, were sent to their *long, long home* and *held it*, and now *hold it*. They kept up their vain attempts to retake the ridge till near dark. But no, the "Yanks" were up there and were bound to stay too. We kept up a continuous fire on them all the time, firing by volley, by company. In the night we straightened out our lines, forming two lines instead of one. We are in the second. Both have put up breastworks, and defy the whole Southern Confederacy to drive us out either. They can't do it.

Gen Ward said we did bully. Now I suppose you would like to know the casualties of the Beloit boys. Co B lost one killed and six wounded. Their names are as follows: John Jacobson (a Norwegian) shot thru the head and killed. Wm Orr shot thru the face, badly, but we think he will get over it. Sumner Nelson shot thru the ankle. His foot has been taken off. He is feeling well. He was transferred from Co C to Co B. Nelson Salisbury, Corp., hit in the right side, slightly. Serg. Fairservice was hit in the back, the ball passing thru his knapsack and all in it. The ball had lost its force and only bruised him. He stayed with us all the time. And one other, Tom Court, transferred from Co C. He was back as much as threequarters of a mile as cattle guard. He was shot thru the right shoulder, not bad.

Co I lost as follows: Henry Hunt shot through the breast, some hopes of his recovery. Ben Hanson shot thru the thigh. His leg is amputated close up. They say he will die. And Bowers, flesh wound in the thigh, very high up, doing well. The regiment lost seven killed, thirty-five wounded and two missing. Lieut. Ball wounded, doing well.[30]

Wm Minot is writing home so his folks will hear. He was not in the fight. For the first time in two years Bill was unwell and had to fall out. He is with us now and feeling better. Nothing the matter with him, I guess, only he ate too many green apples.

There were only twenty-nine muskets in our company when we went in and now there are only twenty-two left. The attack was general the whole length of the line. We licked them at every point.

Our boys have been busy all forenoon burying rebs. Charles Murry and I had the pleasure of covering up the remains of Col Knapp of the 33rd Miss. He was as brave a man as I ever saw. There were three stands of colors taken in our lines and it is reported that our Division took seven. The 26th Wisconsin took one—a nice one too. Our brigade have buried all the dead from our brigade in one place, and fixed up the place as well as possible. We have buried over one hundred and twenty rebs that were killed between where our skirmish line was, and the ravine in which they attacked us—not over twenty rods in width and the length of our brigade. There are any quantity of dead ones in front which we cannot bury. Lots of their wounded fell into our hands and there were lots and lots of them taken prisoners by us.[31]

I tell you what it is—it is a big victory for us. We have never had such a good chance to show what we are, and remember, there were four lines of rebs and only two of us. But it was an open field and fair fight and we whipped them two to one. We can do it every time. Col. Bloodgood behaved well. Cap. Brown ran like a whitehead. He started once and the boys yelled to him to come back, and he did. In a minute he left. If you could have seen those long legs just getting down the hill you would have at least pronounced him a good runner. Now can you expect men to be brave and cheerful and encourage their officers when they are the first to leave, and when it is their place to encourage us? But there is true mettle in what is left of us, and you can depend that they will never give Beloit reason to be ashamed of them.

Homer Miller is detailed again as teamster, so he was not in. His regiment was next to us. I found an old schoolmate in it this morning—Nicholson. Mr. Fisk will recollect him. We have reports that McPherson and Schofield are within one and one half miles of Atlanta. We are within about four or five miles. The mail goes in a minute, so goodbye for this time. I have not had time to read this over to see if you can read it, but it looks awful bad, as my hand cramps and my pencil is not over one inch long.

Love to all. Ed, my boy, I love you. Write me. L.S. Moseley

NOTES

28. Lute's letter of July 21, 1864, described the Battle of Peachtree Creek, another victory that boosted the morale of the entire regiment. Total Union casualties were estimated at about 1,700; Confederate casualties were more than 2,500. American Battlefield Trust, accessed July 7, 2022, https://www.battlefields.org/learn/articles/battle-peach-tree-creek/.

29. Brig. Gen. John Geary, Division Commander, Army of the Potomac.

30. Coburn's Brigade lost seven officers wounded, thirty-three men killed, 169 wounded, and seven missing, making a total of 216 casualties. "The ferocity of the fighting on the front of Coburn's Brigade, from which they emerged victorious, strongly attests to the bravery and fighting qualifications of these soldiers, which were never questioned again. This was their greatest day." Welcher and Ligget, *Coburn's Brigade*, 240.

31. "The real battle came when that field of horror was witnessed. Along the fighting line where the hand to hand conflict had been, the dead and dying soldiers, blue and gray lying side by side, were piled everywhere . . . The Union soldiers in charge of the field gave aid, indiscriminately, to all the wounded, and honorable burial for the dead." *Terre-Haute Tribune*, "Memories of the Civil War," October 15, 1911, from interview with James H. Crabb, Company G of the 85th Indiana.

CHAPTER 5

The Fall of Atlanta and Sherman's March to the Sea

July 25, 1864–December 26, 1864

We don't want to stop until we get Atlanta.

—LUCIUS S. MOSELEY, August 1, 1864

Service: Chattahoochee River Bridge August 26—September 2. Occupation of Atlanta September 2–November 15. March to the sea November 15–December 10. Siege of Savannah December 10–21.

—DYER, *Compendium*, vol. 3, 1682, 1683

Camp near Atlanta—Monday, July 25, 1864[1]

Dear Home,

Last night I received a *good long letter* from you and glad indeed was I. George Perkins gave me this leaf out of an old writing book. I had a good supply of paper when we left Lookout Valley but some of the boys were out and I let them have some and now mine is gone. But you have sent me some, which I think will be here next mail. So I am all right, that is if it comes. My tobacco never got here but I hope the paper will.

I hav'nt much news to write. I wrote you on the 21st after our fight. The 22nd the rebs fell back and we advanced right after them. We are now within two miles of Atlanta, instead of in there. But we will soon be in. They have some awful strong works here—forts, redoubts and lounetts, and they amuse themselves by throwing solid shot at us nearly all the time.[2]

They can't—or at least they don't—hurt anyone. We are behind a hill so they can't hurt us. Most every hour they throw shells at us but they either strike in the hill or they go way over. The chief of artillery said last night that they could not hit us. We can use our artillery very little yet for we hav'nt sufficient protection but before long we will show them the Yankee of it, for we are building works, forts, etc. Then we will get some of our large rifle guns into position and tear them to pieces. I have heard of but two or three being hurt by their shells yet.

We heard a bell ring in Atlanta this morning. I suppose there was some of the worst fighting done on our left on the 21st that was ever done in this department. They drove our men back and then we drove them; they drove our back and ours drove them and held the ground, driving them one half mile farther than at first. They killed Gen. McPherson and Brig-Gen. Smith. It is reported that we killed Gen. Hardee and have his kady.[3] I do not know if it is true. We have built the best kind of earthworks. They can't throw a shot thru them. They are as much as ten or twelve feet thick. In my opinion it will take a regular siege to take this place but it will be a large victory when we do get it.

Old Co. B [Bloodgood] now has twenty-one muskets. Our effective force— three Serg, three Corporals and fifteen men—some less than we left Cincinnatti with. Most of them are detailed tho.

Wm Minot received the cedar camphor day before yesterday. We couldn't imagine what it was but thot it was only a joke of Frank's. But the letter explained the matter. Altho it is useless to try to kill off the lice while we are all the time camping on the rebels old camping ground. When the campaign is done and we go into camp again we can soon get rid of them but never while we are on the continual move. I have to thank Eddie for his extra good long letters. He wrote more news after he was going to close than he did before. I am much obliged to him.

I think you are wrong in thinking that Sile Wright hasn't a bad wound, for the ball went straight thru his arm. He is a good soldier; was hit way out in front of the line and has a worse wound than Pole. We are all glad that he has gone home. If you see him, give him my best respects and tell him he has missed the best part of it. Ask him if he gets plenty of tobacco. Tell him when he is putting those great chews into his maw to think of George and me. Then see him laugh. Ask him if the greybacks bite as hard in Wisconsin as they do in Georgia.[4]

Wm Minot wants to know if those cedar chips are to make coffins for the greybacks. I got poisoned with ivy on the 20th and my face and hands are swollen so I look nice and fat . . .

I have managed to get rid of my three dollars already. I don't know as there is any show for us getting any pay. We won't until we get this matter settled. I don't care if you send me another dollar, and another little thing— if Ed thinks of it when he is down town I would like to have him get a sheet of fine emery paper. When you write just put in a piece the size of the letter each time. It is hard work to keep our guns clean without it and a small piece helps considerably.

I believe the weather is cooler here now than it is in Wisconsin. The nights are very cool; we have to put our tents over us to keep warm . . .

I will write as often as convenient and you must write often. Please thank Miss Minot for sending William so many papers, for I get them to read. I received a paper from Mr. Fisk a few days ago.

The boys are well.

Yours in love, Lucius S. Moseley

NOTES

1. The battles for Atlanta took place between July 20 and July 28, 1864, with the new Confederate commander, John Bell Hood, striking Sherman's advancing army three times: at Peachtree Creek to the north; then just west of Decatur (in what became known as the Battle of Atlanta); and again at Ezra Church to the east. Although Hood lost all three battles, the city remained in Confederate hands. Formidable Confederate works surrounding Atlanta discouraged Sherman for a direct attack, but the hungry, exhausted soldiers defending Atlanta could not hold out once Sherman's armies had cut off their supplies. Ward, *Civil War*, 326–29.

2. A redoubt ("place of retreat") was an enclosed fortification protecting soldiers outside the main defensive line. It could be a permanent structure or a hastily constructed temporary fortification. The lunette is also a protective fortification with two faces and two flanks, open at the back.

3. Brig. Gen. James B. McPherson was killed in the Battle of Atlanta on June 22, 1864. He died in combat while facing the army of his boyhood friend and West Point classmate John Bell Hood. General Hardee survived the war and lived until November 6, 1873. His "kady" was a straw hat or derby, which may have been lost in the field of battle. Brig. Gen. Smith, mentioned in Lute's letter of July 25, 1864, may have been a mistaken name or report of death.

4. "Greybacks": Union soldiers' slang term for body lice, which also likened them to Confederate soldiers in their gray uniforms. Confederates called their lice "blue-backs."

Camp near Atlanta, Aug. 1st, 1864

Dear Home,

Here I come again, with little new or interesting news but with assurance that I am all right yet.

I give you a sort of map of our lines on a small scale. [This map did not survive.] A represents our old lines and B the rebel where they charged us on the 20th. We took those works and they went down and pitched into McPherson, on our left.[5] Where the line is drawn across both lines we advance to the letter C. Their works are very strong inside the line that shows where our lines are. They have large forts and the strongest works. McPherson came around on our right to the letter D, where his force was attacked and had a severe fight. Our division was then set down to protect the flank, and now forms that hook—our regiment lying about where those little marks are. We want to cut that R.R. running nearly south, but it is a very difficult matter as our men found out yesterday. They sent a division out to see and found a swamp between us and the R.R. and a rebel fort to protect it.[6] So you see, we hav'nt got Atlanta yet. As you suppose, it is very easy for people at home to take such places with a pen, but when it has to be done with powder and lead it is a different thing altogether. I suppose people north think we have already used up time enough to take such places but I believe if they were here in the ranks they would be glad to have a few days rest now and then. It is now eighty-six days since we have been where we could hear the explosion of powder and in this climate I think it is time to rest. But we don't want to stop till we get Atlanta.

Yesterday (Sunday) I was on picket. I got your letter then, written the Sunday before. This morning I have been all forenoon cleaning my gun. I hav'nt written as soon as I should. I have received neither tobacco nor paper. I don't know why I can't get such things by mail as well as the other boys. There were a large lot of packages this P.M. but none for me. I *know* the boys have, and *do* receive every day, tobacco by mail from home for eight cents per pound. If mine would only come I would be willing to let it drop.

I don't know of anything new to write. Bill Minot received a stack of papers from home today. I am very much obliged to you for that cedar camphor but there is no use at all trying to keep rid of greybacks while we are camping on a new piece of ground every night. It is the old camping ground of the rebels. We have all had them since we began this campaign. When it ends we will soon get rid of them, I'll tell you.

I am in no writing mood today so guess you will have to put up with a poor letter. I did think nearly every minute of yesterday afternoon that you were writing to me. It rained very hard yesterday afternoon here.

I will try to write my dear good grandmother a letter very soon. Give her my very best . . .

Love, Lute

NOTES

5. Maj. Gen. Oliver O. Howard became commander of the Army of Tennessee following McPherson's death on July 22. In this letter, Lute apparently referred to the forces McPherson had commanded.

6. Large sections of the Confederacy's railroad system had been destroyed. Sherman's army was especially proficient at destroying railroads—and repairing them as well—when necessary to their purposes. McPherson, *Ordeal by Fire*, 443.

In the trenches before Atlanta—Sat., Aug. 6th, 1864

Dear Home,

A few words again from honest old Lute. There is nothing new or important. We came up and took our position a few days ago, just to the right of the Chattanooga R.R. The bridge is completed and the cars run clear down to our lines, so the Johnnies can hear them.

There is a fight somewhere on the lines most every day, the rebs attacking, and in every case getting most beautifully whipped and losing lots of men. They tried the 8th Corps, on the left, last night and were cleaned out. We keep advancing our lines up to them. In some cases they are so near they can't put out skirmishers, but we have them out all the time. Our brigade has advanced our lines and have an awful strong line now, with an abuttice [abatis] in front made of peach tree that they can't get thru.[7] Then we have dug a large ditch just on the outside.

I wish they would try us, for we could whip them nicely. It is reported that in every place we have been fighting our men have buried women dressed in uniform. They say there were nine where we fought them on the 20th.[8]

Frank Kelly has been missing since the 20th and some artillery men report that they buried him. He was a musician and was, of course, in the rear so we did not find him.[9]

The rebs amuse themselves nearly all the time by throwing what we call camp kettles, or large shell at our works. They are six inches in diameter and are about fourteen inches long. But they can't throw them straight and they can't throw them thru the breastworks. I have heard of but one man being hit. He belonged to the 33rd. We are always very lucky.

Cap. Brown had a letter from home last night. He says Mr. Underwood of Geneva wants to sell his place. He asks $600 for it. Cap was telling me what kind of a place it is. Now I was thinking that perhaps you would like to go out and see it and maybe you will like it. I don't know anything about the place, was never there to notice the place, and only speak of it.

Last night I had a letter from you dated April 24th. Rather slow in coming I should say. Our brigade is trying to get the Spencer rifle. It is a nice gun—shoots seven times and does not take as long to load the seven loads as the one in the old gun.[10] We will have to pay $28 for them. That is it will be taken out of our pay, and then when the time is out we can keep them or turn them in and get our money back. They furnish us cartridges. Now I think it is a good plan. I have seen the time when I would give that much money just for the use of one for a little while. What do you think of it?

I find that I am in debt to the government $9.81 on my last account. This will be taken out of my pay. I have tried to be as saving as I could but at the same time I intend to have good clothes. I owe about medium in comparison to the other boys. Some owe over twenty and some the government owe.

All for now, Love, Lute

NOTES

7. The abatis was an arrangement of felled trees with branches facing outward, one of the oldest forms of defensive fortification.

8. An estimated 700 (or more) women disguised themselves as men and fought in Union and Confederate armies. The secrecy of their service has made an accurate count impossible. Their motivations were much the same as those of male soldiers—a need to share the trials of loved ones, ardent patriotism, idealism, thirst for adventure, and financial need. DeAnne Blanton, "Women in the Civil War," *Prologue Magazine*, vol. 25, no.3, Spring 1993, https://www.archives.gov/publications/prologue/1993/spring/women-in-the-civil-war-3. html/.

9. Frank Kelly of Beloit survived the war and was mustered out on June 12, 1865.

10. The Spencer rifle was the world's first military metallic-cartridge repeating rifle. The Spencer Repeating Rifle Company, established in 1862, supplied some 106,000 of the seven-shooters for the Union war effort. Rick Britton, "A New Kind of Firepower that Gave Union Soldiers a Fearsome Edge," July 7, 2022, https://www.historynet.com/anew-kind-of-firepower/.

～

In the trenches before Atlanta, Friday, Aug. 12th, 1864

My dear loved mother and brother –

I shall expect a letter from you when the mail comes today, so I thot I would write my letter this morning and have it ready.

We have advanced our lines again, or have had a laboring party putting up works in front, and this afternoon we are to move out and occupy them.

I am on picket and so if I don't write now I won't have time in two or three days. There has been no fighting now for five or six days, only artillery. This has been most constant. Even now while I write, the roar is most deafening. The enemy have inflicted, as yet, little or no injury. What effect ours will have on them I don't know. We are getting some large guns into position and it is my opinion they will make it warm for the Johnnies.

I heard yesterday that there are 40,000 reinforcements coming to us and Oh! I hope it is true, for I believe the rebels have been strongly reinforced.

Wm Minot and I went along up the line yesterday, as far as the R.R. There is one place where we could see perfectly plain a large rebel fort. We could even see three embrasures and the ends of the guns.[11] But they have to keep quiet as we have some 20 pounders that command it. We could also see the city, which is said by the artillery men to be 15,000 yards distance. Our men throw shell over into it every few minutes. On top of their fort is a flag bearing the stars and bars, which, it seemed to me, was ashamed to float out to the breezes of heaven, but hung shamefully by the side of the staff. It is the only one I have seen put up in sight, while we nearly always display the stars and stripes on our works before each regiment. Our old regimental flag looks the worse for wear. It is some soiled and has a great many bullet holes thru it—one thru the staff, cutting it most off.

The boys are in good spirits but we are all worn out. We are now on duty nearly all the time. We are on picket every three days and the rest of the time we are putting up breastworks. I truly hope we will be able to take this place soon and that they will then give us a rest. I wouldn't be at home and drafted now for a thousand dollars. I am glad that I came when I did. Mother, if I live till one year from today I think we will start home. Our time is not out until the 2nd of September, but it will do to count from this date as we will start from the field as soon as the 12th of August. Two thirds of the time gone and I am all right yet. One short year more. If, after this campaign, we go into quarters and lie around some three or four months, the last year will pass off quickly—but dinner is ready now and I will eat and then finish my epistle.

Well, I have taken a long nooning, for it is now Tuesday the 16th. We are in our new line of works all right and have advanced our skirmish line so that we stand picket very close to the enemy . . . [missing page(s).]

NOTE

11. Embrasures were notches cut in the top of fortification walls through which guns or cannons could be fired.

Camp 22nd Wis., Vol. Monday Aug. 22nd, 1864

Ever dear home,

Will Minot and I have just sat down to a rudely constructed table to write a few lines to loved ones at home. We have both just received a letter from home. Mine contained a splendid piece of emery paper very much needed by me, a one dollar greenback and two stamps, besides a few words from each of you. Now just for a moment imagine how glad a boy is to receive such, when 800 or 900 miles from home with all means of communicating with them at times cut off and with 50,000 men within a few miles and some within a few rods, any one of whom would gladly take his life.

I suppose you are aware ere this that old Wheeler is in our rear, and is doing all the damage to us he can by cutting the R.R. He has succeeded once or twice in cutting it, but not in holding it.[12]

I have not received a letter from you before this for two weeks, so now there is another yet due me. There is but little of importance to write this time as there has been no material change in our lines. We have silenced the rebel batteries along our line so they have not fired a shot in three days. There has been no firing, only skirmishing, and our batteries which throw shells over into the city, and sometimes at the rebel skirmish pits, every few minutes. I was on the skirmish line yesterday but we have got so now we fire but very few shots on the line. The rebs appear to be glad of it, for they fire but seldom.

Bert is alive and getting along first rate. He was not wounded nearly as badly as we first supposed. The ball went in just below the cheek bone on the right side of the face and came out to the skin under the left ear, then followed around under the skin to the back part of the head where it came out. He eats and talks and says he will be back in a short time, but he won't; he will probably get a furlough and come home.

There was a mail came in day before yesterday. I had a letter from Frank Latta. He sent me a newspaper containing some paper and envelopes. He said he would keep me supplied so you see it is worth something to have friends. Bill Minot got a paper with two pieces of emery paper in it—one marked Lute Moseley and the other Wm Minot.

I don't know what to fill up this large blank with, but am going to keep right on scribbling until it is done.

Does Pole have any big stories to tell about us fellows? I'll bet he will spend what money he has got a hold of, but my gracious! If I had only been there to help him in his attack on that chicken pie! I think we would have shown you some military strategy and just overpowered it and swallowed it whole. Yes, I wouldn't be at all afraid to charge one alone, without support or artillery. I'd make a demonstration of the left and then just swing around on the right and flank it completely. I'd come Gen Grant on it—cut loose and let all communications and base supplies go and come up on the rear.

Ask Pole for me if the Johnnies shoot close enough to hit his trees in that country to get behind, and if the enemy uses artillery on the skirmishers. Tell him we have a better way now. We build pits large enough for seven or eight men and pile into it.

The boys are all well. Ed Fairbanks and Aus Smith are playing checkers. Mr. Adams and George Clark are reading. Alec Pope and Corp Traver are writing. Ed Anderson is reading. John Newman and Aus Smith are doing nothing. Ben Kline is company cook—lying in his bunk reading. Chas Crist is reading. The Norwegian boys, Tom Simonsen and John Nelson, are chatting with some friends. Serg Murry is writing. Fairservice is walking the ditch. Corps Minot, Moseley and Traver are writing. Old Cap [Brown] is off somewhere telling his big stories I suppose. Chas Fountain is on picket. So you see what the whole company is doing. Corp Sime Sage, I don't count as a member of the company, *for he has never shot his gun at a rebel yet* and has not been on picket on this campaign. He is a slink and plays off. Corp Getten is playing sick. He says he believes he will get killed and so acts just like an old sick hen, and goes on no duty at all. Dick Radway, the slink, is cooking for the Cap.

Well, I have blacked over the stated amount of paper and will close, altho I haven't told you any news. Am well and hearty. Write often.

Respects to all, Corp Lucius Selden Moseley, Co B, 22nd Reg. Wis. Vol.

NOTE

12. Maj. Gen. Joseph Wheeler ("Fighting Joe") commanded the cavalry of the Confederate Army in the west and was given the task of harassing Sherman's troops during their March to the Sea. The four railroads that centered in Atlanta were of strategic importance to Union and Confederate armies alike.

$\sim$

Headquarters 22nd Wis. Vol Inft., near Atlanta, Wed., August 24, 1864

My dear and loved brother Eddie:

I have another warm long afternoon before me with nothing to do to while the weary hours away, only to sit here and listen to the booming of the siege guns and the rattle of musketry on the skirmish lines. This I have become so accustomed to that there is very little amusing or entertaining in it. So, brother Eddie, I thought you might like to know that you have a brother still, way in the sunny south, who thinks of you and cares for your welfare. Eddie, I spend many and many a lonely hour in thinking of you and others near and dear to me.

I haven't a word of news to write you, but the spirit moved me to write and so I commenced, not knowing where I will find the material to fill up the sheet.

Two years ago today was the last before starting off to try the fortunes of war. In these two short years I have experienced more real hardship than ever before in my previous life, and in fact more than I had ever thought my future life had in store for me. I have one long year yet untried. Sometimes the future looks dark but I still hope to see the end. At all events I am *very glad* that neither you nor our *dear* father will likely be called upon to try your fate in the army. I never could bear the thought of either of you having to go through what I have. I would much rather go myself for another three years.[13]

Tomorrow the 33rd boys that did not reenlist start for *home*, and a happier lot of men you never saw. I would not agree to stay the next three years if they would give me $5,000, for I believe when I serve three years I have done my duty and money would not have the least influence on me.

I expect to spend the next twenty-four hours in a skirmish pit. You can judge a little from this whether there is anything very agreeable in soldiering or not. Supposing you had to go out in the woods and get behind a little pile of dirt, in a hole in the ground, and stay there all night and all the next day with no sleep and only coffee and hardtack to eat. You would think it would nearly kill you but we all have to do this once in four or five days. I do not write this to excite your sympathy but only to let you know what a soldier has to do. It is what we have been doing for the last three months. I cannot see that we are any nearer occupying the city of Atlanta than we were two weeks ago, but for all this we may be. A corporal has very little means of knowing what great things are being done on the lines.

Eddie, you said you had a new suit of clothes and you were going to send me your picture. You have no idea, my dear boy, how gladly I will welcome it. Yes, I will be a great deal happier to see your picture here and know that *you* are at home and improving your education than I would to see you down here. You will surely never regret it if you get a good education and now is the time. Mr. Fisk is the man to go to school to. He is a good teacher and a friend of mine. If he inquires for me, tell him I am well and have not forgotten his teaching. Give him my best respects.

Well, Ed, I don't think of anything more. Sime Sage went to the hospital this morning with the scurvey and I have unmistakable signs of it coming out on me, but it don't amount to anything, for if it gets bad I shall go back and thus get a rest.

Now Ed, just think of the days when we used to cob each other and the fine old times we used to have.[14] I have been right at my post every time for two years and have only one more to serve so let us hope to see the time when we can throw not cobs but happy glances and smiles at each other again. Not only hope for this but hope to see our country restored to peace and quiet. Oh! If we only had that last call in the field, I believe we could crush this rebellion in a very short time.

But my paper warns me to close. Give my love to our dear parents.

Your loving brother, Lucius S. Moseley

NOTES

13. Lute expected that his father (age 53 at this time) and brother Eddie (age 16) were not likely to be called into army service. The third Federal Conscription Act, enacted on February 17, 1864, extended the draft to able-bodied men aged 17 to 50, with no occupational exemptions. However, drafted men could either provide a substitute or pay a $300 commutation fee, which caused outrage by many who declared this "a poor man's war and rich man's fight." McPherson, *Ordeal by Fire*, 355–57.

14. Lute referred to the fine old times when he and Eddie, his younger brother, used to "cob each other"—a playful fight involving corn cobs.

In the trenches before Atlanta, Wed., August 24, 1864

Highly esteemed and respected grandmother–

It is a long, long time since I have written to you but this is not because I have not thot often of you. We have been in such circumstances that it was very difficult to write. But I am not going to make excuses until one half of my paper is written over. I have been writing to Eddie and thot I would write a little to you and send with his.

We are now behind a heavy line of earthworks, within one and one half miles of the city of Atlanta, and have been here since the 2nd of this month. We have been for the last four months lying behind works, marching or fighting every day, and we are getting tired of this kind of a life. Yes we long for a rest but will not get it for quite a time yet.

I hear that your health is poor. You do not know how much I want to see you. If I were in Beloit it would not be long before I did see you too, but only think of the miles and miles between us, and besides Uncle Sam claims my services for another long year. Just two years ago today was the last day I had at home before trying the fortunes of war. I have seen two years of hard service. I have a great deal to be thankful for, for I have not been sick so as to have to go to the hospital, and have not been touched by a bullet, altho I have been in as many as five hard fights, and on the skirmish line as often as once a week during this campaign. Our company, which had 92 men two years ago, now has only twenty left for duty and one whole year to serve yet.

There is very little of importance to write. I received a letter from cousin Fannie a few days ago. She sends love to you. She writes a most beautiful letter. I am almost ashamed to answer them, for mine are so poor.

I expect to spend my next twenty-four hours on the skirmish line and will be glad when it is passed. We go out about thirty rods in front and six men and one corporal stay in one post. We can see the rebels perfectly plain in their skirmish pits, not over thirty rods from us. We used to shoot at each other. Lately we remain there, both in plain sight, and do not fire a shot, but they won't talk a word with us.

In the morning the 33rd Indiana—belonging to our brigade and have been with us ever since we came out—are going to start home, their time being out. I tell you if they ain't a happy lot of boys, I never saw any. It makes me a little homesick and I can't help it. Only think—go home and know that they have done their duty and won't have to come again. If I ever live to see that time I will be a happy boy. I believe I could enjoy a citizen's life where I could know that I would'nt get marching orders in less than an hour, and could come and go at will. But I must hasten, for it is nearly time for the Post Master to call for the letters. He is now coming so I must close.

So with love to all, I subscribe myself your grandson, L.S. Moseley

Headquarters, 22nd Wis. Vol., near Chattahoochie, Monday Aug. 29, 1864

Dear parents and brother,

I believe it is now a week since I have written so I will try to enlighten you a little on my whereabouts, etc.

There has been a grand move of the whole army. The old 20th Corps is left here along the river. The first Div. is at the RR. Bridge, the second is at a ford above, and the third (ours) is at a ford below. The rest of the army has moved to the right. We don't know where they are, but I suppose they have gone clear around to the right and will ere long come up in the rear of Mr. Johnnies, and they can't come this way, for we are guarding all the passes across the river so I think it will be very uncomfortable for them.[15]

We are, as I told you before, within some 80 rods of their breastworks, and to leave and get away without their pitching into us was no very small job. We put out our skirmishers as usual. After dark we moved back very quickly and had our bugle blown as usual for roll-calling, etc., in the old works. The pickets remained until about 4 o'clock in the morning and then fell back. There was a heavy fog on. We were off to the river and putting up works by this time. In the morning the Johnnies thot strange that we fired no artillery as we have done every ten minutes, night and day, and no picket firing. So they began to shell our old works and finally charged them. I suppose they had thought we had gone clear to Chattanooga, but they soon found out their mistake. A force followed us and at noon Saturday drove in our pickets and opened a battery on us, throwing shells in every part of our lines. Finally we heard their bugle sound charge and a few of them came in sight of us. We put a few shots at them and away they went. Our artillery fired a few shots at them, dismounting one of their guns. We lost two men killed and four wounded and one or two prisoners. We don't know their losses, for of course they took them off with them. We may expect to hear of a big battle soon I think. We are lucky to be sent back here to guard the fort instead of going with the army.

The last day we were over in front of Atlanta, I was on picket. We were in plain sight of three of their pits. We had stopped shooting by mutual consent. We sat up on the top of our pit and they sat on top of theirs and looked at us. They had orders not to talk with us, so they wouldn't. We hallooed "Good morning, Johnnie" and they took off their hats and shook them. Dan Cunningham of Company I took a couple of newspapers and went half way to them and stuck the papers on a bush and came back. Then one of them came out and got the papers. Bill Minot came down from camp and carried a paper out and told them to bring one down and get it. So after a while one came and left an extra, which William [Minot] sent home. We met the Johnnie when he came after it and asked him if they were not allowed to talk with us. He shook his head.

I have not had a letter from you since one dated the 7th, but since I commenced to write this one came dated the 14th. I was very glad to hear from you again. Mother did not understand when I spoke about the cedar camphor. I certainly did not for a moment mean to make fun of you, my dear mother. No not in the least. I beg your pardon a thousand times. I don't wonder tho that you thought so. I did not think what I was writing. But even Angamton will not kill or destroy these lice.[16]

Yesterday was the first day in 113 days that we have not heard cannonading. Today it is still and quite a relief. Yes, what would those 100 day men think if they had to be where they could hear artillery day and night the whole length of their time. I think they would sing a different song. We saw a letter from the 40th Wis. that said they had to draw raw meat and some of it was even maggotty. Now we think if they had been in our place they would have been very thankful to get it. They said the boys refused to take it. Ha! Ha! And then sent to the state for a few delicacies. Now we hav'nt seen one speck of sanitary on this campaign, but we think the poor 100 day men ought to have it. They said that regiment was the best E-d-u-c-a-t-e-d and the smartest lot of men Wisconsin had ever sent out, but I wonder if they will put down any more of the rebellion in their 100 days than the 22nd in their three years. I understand tho that they have had a chance to try a little lately. Well, enough of them.

Now about the commission: I have made up my mind I would rather serve my one year as a corporal and then be done, than to take even a Captain's commission and remain three years longer, which I would have to sign up for. About coming home, there is no more show for me to come home than there was a year ago. If I got a commission I thought I could stop home a few days while going to my new regiment. I don't know as I would care to come home if I had to go back again. I want to stay the next time I come home.

I have been feeling quite unwell for the last few days, but it is all owing to being up so much nights and working so hard to get our works completed. You see the night of the 25th I was on picket and had to be up all night. I was on duty all day the 26th and marched all night, then went back to work to fortify. Was on guard or camp watch the night of the 27th. I have the scurvey a little and have drunk so much coffee and eaten so much hardtack and bacon that my stomach is a little out of order. Capt. gave me enough tea for two drawings and Wm. Minot has gone off after some green beans today and I am to have some of them. I bot two pounds of dessicated potatoes and I think it will make me come out all right.

Chas. Murry and I tent and live together. Each of us will send home for a quarter lb. of tea and one of us will likely get it. So you may please send me some by mail. The paper you sent me will last me.

They are making out our muster rolls so I hope we will get paid before long. The most important thing is my health and I am going to do all I can to keep it good, if it costs considerable.

The weather is getting cooler and I am glad of it.

I had one great shot at the Johnnies Saturday when they came up here to see us. That is more than Sime Sage has done in the two years he has served. He is now back in the hospital and he isn't any more sick than I am with the scurvey. I have two sores on my ankles as big as a quarter and he has only one. Well I don't think of anything further to write. Burt Bullock is doing well.

I certainly feel very much obliged to you for writing so punctually every time. Perhaps I write more than is interesting for I know I always string my letters out long without telling you much.

Love to each of you and respects to all. L.S. Moseley

NOTES

15. Harvey Reid's letter of August 26, 1864, further explained the military strategy near the Chattahoochee River: "The 20th Corps is ordered to take position along the south bank of the Chattahoochee, covering the bridges and fords while the remainder of the army, cutting loose entirely from the railroad, moves by the right flank so as to cut the two Southern railroads . . . If this flanking movement is successful it must force the evacuation of Atlanta." Reid, *Uncommon Soldiers*, 180.

16. Various compounds were used to try to destroy the body lice that plagued the soldiers, none with much success. Soldiers would boil their clothing when possible or wear their clothes inside out for temporary relief. "Skirmishing" for lice (picking the tiny insects off clothing and bodies) was a time-consuming method, but temporary in effect.

∼

Atlanta, Sunday, Sept. 11, 1864

Dear ones at home,

After two weeks of waiting and wishing, I received a mail this a.m. I was indeed very anxious to hear from you. I assure you there is very little of interest to write, for our RR has been cut and there have been no papers here for quite a long time. It is reported here that Morgan is killed.[17] Now if we could only be fortunate enough to use Forrest and Wheeler in the same friendly manner, I would be very glad.

I suppose you expect an interesting letter now that we are in the key city, so long fought for and so much coveted by the Yankees.[18] But the truth is

UNION RALLY

The Union Men of Beloit, in favor of a vigorous prosecution of the war as the surest way to secure peace, are requested to assemble at Hanchett's Hall this Saturday evening, at 7 1-2 o'clock, to organize a **Lincoln & Johnson Club.** Every true union man in town should be there.

Beloit, September 10, 1864.   **BY ORDER.**

Union army handbill, Beloit, Wisconsin, September 1864 (courtesy of Wisconsin Historical Society)

that the citizens, after having invited us for the last year to come on and fill Yankee graves, now that we are here, have all taken their knitting work and gone south to see their kin and to stay a while. Now the city is full of live Yankees and a few colored population.[19] We intend to stay a short time.

We have orders to prepare for another immediate and active campaign. We will probably lie still for six weeks and then go at them again. That suits me, for now is the time to keep the ball in motion and not wait for them to get ready.

You certainly don't know how much you have to be thankful for, that our lot was cast in the North instead of this part of the world. Most of the citizens have gone south with the Army and what are left are said to be bad characters mostly. Gen. Sherman says that everyone not in government employ should leave the city. There are lots of women here who have had their husbands killed in the Rebel army and I suppose have actually been obliged to disgrace themselves to obtain a living.[20]

Yesterday I went down through the city. It has been a pretty place but there is not a nice dwellinghouse left here, as I expected to see. The destruction of property has been large. In the north half of the city every house is torn by Yankee shells. Everyone in the city has what we call "bummers" holes, which consist of a hole dug deep in the ground and covered over with dirt from three to nine feet deep, where they lived. How would you think you would like such a dwelling place?[21]

I received a letter from you today dated Aug. 28th. I have not received the paper and envelopes yet. Bill Minot received a stack of papers and then some emery paper for me. I was very glad of it, for now we will be having inspection every day or so and a clean gun helps some.

The boys are reading some of the speeches made in Chicago. What traitorism! Why I had no idea it had got so bad. Oh if we soldiers could only have our say—if we could only get hold of those drunken traitors—we certainly would soon stop their spouting.[22]

But I must close. Give Pole my respects. He was a good soldier sure. The boys all say so and we hope he will get well. So with love to all of you. I feel anxious about Mother, for I am afraid she will make herself sick. If Grandmother still lives tell her I love her and wish I could be there to see her once more.

L.S. Moseley

NOTES

17. John Hunt Morgan, the Confederate brigadier general, was killed during a Union raid in Greenville, Tennessee, September 4, 1864.

18. The population of Atlanta was approximately 22,000 in 1864. Capture of the "key city," an important railroad hub and manufacturing center, was a major turning point, changing antiwar sentiment in the North and giving President Lincoln a crucial boost to his reelection campaign. McPherson, *Ordeal by Fire*, 443.

19. On September 1, 1864, the Confederates evacuated Atlanta. As Union troops poured into the city, Sherman declared in a telegram to President Lincoln: "Atlanta is ours and fairly won." Commager, *Blue and the Gray*, 947. William H. McIntosh wrote that many inhabitants were given the choice of going north or south. "Those electing to go north were given transportation by rail, and those going south by wagons . . . A truce of ten days was arranged with Gen. Hood and deportation began." William H. McIntosh, *"Annals of the 22nd Wisconsin,"*110; unpublished manuscript, Manuscripts Library, Wisconsin Historical Society, Madison, WI.

20. Most of the civilians remaining in Atlanta were there due to poverty, "having no means to remove, nor place to seek another home. Their condition was pitiable." James M. Calhoun, the mayor of Atlanta, sent a message to Brig. Gen. Ward, Commander Third Division, Twentieth Corps, on September 2, 1864: "Sir—The fortune of war has placed Atlanta in your hands. As mayor of the city, I ask protection to noncombatants and private property." McIntosh, *Annals of the 22d Wisconsin*, 106.

21. Confederate troops contributed to the destruction of Atlanta. Railroads, depots, roundhouses, factories, and foundries were blown up so they would not fall into Union hands. Private homes were not supposed to be touched, yet many were raided, riddled with bullets, and burned in the chaos. As Sherman rode out of the city, he looked back to see it smoldering and in ruins. He justified the means with unwavering ends—bringing the war to a close and thus restoring the union. "We cannot change the hearts of these people of the South," he said, "but we can make war so terrible . . . and make them so *sick* of war that generations [will] pass away before they again appeal to it." Ward, *Civil War*, 242.

22. Here, Lute referred to speeches made in Chicago at the Democratic Convention in 1864. During the months leading up to the election, political views in the North were increasingly divided and often vicious in tone. Many soldiers were incensed by the antiwar Democrats. George B. McClellan, the Democratic presidential nominee, drew support from the antiwar "Copperheads of the North." See also Wells, *Wisconsin in the Civil War*, 75; Catton, *Reflections on the Civil War*, 114–16.

༄

Atlanta, Wednesday, Sept. 21, 1864

Ever dear home,

I received your very kind letter, bearing date of 11th, on the 19th, which brought to me the sad news of grandmother's death, and although it had been so long expected it cast a gloom over me. I have felt very sad ever since.[23] We were out on inspection when the mail came and were no sooner dismissed from it before I was detailed for picket. I went out and spent that night and the next day on the sentry's post. Everything was very still and quiet, which contrasted so deeply with our duty for the last four months, that it gave me an opportunity for thinking. I thought of home a great part of the time. I ought not to feel discontented or homesick, but I have somewhat. I am thankful I have been spared these last two years. We had had as hard a life and narrow escapes as most anyone ever passed. Eleven more months to serve!

I am in the same fix you were, for a recital of the ruins of Atlanta would not be interesting and there is no news. We are having a cold wet and nasty time. We do not have comfortable quarters.

Col. Bloodgood puts on considerable style but it is only for eleven months and not three years.[24]

You say you do not get my letters. I write at least once a week. Col. Colburn [Coburn] has been here to bid us farewell. His time is out and he starts today for home. He has commanded our Brigade for the last two years, and a better, kinder, more impartial man never had the honor to command a brigade. He said Wisconsin has the greatest reason to be proud of the 22nd, for he said there is none better. After leaving us he went to the 33rd (Indiana), his own regiment. He could not say a word, only God bless you and goodbye, then he cried like a child. He told us that he thought the 22nd Brigade justly merited the honor of first occupying Atlanta and the honor of being in advance, which it had. Now we have lost, since we started, our Corp commander, Col. Colburn [Coburn] and our Battalion commander, Col. Utley. We have in their places Gen. Slocum, Corps; Gen. Ward, Div. ; brigade not known; Col. Bloodgood, Battalion.

The Col. said he thought our heaviest work was done. He did not think there would be much more fighting to be done here. I hope he is right. I expect now we will be put in some other brigade, as we have no Col. to command. I must close.

With all love and affection of a would-be dutiful son, I remain, L.S. Moseley

NOTES

23. Lute's maternal grandmother, Dolly Chase Gage, died earlier in September in Beloit at the age of 77.

24. Col. Coburn was mustered out on September 21, 1864, when his term of service expired. Following his departure, the brigade came under the command of Lt. Col. Bloodgood.

∽

Atlanta, Ga., Oct. 20, 1864

Dear parents and brother,

I presume you have not heard from me in three or four weeks, for as I suppose you know, the rebs are in our rear, and the R.R. is cut. We don't know anything of what is going on north of Chattanooga. I have received two letters from you in this time, one dated Oct. 2nd.

Charles Fountain has a furlough, and is going to start home tomorrow, so I will send it by him. My health was never better than now. I am well of the scurvey. We have plenty to eat so far, but I have to work like sixty, for we are fortifying the place very strongly. Half of the men work one day and the other half the next.

The 15th, our brigade, with two others from the 1st and 2nd divisions, and 750 wagons went off foraging. We went southeast, and filled our wagons with corn, and the boys put a great many dead hogs, sheep, chicken, geese, ducks and sacks of sweet potatoes, jugs of sorghum, cans of lard etc. on top of the wagons. Chas Murry and I brot in one canteen of sorghum, eight pounds of dried apples, two chickens, one year mutton, a little pork steak and four good messes of sweet potatoes. We were gone four days. I guess old Hood will not starve us out of Atlanta! Ha! Ha! Four hundred wagons went before and came back all loaded. Tomorrow there is another train going. Sile Gibbins is Brigade forage master, and he goes. He just told Captain that if he would let two men go from our company, he would let them have a team to haul in all they could get. So Bill Minot and Sime Sage are going. We drove in some sixty head of cattle and some sheep, horses and a few mules. In fact we are stripping the country of every thing. Besides we captured two or three Johnnies. There are some few rebs here, but they fall back as fast as we come up. We will not starve as we have rations to last us a good long while.[25]

I got the tea you sent me, and oh man! It is good. I have not yet received the paper. We have had but one mail since the latter part of Sept. The R.R. is all torn up for 25 miles and they tell us it will be ten days before the mail can pass. Chas. Fountain will have to walk that 25 miles, I suppose.

We have at last signed the payrolls, we should get paid before long. They will owe us for ten months on the first of Nov.

If Chas gets thru alright I want you to get me a new diary for 1865, if you can. I will send one home, which I wish you to put away with the other. I also need a good gold pen. I have had to borrow one for the last 5 months. Chas will bring them back for me. Ed will have to get them to him, for he will not feel much like running around. The poor fellow has lost his wife, and of course feels very badley. He is a fine young man.

I guess this will be the last lot of stuff I will have to send home for. I did think about sending for boots, but I think my shoes will do in this climate. My old boots would have lasted me this winter, but when my ankles got so sore with the scurvey, I couldn't wear them and traded them off for a pair of shoes.

I certainly never saw such a splendid fall. The cornfields are poor, only average one ear to a hill, Irish potatoes don't grow well either but they sure can grow cotton and cane. Give me the good ol north anyday!

Hope this note will find you in good health and happy. Yours in love, L.S. Moseley

NOTE

25. Harvey Reid wrote to his sister on October 24, 1864, from Atlanta: "These foraging expeditions are a terror to the country and really a curse to the army, for all discipline seems to be laid aside. The men take everything that is fit to eat, leaving families nothing to make another meal of—they kill chickens, pigs, sheep and calves, take the last particle of corn meal, flour and so forth that they can find and some even go so far as to take bed clothes from the beds, knives and forks and crockery and so forth. Such conduct is condemned by all but the worst sort of the men, but it is too often winked at by the officers."(Reid, *Uncommon Soldiers*, 197, 198.)

Atlanta, Ga., Oct. 30, 1864

Dear Parents,

We have just returned from another foraging trip and feel somewhat tired and worn, as it rained full half the time we were out. On returning I found a letter for me from you. I suppose you knew our communications were cut. You see the enemy are and have been at our rear for about a month and the track has been torn up. We hav'nt had mail for a month.

I hear this morning that we have marching orders and are going to start on another campaign.

There is a fellow here that I have got well acquainted with. He belongs to the 7th Pa. cavalry. His time is out and he starts for home today—three years in the service. It makes me feel homesick sure.

What a lot of marriages you are having at home now. I have heard of seven lately. It seems the war doesn't make much of an impression on some people. Those fellows should be taking their turn instead of getting married. The government hasn't paid us for ten months, but comes around and pays officers and some soldiers and lets other go. I don't like it. Well I have the blues a little this morning. I suppose that is all that ails me.

We had three men shot when we were out foraging the last time. None of them were killed. One was shot in the hand and another in the shoulder, don't know where the third was hit.

Nov. 3. I will continue.

It is one of the most uncomfortable, disagreeable days we have had since we came here. Cold, rainy and nasty. Tuesday night I was on duty on the vidett post.[26] It is situated about thirty rods outside the picket line, on the road that runs south from the city, and up on a hill. The storm commenced that day, and that night was, I think the worst I have spent in the last eight months. My rubber blanket was torn so it was of little use to me, and in fact, everything combined to make the hours pass very slowly, and to remind me of the horrid night I spent at Tullahoma while in the hands of the enemy. But that, as all other nights, at last gave way to day, which was little, if any, better. But at nine in the morning we were relieved, and went to our good and comfortable quarters. But I cannot help, as I listen to the roaring wind, and driving rain, to think and pity those that are out now.

We received another mail today. I, of course, felt certain of at least a letter from you, but none came, so now perhaps I am paid in my own coin for letting so long a time pass without writing, but as I told you in my last, I thot it of no use to write, for I supposed as we got no mail, it would'nt go if we sent it. But I will try and be patient.

We have been on another foraging expidition. As there seems to be nothing else to write about, let me occupy a few minutes of your time in reading an account of it.

On the 25th we received orders to go the next morning at 5 A.M. We were up and ready, and at five fell in, and marched out about a mile where we stacked arms, and as is customary in all military movements, waited some two hours, during which time one of the 85th boys accidentally discharged his gun, the bullet hitting him just above the left eye, and inflicting a bad wound, which was not thot mortal, however. We fell in, and as the train consisting of 700 wagons passed; we were placed, one regiment at a time, between each 100 wagons. The rest of the force acting as advance and rear guards. We marched to the eastward, thru the town of Decatur eight miles from Atlanta and on and on, till nine in the evening, we found ourselves just north of Stone Mountain. Twenty-five miles from Atlanta, hungry and tired. We ate our hardtack and beef, then spread down our rubber blankets and lay down with our tents for covering and our cartridge boxes for pillow. You may think this a hard bed but we liked it so well that when morning came we were indeed, very loth to give them up.

About eight o'clock the three right companies, A, F, and D, were sent off to pick corn, and we were left to have, as we thot, an easy time. But about nine it commenced to rain, and continued all day. We sat around our fires, built of the rails belonging to some old reb, until four. Then we and seven companies of the 35th were ordered off some where. We went around to the east side of the mountain and camped. We had 150 wagons and two pieces of artillery with us. In the morning the rain had stopped, and we went on to load up, driving some ten or twelve Johnnies off before us. Companies E and B were sent about one half mile ahead to the cross roads, to keep the rebs off while the rest picked their corn. Our wagons were soon loaded, and came up where we were, and went into park. After waiting till dark the rest of our train was ready, and we went on right around the mountain, and about twelve in the night joined the rest of the train at a little town called Gibralter. Two of our party were shot this day by bushwhackers, but not killed. The day before a Lieutenant and some eight men and some mules were taken prisoners, and were found hung up by the neck in the woods. Gen. Geary told the citizens that if his train or men were shot at, or hung any more he would burn every building within ten miles, so we were not molested farther.

The next morning we started out in advance. At every crossroad or clear place, where cavalry could get thru to molest the train, men were taken off of our regiment, and posted as pickets, and fell in as the rear of the train passed, which was, I should judge, fully nine miles long. We got into town about nine in the evening. Well, enough for forage.[27]

Just as I turned to this side of the sheet, Frone Herrick came in with some more mail—two letters from my own dear home for me, so now I have heard from you and I am so glad that Ed takes an interest in studys. Yes sir! You have improved very much in your writing. As to spelling, you must know by my letters that I am shockingly deficient in that myself. I am trying to improve.

I must write two or three other letters tonight so I must hasten, but as soon as I can, I will write you a letter, Ed.

We are expecting every day to move somewhere from here. I don't know where or which way. We have mustered for pay again. Ten months more due us, and as ever they tell us "next week or very soon." I am not in very great want of money, but hav'nt a cent. There is no chance to buy if I had, only occasionally a little at the commissaries. Charley has money and he buys for both. And when I get some and he is out, I do the same. He is a good boy and a friend of mine. We share alike in everything.

Chas Fountain has not started home yet, but expects to every day. But I will close for the present. Write again soon.

So with love to each of you, I remain, your son and brother. L.S. Moseley

P.S. I bot one quire of this paper off one of the boys on tick. What you sent has not come. My tea came and you bet, we use it spareingly, but often. No currants have yet reached me. Bill's all came right. Only nine month's more of duty for me, and then, if alive and well, I can come home.

NOTES

26. The vidette was a sentry post, usually mounted, stationed in advance of a picket line, closest to the position of the enemy.

27. Gibralter, GA, is located near Stone Mountain, GA, some 13 miles east of Atlanta. Again, Lute wrote of the extensive foraging by Union troops, which included stealing crops, livestock, clothing, and household goods from civilians. General Sherman reportedly told his troops to "forage liberally" when they had the opportunity. This strategy kept the Union Army well supplied while decimating and demoralizing Confederate soldiers and civilians, resulting in long-lasting hostilities. Joseph T. Glatthaar, "Forage Liberally: Union Raiding Strategy During the Civil War," Hamilton College, Nov. 12, 2014, https://www.hamilton.edu/news/story/forage -liberally-union-raiding-strategy-during-the-civil-war/.

Atlanta, Ga., Nov. 7, 1864

To my highly esteemed and much loved brother Ed,

Having an opportunity to write a few lines. The truth is, Eddie, I had almost began to dispare of ever receiving another letter from you, and when it did come, you can imagine my joy. I looked at it before opening it, and wondered who it was from. Your writing has improved so much. It gives me such pleasure knowing you are improving so much. I can see now the use of a good English education.

You ask what time I usually go to roost. It depends very much on circumstances. When we are in camp, taps sound at nine, but when we are on the march we usually don't quit until nine. Then we have to get wood and water and get our supper. Sometimes we march all night and get no sleep. A soldier has to eat and sleep just as he can. I tell you people at home don't know what a soldiers life is. I know this by the new soldiers coming in. They think our first rate times are awfully hard.

I send you, Eddie, a $5 greenback as a present. It is only a small token of my esteem and love. I want you to use it as you see fit. I often think of you, be happy and good, but educated and useful. Write often and I will answer any letter that you write. I cannot write more now.

The above is from your absent brother, L.S. Moseley

∼

Atlanta, Ga., Monday, Nov. 7, 1864

My dearest Mother,

I have just been writing to Ed, and now will address a few lines to you, my dear mother. I sent a letter home yesterday, and you will be surprised to receive one today, dated Atlanta. I will explaine it to you. We marched out four or five miles on the Macon Rd., expecting to go on, but for some reason or other the order was countermanded, and we were ordered back to our old camp. We very fortunately left our "house" standing, and found it ready to move into. Some of the boys burned theirs when we left, and now have none.

The rebs made a dash at our picket line while we were on the road, and killed one man belonging to Co. B, 33rd Indiana. He was on the Vidette post, on the road. I don't know the reason we were ordered back, but suppose it was because everything was not ready. We now expect to start again in the course of a week, and go to Savannah and perhaps Mobile. Then we will have marched from the Ohio river to the Gulf of Mexico. I like the plan first rate, but hate not hearing from you.

Wm. Minot is in the hospital in town. He will go with us when we march, for his shoulder is about well. I am glad, for it would be lonesome without him. We have both been in the regiment all the time, so far. He is a fine young man and my friend and has such a good disposition.

I sent Ed a small present, and I also sent you $5, which I want you to use for your own comfort. It is realy only a trifling token of my love to you. Hope it reaches you safely.

Chas. Murry and I were talking last evening about what we are going to do when we get home. His father gave him an eighty, and he says he is going to farm it. I told him I guessed that father and I would get us some land and try the same. Now what do you think of it? I hav'nt written to father but tell him I love him and that when my time is out I am coming home, and try with him to make ourselves happy. This is all for today.

As Ever your Son, L.S. Moseley

Write as usual and direct as before.

Nov. 8th—I have just received your letter of the 30th, containing $1. Every man in the company voted for Abe.[28]

❧

Still at Atlanta, Ga. Nov. 9, 1864[29]

Dear home,

Last chance to send mail, so I will scribble you a line. I think by what I see that we are going to destroy this place. By tomorrow this time Atlanta will be among the things that were (I think) . . .[30]

It seems hard to be so far away from you, and not able to hear from you, so I will write every opportunity. Don't send me anything by mail until you hear from me. I don't know where we will go. Maybe we are only going to make a raid and come out at Chattanooga, or it may be we are going to Savannah and down thru that way. So with all the love and affection of an absent son, I am obliged to bid you goodbye for a little while, maybe as long as forty days.

Now I beg of you not to feel uneasy about me. Don't fret and lie awake nights thinking about me, I shall come out alright. We are going thru this Confederacy like a dose of oil . . .[31]

NOTES

28. The men of the 22nd Wisconsin cast 372 votes for Lincoln and ten votes for McClellan. Reid, *Uncommon Soldiers*, 198.

29. On this date, Sherman issued a special field order, dividing his army into two wings about thirty miles apart—a Right Wing commanded by Oliver Howard, and a Left Wing, commanded by Henry Slocum. The 22nd Wisconsin Regiment (commanded by Edward Bloodgood) was part of the Twentieth Corps (Alpheus Williams), Third Division (William Ward), and Dustin's Brigade (Coburn's old brigade, now commanded by Daniel Dustin, formerly a colonel with the 105th Illinois). William's Twentieth Corps was directed to begin the destruction of railroad tracks between Atlanta and the Chattahoochee River bridge. Welcher and Ligget, *Coburn's Brigade*, 277–79.

30. William H. McIntosh, Company A, 22nd Wisconsin, described the scene that he and other rank-and-file soldiers witnessed on November 15, 1864: "Along in the evening, a grand scene was presented to our view. Atlanta was on fire . . . and when morning came there was little left but dwellings and churches aside from smoldering ruins . . . Our last view of Atlanta presented a ruined, depopulated, fire-scourged city from which clouds of smoke were slowly rising and through which the soldiers were silently marching with thoughts fixed upon the future." William H. McIntosh Papers, Wisconsin Historical Society archives, as published in appendix of *Uncommon Soldiers: Harvey Reid and the 22nd Wisconsin March with Sherman*, 253, 254.

31. In mid-November, Sherman's troops began their March to the Sea. Cut off from supplies or contact with the North, they devoured or destroyed whatever lay in their path. Although Sherman had instructed the soldiers not to plunder private homes and properties, few took the order seriously. Ward, *Civil War*, 242.

Camp on the 22nd Wis. —on the banks of the broad Savannah—
Fri, Dec. 16, 1864

As you see I didn't get the above letter mailed. I will cont.

I will begin with our trip, hoping it will be interesting to you. On the 14th of Nov we were ordered to be ready to march. The whole of the day and night being used to destroy the great City of Atlanta, and I assure you it was destroyed too, hardly one stone left upon another.[32] At five in the morning of the 15th we started—none of us knew where for. We marched all the first day and night until nine o'clock on the 16th, and camped two miles south

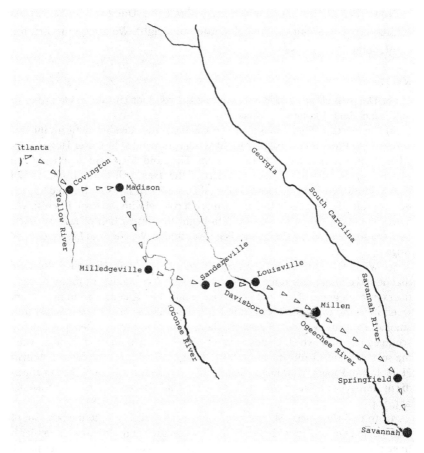

Sherman's March to the Sea (courtesy of the Moseley family)

of Stone Mountain. We rested there one hour and then went on. We got to camp at dark, sore, tired and sleepy. I was detailed for picket; never hated to go so bad in my life. On the 17th we started at six and marched all day until 3 the next morning (cross and out of patients). The 18th we marched 18 miles—thru the town of Rutland, and went into camp about dark. There we got sweat potatoes aplenty, and have all thru. It rained a little on the 19th. We went to tearing up the R.R.[33] We marched thru the town of Madison, a splendid place. Eight miles from there we camped. On the 20th our brigade was train guard.

Aus Smith and I went into a yard to get some peanuts. We found some sheep so we stopped and killed one. We were some twenty minutes late into camp with it, that is, we did not get there quite as quick as the regiment, and ol Brown put us on picket for it. It was raining and I did not want to go. So I went to the Col [Bloodgood] and told him; he excused us.

Bill Minot picked up a negro, and we took him to carry our cooking tools and cook for us. The 21st Bill Minot and Weaver went off foraging. It rained steadily all day. We marched 14 miles. I am on camp guard the 22nd. Change in the weather, it is very cold. One of the Colonel's pack mules was stolden last night, and he is very mad. He put me and all the rest of last nights guards on extra duty, which I hope to live long enough to pay him for, for I was not to blame for the mule getting away, and he knew it.

About dark we started, and crossed the yellow river on pontoons. We marched to Milledgeville, and got to camp about 4 in the morning.[34] The 23rd, we did not march, so I went down to see the place. On camp guard, the extra duty the Colonel put me on—the first I ever had to do. 24th, Thanksgiving day. We cross the river, are train guard and march only nine miles, but it takes until three the next morning, for it takes the train so long to lock down the hills, and cross the mud holes. The 25th we march miles and turn in for dinner, and then find the bridge across Buffalo Creek is destroyed, so we lie here all night and have a good nights sleep. On the 25th we help the teams cross, and at two we march nine miles. Co G and B are rear guards. We camped at Sandersville, where our advance had quite a skirmish.

On the 27th old Ward took us six miles out of our way.[35] We marched some 18 miles and camped at Davisborough. The 28th our brigade was in the advance, and such foraging you never saw. We had honey, sweet potatoes, and about every thing you could eat. We marched 9 miles and had to stop for a bridge, and the 33rd Indiana were skirmishing with what they thought to be rebs, but proved to be some of the 85 Indiana, belonging to the 14th Army corps. The 29th we stayed there until night. The whole train crosses and after dark we cross in mud clear up to our knees. The country is all swamp from there to Savannah. We went into camp. The 30th we lay in camp until dark, then started out marching thru Louisville and on and on. I can't believe there was ever a darker night or worse fog. We had to cross sleughs and creeks, and got to camp at 1:30 in the morning.

The next day we waited until dark before starting across those awful mud holes, and it was only to give the train time to cross. You have no idea how hard it is, or how long it takes to get a very large army across a small creek. You see we had to be very careful to keep a sufficient force all along the train to protect it. It is the worst work a soldier has to do. Dec. 2nd we marched early and fast, 18 miles. The next day, 12 miles, a little to the left of Millen, where the rebs kept our prisoners. Some of the boys went over to the pens.[36] The 4th we marched 5 miles and camped. The 5th, 16 miles and stopped at dark. We had an awful time finding wood and water. The next day it rained all day, marched 12 miles thru miserable pine swamp. Camped about ½ mile from Springfield. The 8th we marched 5 miles. The 9th we heard cannonading in the front. The roads were blockaded with big pine trees felled across. The pioneers began to clear it out and the rebs opened fire on them with cannister shot, we soon put them to flight. I am on picket the 10th. Next day we marched 10 miles within 4 miles of Savannah.

On the 11th we were sent out to the river to support a battery, to keep the rebs from running boats on the river. The 12th—last night I slept on a bed of Spanish moss—known at home as mohair.

Chas Murry, Ed Fairbanks and I were paddling up the river in a canoe, just for a ride, when we saw 3 steamers coming down. We went to shore. The steamers came right on and were soon . . . [last page of letter missing.]

NOTES

32. Sherman told the mayor of Atlanta, "War is cruelty and you cannot refine it." He is also reported to have said, "We don't want your Negroes or your horses or your houses or your lands . . . But we do want, and will have, a just obedience to the laws of the United States." Robotham, *Civil War Album*, 222.

33. To maximize the damage, Sherman's men heated rails and tied them around trees. The twisted rails became known as " Sherman neckties." Robotham, *Civil War Album*, 222.

34. Milledgeville was the state capital of Georgia until Reconstruction when the capital was relocated to Atlanta in 1868.

35. William T. Ward served as a brigadier general in the Union Army, took part in the Atlanta campaign, and distinguished himself in the Battle of Peachtree Creek. He led the 3rd Division of the Twentieth Corps in Sherman's March to the Sea and through the Carolinas.

36. Camp Lawton/Millen Prison near Millen, GA, held approximately 8,600 Union prisoners. The stockade opened in October 1864 to relieve the horrendous overcrowding and high death rate at Andersonville Prison, needed to be evacuated quickly due to the advance of Sherman's army. Robert Knox Sneden, "Camp Lawton at Millen, Georgia: About 8,600 Prisoners Confined Here November 14th," accessed July 8, 2022, https://www.loc.gov/item/gvhs01.vhs0054/.

Savannah, Monday, Dec. 26th, 1864

Dear parents and brother,

I have written you once since we came before this place, and should have written you again before this, if it had not been for moving and the coldness of the weather.

We are now camped just in the edge of the city, the Johnnies having *vacated*. They left on the night of the 21st in somewhat of a hurry too, for they left all their heavy ordinance *with us*. I have heard that they left 260 cannon, but I don't know if it is so.[37] I hav'nt been in the city yet, as private soldiers are not allowed to go there. The men that do the work: the ones that win the prizes are not allowed to go down and see it, but are ordered to stay in camp. Well, so let it be for eight months and five days, and then, if Heaven spare my life, Lute Moseley will go to town or wherever he chooses without asking such as man as Cap Brown if he can.

Saturday we moved down here, and yesterday (Christmas) we lay around until nearly night, when we were gotten around where they wanted us, and commenced to put up our tents. We, that is Chas, Bill and I, have ours nearly done. They have gone off to see if they can find some boards and nails, so I am writing in their absence.

I received a letter from you bearing the date of the 4th. I was very, very glad. It was the first letter from Beloit in our camp. All were anxiously waiting for me to read it, to see if there was anything in it about their folks at home. I don't suppose you feel any more anxious to hear from us that we are to hear from you. Ed Fairbanks feels very uneasy concerning his folks who were at Nashville. His father was carrying on a piece of land ten miles from there, and old Hood has been making mischief around there, so Ed does'nt know how his father is getting along.[38] I have always been sorry till now that father did not go there with him, but now I feel as tho if I ever get out of this, I will stay away as far as I possibly can.

Last night it rained as hard as it could pour, and today it is still cloudy, but don't rain. It is warm enough to go in shirt sleeves. We have had two cold snaps, each time it was cold enough to freeze water over in a pail. But I say confound such a country as this. Before we have always been in a country so hilly that I didn't like it, but this country is so level that it is covered with water—at least half of it is. I don't wonder that the inhabitants seceded, for anyone that would live in such a place would, I suppose, be mean enough to rebel or anything else that is mean.

I suppose you would like to know how we get along as to *grub*. Well, we get a plenty. I can't say that I like it, for it is nearly all rice, and you remember that I am not particularly fond of it. We get neither hardtack or sugar, but I guess we will after a while. I can get along without it first rate. By the way, the rice we get here is different from the old stored riced you have. We have to thresh and hull it ourselves—have regular steam mills on purpose. There are thousands of acres of rice swamps around here. It is inundated by flood gates when the tide comes in. And there are thousands and thousands of what I suppose are called niggers, but they are as much below the Negro of Wisconsin as he is below a good smart white man. They all, men, women, and children lie around on the ground like so many great, lazy dogs. They talk differently from others I have seen. Some of the boys think it is part French and others think it is the regular African *brogue*. It is "yes sir, yes sir" to everything you say to them. We have a smart, fine young fellow to cook and wash for us. Cooking, washing and mending in a boarding house have been his business. I am teaching him to read, and you ought to see him study and try. I wish he was north some where, where he could get a good place to work.[39]

Say, the boys here have heard that Pole put a copper cent on his wound to keep it sore, so he would not have to come back. Now is that so? He was a good, brave man while with us.

Sam Smith, old Hoshier and Sam Miller are the men who can't bear to hear the bullets whistle, and they are the ones to get the furloughs. Such a man as Bert Bullock can't get one. At Thompson's Station he was shot thru the arm and leg, was hit on the breast buckle, and in the breast, the bullet lodging in a pack of cards. Besides he was hit a number of times thru the clothing, knapsack etc. At Atlanta he was shot thru the face or head. He has never been home, and he can't get a furlough to save his life.[40] Well, the boys have come back, and I must help finish the tent. I will write again soon. Write often, and direct as you did before, to Savannah.

Love to all, L.S. Moseley

NOTES

37. The city of Savannah was undefended when the Union troops arrived. On December 22, 1864, Sherman sent Lincoln a telegram: "I beg to present you, as a Christmas gift, the city of Savannah, with 150 heavy guns and plenty of ammunition; also about 25,000 bales of cotton." Ward, *Civil War*, 348.

38. John Bell Hood, a Confederate brigadier general, was severely wounded at Gettysburg and again at Chickamauga. Despite a useless left arm and the amputation of his right leg, he assumed command of Johnston's army in July 1864, fought to defend Atlanta, and led battles in Tennessee where he again met defeat.

39. The black population of Wisconsin in the 1850 census was 1,171, with a total state population of 774,710. Beginning in 1862, additional black residents moved into the state, coming from various "contraband camps." They paid taxes if they owned property but could not vote or join the state militia companies. In June 1861, the U.S. Congress authorized the employment of black men in the army, "as laborers, or in whatever capacity they are competent." This action served as the basis for raising black troops for the war. By the end of the war, 353 black men were officially credited to Wisconsin's roster of military service. Klement, *Wisconsin in the Civil War*, 93–97.

40. Furloughs, for both Union and Confederate soldiers, could be granted by commanding officers attached to the soldier's company or regiment when periods of inactivity permitted. Furloughs were a privilege, not a right, for enlisted men, and according to common complaints in soldiers' letters, the granting of furloughs were often influenced by personal relationships.

CHAPTER 6

The Road to Washington

January 6, 1865–May 6, 1865

We can stand most anything now.

—LUCIUS S. MOSELEY, April 14, 1865

Service: Campaign of the Carolinas, January to April 1865. Lawtonville, South Carolina, February 2. Taylor's Hole Creek, Averysboro, North Carolina, March 16. Battle of Bentonville, March 19–21. Occupation of Goldsboro March 24. Advance on Raleigh April 10–14. Occupation of Raleigh April 14. Bennett's House April 26, surrender of Johnston and his army. March to Washington, DC, via Richmond, Virginia, April 29–May 19. Grand Review May 24. Mustered out June 12, 1865. Regiment lost during service 2 officers and 75 Enlisted men killed and mortally wounded and 3 officers and 163 Enlisted men by disease. Total 243.

—DYER, Compendium, vol. 3, 1682, 1683

Camp 22nd Wis., S.Car. Jan. 6th, 1865[1]

Dear Home—

Mail goes at twelve, so they say. Well, I will try to have a short one ready to go.

It is a miserable rainy day and everything seems gloomy and dull. You may like to know how I spend the Holidays so I will give you a brief account. On the 24th we had our tents staked off and were waiting for lumber to put them up. You see, we had been up on the river. We had carried lumber some half mile to put up our tents and had just got them up when we were ordered to march. We took two old scows and put our lumber on them and ran them down the river. But we found when we got there that we were a mile away from the river. But there was an old canal that came up within a few rods. One of the boats could run in it: the other that had our lumber on it could not. So the boys ran the little one up and unloaded it. Then we loaded it on to the small boat. By this time it was dark. We ran down the river and got into the channel but the tide was running out and it was so muddy we could'nt pole our craft. We could'nt land, for it was so swampy. So we worked until nearly twelve at night and finally got where we could get out and then only about a third of the way. We tied up and left it till morning. So you see how I spent my Christmas Eve. The next morning Bill Minot, Weave Schoening and I went down and ran it up easily as the tide was coming in. We backed it down and put up our tent. We had a good dinner of nothing but boiled rice. On the 26th we finished up our tent and then they ordered us to drill. It was rainy and cold. On the 29th we drilled and had dress parade. You see, *they are letting the boys rest now.* The 28th we drilled nearly all day. Still rainy and cold. The 29th we were ordered to prepare for a review so we cleaned and rubbed and scoured. The after-noon we had what they called a mock review.

It is what we call awful cold. At home it would be very warm for this time of year. But you see, we threw away all the clothing we could do with-out when we left Atlanta and we hav'nt drawn any yet. I never was clothed so poorly before in my life, but we expect to get clothes today or tomorrow.

On the 30th the grand old 20th corps was reviewed in the streets of Savannah by Gen Sherman. It was a splendid sight to look at and I never saw men march in such good order. We were very highly praised by our commanders. After we passed the General we were double-quicked off out of town.[2] The 31st we were ordered to march. We started at seven and went across the first part of the river on to an island, or a rice plantation. We crossed this, about two miles wide, on a dike, and came to another river. There was a rebel force on the other side. They wounded three of our men, or three of the 102nd Illinois. We got a battery into position and very soon shelled them out of it. The wind blew so hard and the river was so wide that we could not lay our pontoons, so we went back to our starting place and camped for the night.

On the first of January we went the same road over again and camped right where we were the day before. We could not yet get a stick of wood for there was none on the island. I tell you, if we weren't cold that night! In the morning we got up, and if you will believe me, we went straight back to Savannah—some of our gallant old Kentuckian's (Gen. Ward's) sharp moves. Then we were loaded on to a steamboat. It was the steamer that Robert Small [Smalls], a Negro, ran out of Charleston. He is the Captain of her now and has some smart looking white men under him. But I tell you, he is smart.[3] We went around the island and landed on the shore of South Carolina. We lay there all day, and the next. On the 4th we marched out here, some seven miles from the river. We are in some old fortifications. Some say they were built in the days of the Revolution and some say they were built at the beginning of this war. I don't know which is true. They are not built as we build them now and they look as tho they had been built more than four years ago.

Yesterday we went and backed lumber again, one and one fourth miles, and put us up another house. So you see we get exercise enough.

I don't know whether you ever saw a rice field or not but it is quite a trade. In the first place it costs thousands of dollars to prepare the ground, as it has to be ditched off into beds about four by fifteen rods, the ditch being about five feet deep and four feet wide. Then there has to be a dike built all along the river to keep the water off. Then there has to be large races cut to let the water in and to run flat boats on to carry off the rice. Every ditch has to have a floodgate in it. They plow the ground, then mark it out the long way of the beds, the rows about six inches apart. Then the darkies sow it by hand, one row at a time. Then they open the gates and let in the water. The rice is cut with hand sickles and bound and toted out to the races on the darkies heads. It is then carried to a mill, generally run by water. They let the water in when the tide comes in, and then close the gates till after it has started out. They have water enough to run until it starts in again. It is threshed off the straw, using six cylinders, like those on our machines north. Then it goes to a hulling mill. The hulls stick so tight it is almost impossible to get them off. It is put into morter, and a beam six inches square and ten feet long, lifted by water power keeps falling into it till it is nearly all hulled, then it is put thru a fanning mill.

I received a letter from you, dated the 20th, the last I have heard. I have written as often as I could. Have you ever received two letters from me written at Atlanta, and containing $5 each?

Write often and direct as before to Savannah. L.S.M.

NOTES

1. Lute gave no location here, but his brigade (Colonel Dustin's Second Brigade of Brig. Gen. Ward's Third Division of the Twentieth Corps) had moved across the

Savannah River. According to Harvey Reid's letter of January 5, 1865, they were now encamped "about five miles from the river in a position commanding the only road by which the river between Savannah and the coast can be reached by the rebels, this being the object of our move." Reid, *Uncommon Soldiers*, 219.

2. Sherman reviewed the Twentieth Corps on December 30, probably to strengthen a sense of pride and confidence in the men, which his presence inspired. Welcher and Ligget, *Coburn's Brigade*, 313.

3. Robert Smalls (1839–1915), the pilot of the *Planter*, became a naval hero for the Union. On May 13, 1862, he commandeered the Confederate steamship and delivered sixteen "Negroes" past the Charleston forts, beyond Confederate waters, to freedom. After the U.S. Congress granted Smalls and his associates the ownership of the *Planter*, he was employed by the Union Army, furnishing valuable information about navigating coastal waters. Smalls was also influential in persuading President Lincoln to recruit free black men for service in the Union military. He went on to become a congressman from South Carolina during Reconstruction. Benjamin Quarles, "The Abduction of the Planter," *Civil War History*, vol. 4, no. 1, Kent State University Press, Kent, OH, March 1958, 5–10. Project Muse, https://www.jhu.muse.edu/article/415464/summary/.

Camp at Goldsboro, N.C., March 31, 1865[4]

Ever dear parents and brother–

Once more I have the pleasure of being where I can communicate with you by pen and I have so very much to say that I don't know where or how to commence. As you probably know (by this time) we have been on another long hard campaign. We did not know ourselves that we were again to leave our cummunications, else I should not have left you in the dark, which has doubtless been to you, as to myself, the cause of much anxiety.

The last letter I received from you was dated December 21st, until the 25th of March. Then I received nine letters from you, the latest dated Feb. 27th. So you see I have not heard from you very lately. We are not in anything of a settled condition yet, so I shall not try to write anything, only to let you know that I am "O.K." yet.[5]

After we got here our regiment was sent on guard for the wagon train to Kingston—thirty miles—and we got back only two hours ago. We have no tents up and the wind blows so it is almost an impossibility to write a legible hand. I have had the best of health on this trip, am well and feeling good now, only I guess if you were to see me you would hardly own me as your son and brother, for I am *ragged and dirty*, sure.

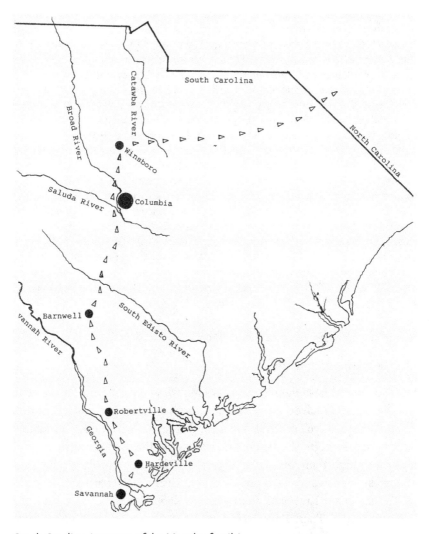

South Carolina (courtesy of the Moseley family)

On the third of March I was detailed to forage so I got me a mule, or donkey, and have been at that business until now. Our regiment had but one fight. We foragers (or as we call it, "bummers") skirmished with the rebs nearly every day. They captured some of the foragers but I was always lucky enough to get away. They drove me from one house with only my gun and mule once, leaving my saddle and forage, but we went back afterwards and got it.[6]

I would like to sit down some of these evenings and tell you about it but you just wait five months and I will. You inquire after the rest of the boys—all are well, but George Wheeler. He was captured. Lieut. Knowles and son of company C, Preshure of company G, and George were all taken at once. That is all. Drewery is all right. But I must close. I will write again soon. Write and direct to Goldsboro, N.C. Respects to all, and love to you, L.S. Moseley

As I failed to get my letter into the office in time for it to go yesterday, I will write a little more this morning. We have at length been lucky enough to get rid of old Cap Brown. He was, as he claimed, stepped on by a mule, and was not able to go into the fight on the 20th. Colonel Dustin, commanding our brigade, preferred charges of cowardice against him and he is now a citizen. He was in command of the regiment. We are all so glad. Lieut. White of company A is now in command of our company.

It is a fine morning, reminds me so much of home. I would like to go out and plow. I am going to have a new suit of clothes today and then I hope to look and feel a little more respectable. I must stop writing . . .

L.S.M.

NOTES

4. After Sherman seized Savannah, he turned his troops (60,000 officers and men, and 68 guns) on a muddy, swampy, and exhausting march through the Carolinas. The troops were accompanied by some 2,500 wagons containing forage, provisions, and ammunition, with six mules for each wagon and about 600 ambulances, each drawn by two horses. Welcher and Ligget, *Coburn's Brigade*, 316, 317. Sherman's men were even harsher in South Carolina than they had been in Georgia. Because South Carolina had been the first state to secede, many felt that it was chiefly responsible for the war and should thus pay a heavy price. Commager, *Blue and the Gray*, 959.

5. The unusual gap between Lute's letters to his family (Jan. 6–Mar. 31, 1865) was likely due to the long and exhausting marches of the Carolina Campaign. The troops had to navigate swamps, swollen rivers, nearly impassable roads in miserable weather, engaging in desperate foraging, skirmishing, and violent destruction along the way. Harvey Reid's lengthy letter dated April 1, 1865, describes this period in vivid detail. Reid, *Uncommon Soldiers*, 224–28.

6. "Bummers" was a nickname for Union soldiers who stole food and supplies from civilians. Large foraging expeditions were authorized by commanding officers in order to keep the armies fed, but small groups or stragglers who called themselves "bummers" also went marauding on their own.

Sunday, April 2nd, 1865 [Near Fayetteville, N.C.]

Dear parents and brother,

I have so much to do and so many letters to write, that I hardly know what to do first. We have no conveniences for writing, so I hope you will make all allowances.

We started from the Savannah river on the 29th of January, and marched fifteen miles. On the 30th we marched but eight. The 31st we did not march. In the evening Alex Pope and I were scuffling, and I threw him on to a stump and broke his leg, and I was very sorry.

On the 2nd of February we ran on to the Johnnies at Londonville [Lawtonville]. We formed in line and advanced on them and they dug out, double quick. We reached Graham on the 8th. The 9th and 10th we tore up R.R. On the 12th we waded the South Edisto river, and oh man! If it was'nt cold. It was about forty rods thru, and I just thot I would "go ded." On the 16th we reached Columbia—or to within two miles of it, as near as we went. The 18th we crossed the Saluda. The 19th we crossed the Broad river; the 20th we reached Winnsboro. On the 22nd we marched 22 miles and camped on the banks of the Catawba. At twelve in the night they call us up, and we sat around until nearly morning, then they set us to carrying rails to corduroy the road so the train could get across.[7] We then marched four miles and camped—tired and hungry lot of boys. Now comes the rain. The 14th and 20th corps have to cross on the same pontoon, and you have no idea how long it takes to get so many men and wagons across one bridge. We have to lay still the 20th, as it continues to rain, and we of course get nothing to eat on account of not moving so the foragers can find the stuff. It looks rather black to us, and I don't wonder. Look at our condition: no rations to eat, our train mud bound, so if we are to stir a wagon it would go down in the quicksand to the hubs; the enemy in the front and on our flanks, and no chance to forage until we move again, the rain still pouring down. One thinks we have undertaken more than we can do. Another thinks we will have to abandon our trains etc., but "old Billy" runs this institution.[8] He sets us to carrying poles and rails, and making a road, and get the trains onto it, so the next morning we move on—the men making what we call railroad every step of the way. So you see how I spent my 22nd birthday—wet to the skin. It was here that Lieut Knowles and son, Wheeler, and Preshure were taken prisoners. They were foraging. Marian Ryons got away, he was with them.

I have not kept a diary since the 26th, for I had none and no way to get one. So I cannot give you a correct account of our trip from that time.

Lieut Morse went in charge of the foragers after Knowles [Stephen Knowles from Linn, WI] was captured. George Perkins went from our company. The rebs were so thick that Cap Brown who was commanding the regiment, ordered two men instead of one from each company. I commenced on the 3rd of March. I picked up an old lame gray mule, gave $2 for a saddle, and borrowed a bridle. I rode old gray two days and got tired of him. So one night after dark I went over to the wagon trains and found a wagon with an extra mule tied to it. So I untied the halter and led him home with me. I should have spoken to the teamster, but was afraid he might object to letting me have him. Then I traded him off, and got one of my own. We would ride out some twelve or fourteen miles in front of the army, and camp at some house until morning. Then we would get some old fellow's wagon, and load it with meal, potatoes, etc., and go to camp with it. George and I captured five fine mules one day, and we took the best ones for ourselves and turned the rest over. On the 13th we (the foragers) crossed to the road that the 14th corps was marching on, and camped in front of them, within eight miles of Fayetteville—some twelve miles in front of our corps. The next morning the 2nd division of the 14th corps foragers, under command of an Indian (Major Holmes) came up and we went with them. We had gone but a mile before we came right on to the Johnnies' camp. We had to fall back a little, then we formed in line and went for them. We "the bummers," or as we are called here, "Sherman's buttermilk scouts" drove twice our number out of their works, and ran them all the way to town. Then they made another stand, and hit four of our men. But we chased them out of town, and then we went for the mills, storehouses etc.⁹ It was some fun and some exciting, to go thru a city as fast as our mules could run, and just as we turned one corner the rebs would be turning the next one in front. Every time I shot my gun my mule would jump as high as I wanted him to. At all events, we stayed in the city that night. In the morning, Lieutenant [Morse] sent me out to camp after a wagon to get our flour etc. Here is where we got our first communications. A small boat came up to us.

On the 16th our brigade had quite a fight—driving the rebs. Ed Parkhurst, Co I, was slightly wounded by a piece of shell. It is well now. He is the only Beloit boy that was hurt. On the 19th the rebs tried to whip us by detail as we came up the road. Our Division was guarding the rear. They charged the 14th corp, flanking them and breaking their lines, but the 1st Division of our Corp came up just then and drove them back. The 3rd Brigade of our Division was in the fight some too. Our Brigade was not in it but was on the line.[10]

We foragers drove the rebel pickets into their breastworks one morning before the column came up. I was in a house within eighty rods of them. I did'nt suppose then that there was any force there. They sent a force around behind us to gobble us in. They went too far around and ran into our column, so of course they had to get out. If it had'nt have been for this they would have probably taken your Lute off with them.

We had a hard fight here. They charged our line eight times. They would come up near, and lie down and rest. Then they would come on again until they had enough, then they would run back. While they were fighting, we were about a mile and a half back at a house getting our dinner and feeding our mules. We had our saddles off, and were in a grainery, shelling corn to carry to camp for feed, when another squad came up to the house on a run, and the rebs after them. I got my mule and started off. We went a few rods and made a stand. We stopped them and went back after our stuff. I have been driven away from three houses this way. Twice I thot I sure was gone, but here I am O.K. yet, with only 152 days to serve—will soon be a 100 day's man.

I have been lucky so far, for sure, and I hope to be fortunate enough to go thru the next five months.

Father says as soon as he hears from me he will write me two pages, so I shall expect it. I don't wonder you thot hard of me if you did not know why I hadn't written, but it made me feel badly in reading over your letters when I came to where you said that perhaps the reason I didn't write was because I didn't receive your letters, and was bound to wait until I heard from you. Some of the boys do that way, but not Lute. You said you would write and I always believed that you did, whether I got the letters or not, and I always write if I am where I can.

They say they are going to let us rest a few days, but it won't be much of a rest to us if they do as they have done so far. There is either a drill, inspection, or review every afternoon, and old soldiers as we claim to be now, it is hard for us to go out and drill over and over again what we had learned two years ago. It is in my mind an imposition on good nature.

There are already grape vine reports in camp that we are going to move again in a few days. Of course, there is no use in listening to them.

Gen Williams [Brevet Maj. Gen. Alpheus S. Williams] who commanded our corps is relieved, and Maj. Gen. Moore [Joseph A. Mower] takes his place.

[The final portion of this letter is missing.]

NOTES

7. The corduroying process consisted of cutting poles as long as the width of the road and laying them close together to form a rough but supportive surface that would support wagons, artillery, horses, and troops. Fence rails were also used when available.

8. "Old Billy" was a nickname for Maj. Gen. William T. Sherman, whose forces in the Carolinas Campaign outnumbered the dispirited Confederates by a ratio of nearly 3:1.

9. Welcher and Ligget provide an account of foraging in Georgia by "Sherman's 'Bummers'": "In marching across Georgia, Sherman's men left behind a path of destruction and desolation. They burned homes and buildings, destroyed fences and gardens, took all the horses, mules and livestock, all the buggies and wagons that were needed for transportation, and left little or no food desperately needed by the people remaining in the region. They also allowed most of the slaves to follow the army from the plantations to seek their freedom. The immediate future for the residents in that part of the state was bleak indeed." (Welcher and Ligget, *Coburn's Brigade*, 307.)

10. The Battle of Averasboro (also spelled Averysboro) took place on March 16, 1865; the Battle of Bentonville began on March 19. Reports on Wisconsin 22nd Regiment's involvement in both battles are found in E. B. Quiner's *Military History of Wisconsin, Volume 3* (Chicago, 1866), ch. 30.

Co B, 22nd Regiment, Wis. State Vols., 3rd Div., 20 Corps. Camp near Goldsboro, April 9, 1865

Ever dear home:

I was very glad again to hear from you, the letter bearing date March 26th. I have written twice since I came here—hope you have received both.

Of course you hear all the glorious news. I wish you could spend one night with us in camp. I presume you would hear more cheering and rejoicing over Grant's victory than you ever heard in all your life before. We have learned a new way of making a big noise. We will fill a canteen with powder, then bury it in the ground with a slow match attached. It makes a loud report. Nearly every company fixes one every evening, and then such cheering and yelling was never done by civilians, or less than 75,000 men.[11]

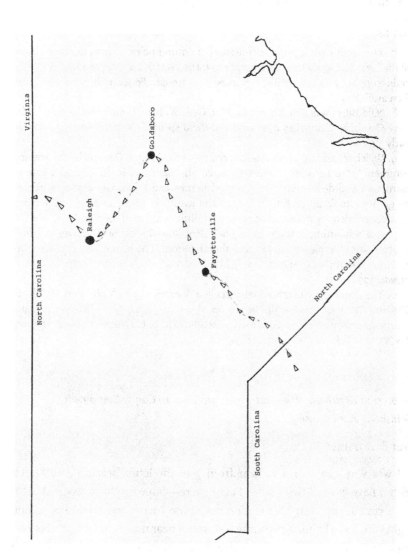

North Carolina (courtesy of the Moseley family)

As I wrote you before, we have been having what they call a rest—that is—we have slept in the same camp every night, and every day we have either been in drill, review, inspection or something else. To cap it all off, we are to start tomorrow or the next day on another thirty day campaign.[12] So this is the last you will hear from old Lute again for thirty days, and I never felt more like going more than I do this time, for I feel as tho we could just more than make the Johnnies hunt their holes, and cry for quarter. Peace will be declared within the next six months, and not much short of that I believe.[13]

Camp rumor says that gen Grant sent word to "old Billy" to pitch after Hood as soon as he could. He said "let's end the fuss now, right off." "Billy" said that in less than four months he would discharge the best army that ever trod the earth and I think he don't tell much of a lie, for we have done as much as any part of the army in putting down the rebellion. What do you think about it?

The boys are all feeling first rate. We aren't in the least afraid of old Hood. If he is all we have to handle, by cracky, we will just show him what for we came down here.

News is something we do not have here. Papers four or five days old find quick sale here at 25 cents a piece.

We are all feeling as good as men can feel, and expect to see the *end*, and then go home and enjoy it. Just two things I hope for now. First, that mother's health will improve, and second, that father will be able to win his suit with the school district, so as to make us all comfortable, and get you a good, quiet, snug home: then I will be happy.

A squad of convalesents have just come up from Nashville and vicinity. Among them is Alf Bond: one of the best boys I have ever met. He was wounded at Dallas Woods. Chas Fountain is also with them besides one recruit. We are very glad to see them for they are good men, but we do not want to see some of the rest come up. There is Frone Herrick. He holds a sergeants position, and has never been in a fight, and it is just so with over half of our company. They lie in the rear enjoying themselves, and drawing just as much pay and more rations than we, and we are doing all the fighting and hard marching. It isn't right and some body is to blame, sure. But it is only 144 days more at all events for me. That is sure, whether the Johnnies are whipped or not. I have strong hopes of their being well whipped by that time. Sherman says that we will just keep on whipping them until they say they have enough.[14]

It seems to me as tho I was free now for old ___Cap Brown is gone. I hope he will meet with his reward before he meets with Co B [Bloodgood] in Beloit, for I just believe he will get toughly handled. I owe him more than I owe old Rogers, and I believe I have got just rough enough since I have been soldering to pay off some of those old scores when I get back. I have heard too many bullets to be easily scared at smaller weapons. But I don't want you to think by this that I intend to be a fighting character or rowdy, but only to get square with the world.

We may not go as soon as I said, but I thot I would be sure and let you know that we are going this time. I wish you would write as soon as you get this and put in some black thread and a needle, and then the next time put in a fine comb, so I can mend up when we stop again. You see we cannot get such things here any more than we could in the middle of a large forest.

Just to show you how we are imposed upon, let me give you the prices of about all we can get here at all. Cheese is $1 per pound, and what you get for a pound will fall short of a half. Thread, the poorest, 50 cents. A tin plate, 50 cents. They will stick a stick into a tub of butter, and then rub it on a piece of paper for 50 cents etc. We haven't received our pay yet, and I don't care if we don't till my time is out. I haven't any money, and I don't know as I want any, for if I had it I should have bot some things at these big prices, and I would rather go without.

I am glad to hear that father had sold his little pony and has a team that he can do something with. If I live to have use for a horse, I will have a good one.

I expect Ed is getting to be quite a boy, or man. Perhaps he thinks he can take his big soldier brother down. How is it, my boy?

... Well, I ought to write two more letters today, so I will close. It is hard work for me to keep still in one place long enough to write, since we have been on the go, and especially now when there is so much excitement over victories, and expectations about marching.

I would like to have you write as often as convenient, and direct as before, for I don't know any more than you do where we are going.

Yours with respect and love, L.S. Moseley

Respects to all.

NOTES

11. U.S. Grant's forces had been putting relentless pressure on the Army of Northern Virginia. Robert E. Lee was forced to evacuate Richmond on April 2, 1865, which resulted in rowdy celebrations by the Union troops.

12. "On April 10, Sherman's forces left Goldsboro on their march toward Raleigh, North Carolina. Colonel Dustin (now commanding the four regiments of Coburn's Brigade) reported that his men had been on the march forty-seven out of fifty-four days since leaving Savannah. They had covered approximately 475 miles through enemy territory, and destroyed about five miles of railroad, and they had taken an active part in the Battle of Averasboro on March 16 and supported the Fourteenth Corps at the Battle of Bentonville. Casualties (killed, wounded, missing) totaled ninety officers and men. The brigade had captured sixty-six prisoners, one piece of artillery, fifteen horses, seventy-seven mules, and 325 head of cattle. Now they were on the march again." *War of the Rebellion: Official Records*, vol. 47, part 1, 785, 809, 810.

13. By early April, General Lee had somewhere between 12,000 and 13,000 armed men surrounded by 70,000 to 80,000 Union soldiers. He had no choice but to surrender to Grant, thus ending the Civil War. Catton, *Reflections on the Civil War*, 121.

14. Lee surrendered to Grant at the McLean house, near the Appomattox Courthouse in Virginia on April 9, 1865, a date now considered to be the end of the Civil War. There were several Confederate troops still in the field, and it was several weeks before all had surrendered.

∾

Raleigh, N.C. April 14th, 1865

Dear parents and brother–

I dare say you little thot one year ago today, when we were lying at Nashville, that today I would be in the capital of North Carolina, writing to you, and much less four years ago today when Sumter was fired on, and I was attending school. But strange things come to pass in these days and here I am in Raleigh, writing to you.[15]

We marched about nine miles today and came in about eleven o'clock. But the most surprising this is that the rebs destroyed the R.R. and bridges from Goldsboro to here, yet a train leaves here tonight. The rebs made Yankee prisoners tear up the R.R. I suppose the reason was because they were short of men.

The 22nd was detailed to guard the wagon train thru while the rest of the army pushed on as rapidly as possible, hoping to catch old Johnston here, but he travels faster than we can.

You have doubtless heard of the awful big news—how Grant and Sheridan have been putting old Lee over the coals. It is true that lots and lots of Lee's men came into our lines.[16] Old Johnston's men don't seem as willing to give up, altho they tell the citizens along our route that they will never fight us again, but they hate to surrender to "Wm Sherman the brute."

I am too tired to write much, only to let you know where I am etc., and then we boys do *feel so good.* Well, if *we* don't feel good, who should?

Father, I want you to put in a big crop, for I am coming home to help you harvest it. We probably have some hard marching before us to catch the enemy but we can stand most anything now. If we won't be the best feeling lot of boys you ever saw if we gobble old Johnston pretty soon and then come home. I am afraid the boys will make old Beloit quake. I have slept but little in the last four days and nights, for it has been twelve o'clock every night before we reached camp. So I will not try to write more at this time. The boys are all well, and so I am feeling bully.

L.S. Moseley

NOTES

15. "Raleigh was evacuated by Johnston's infantry two days before we reached it . . . It does not belie its reputation of being almost a Union town. It is a very pretty place, but not large. The Capitol, Insane Asylum and Deaf and Dumb Institution are all magnificent buildings." Reid, *Uncommon Soldiers,* 242.

16. In the final months of the war, with Union victory imminent, Confederate desertions increased as some soldiers sought protection with the Union army. Actual numbers are unknown, likely higher than official records.

∾

Camp 22nd Wis. Vol, near Raleigh, North Carolina, Monday, April 16, 1865

To my dear parents and brother:

. . . As I wrote you from Goldsboro, we were ordered to start on a campaign of thirty days. We expected then to have at least one severe battle before we reached cummunications. And let me assure you that I wrote that letter with no small amount of foreboding for the future. We heard that Lee had surrendered, and that Johnston, who was then in our front, had no idea of surrendering to "that brute of a Sherman" as he calls him. We knew very well that Sherman would pounce upon him at the first opportunity. We know that we out numbered him and could whip him. But I thot he would hold out as long as possible.

Our regiment was detailed to guard the wagon train thru, while the rest of the army pressed on as fast as possible to over take the enemy. We occupied Raleigh without any engagement, and find the citizens apparently glad to see us, and anxious for peace. We expected to go on after the Johnnies the next morning—and even fell in and started, but went out some four miles when we were ordered back to camp. It was reported that Johnston had come to town and was willing to surrender. We have layed here ever since, and as yet there is no prospect of marching. We have not been officially notified of Johnston's surrender, but it is not only reported, but believed by us to *be so*. No mail has been allowed to go out for the last few days, and this makes me think that it is so, and Sherman don't want to announce it yet for some reason or other. In fact the editor of the Raleigh Progress told me it is true, but that Gen Sherman had ordered him not to publish it yet. The major said it was, and Gen S. and staff went out to the front, some fourteen miles, yesterday. Gen Hardee was here in town the other day under a flag of truce, so of course there is something of the sort going on. Surely Gen Sherman would not lay here idle and let Johnston either fortify or get farther away, if it was'nt for some such an affair.[17]

The future looks brighter, and surely I have strong hopes of being allowed the great enjoyment of once more returning to your kind and loved society, which I must confess, I have at times nearly despaired of. Yes, there have been many times when I thot it looked very critical. Sure, I thot some would get home again, but it is almost a miracle how so many of us could be spared thru so much danger and hardship.

It was officially announced to us this morning that Pres. Abraham Lincoln was assinated [assassinated] at the theatre in Washington. I don't believe it yet. There is a report this afternoon that it is not so. I hope it will prove untrue, surely.[18]

I don't see why we can't get mail. When the Potomac army went without mail for three days, there was an awful blow in the paper about it, but we can go without three months and not a word be said about it in the papers. But that is'nt what I care the most about. I want to hear from my home. We have R.R. cummunications, and why can't we get our mail. We have gone with less of such accommadations, and with less rations and poorer ones than any other army, and I believe there is less said about it. I don't want to complain, but I will bet all I am worth, that the Potomac army never had as poor rations as we have now, only crackers, coffee and a very little of the poorest beef you ever saw killed for a man to eat. I don't want you to say anything about it, for it is the mark of a poor soldier to hear one complain of poor living.

I haven't the least expectations of getting home now before the first of September, for if peace was declared today, it would take some time, you know, to disperse so large an army from here. We may be the first to go, and we may be the last. But I feel so good over the news—isn't it good?

I wish you would write as ever, and direct to Raleigh, while I am as ever the same.

Corp L.S. Moseley

I will pop in and help you eat some of your garden sauce one of these days—tomatoes, green corn, etc. etc.

NOTES

17. A meeting had been arranged between Johnston and Sherman to draw up terms for surrender when Sherman received notice of President Lincoln's assassination. The meeting was held on April 18; terms of surrender were signed and submitted to civil authorities for approval. Jefferson Davis, the Confederate president, reluctantly agreed, but Andrew Johnson, the newly installed US president, and his cabinet disapproved the terms as written. A military truce was in effect during this period. Welcher and Ligget, *Uncommon Soldiers*, 367, 368.

18. President Abraham Lincoln was shot by the actor John Wilkes Booth at Ford's Theatre in Washington, DC on the evening of April 14, 1865. Lincoln died the following morning. Booth was part of a larger conspiracy motivated by revenge and hopes of reviving the Confederate cause. The news took two days to reach Lute and his comrades in North Carolina, but because they were accustomed to rumors, this information was not readily trusted.

∾

Camp near Raleigh, N.C., April 21st, 1865

Brother Ed:

. . . The last letter I received from you was dated the 3rd of April. You had not then heard from me. I wrote, as you probably know by this time, just as soon as I could . . . I am in strong hopes now to be where I can tell you about my soldiering before long. I believe that by the middle of June we will be at home. I don't think it will be longer than that—and boy! What a glorious thot! I can hardly appreciate it, and surely, no one can if we can't. Only think, peace once more—some thing to eat besides hardtack and lean beef—clean clothes to put on, with no greybacks. Oh man! And to enjoy society again. Just think! Where we can lie down and rest secure, and feel that we can sleep till morning without being molested or hearing that old bugle blowing for us to pack up and leave. Surely, you cannot know how to appreciate it, altho I know you will be glad to welcome me back again, and have the war closed.

I feel as tho I would be awful akward and green, come to go back again into society, for you must know that three years in the woods, living as we have, will be a big drawback on manners etc. But I trust you will make due allowance for me, won't you?

Tomorrow we have a grand review in heavy marching order and I hope it is our last one. It is a splendid sight to look upon, but not so splendid to be in the ranks, and march thru the dust to be looked at. But that is but one of the disagreeable duties a soldier has to perform. But Ed, thank God, we are nearly done with it, and I think I have been extremely fortunate in getting so nearly thru with a hole hide, and a strong constitution, don't you, Boy? And I am not sorry I enlisted, and, too, that I have stayed until the war is ended, and I guess you are not. It was hard to leave you, surely. I have lots to tell you when I get back. But, Ed, the hardest battle I ever fought was on the first of June, 1863, and I expect on or about the first of June, 1865, to fight the easiest. The first time I cried with sorrow, the next I expect to cry with joy.[19]

Ed, when you hear of the regiment coming to the state (I don't know whether we will come to Madison, Milwaukee or Racine, but you will probably know) then I want you to come out and stay with me and soldier with me till we are discharged, and then go home with me, if it is so you can, will you?

I don't know how to fill up the paper, for there is, as I said before, nothing to write. There is enough to say tho. I hope you will have lots of tomatoes, for I expect to board with you a while when I get back . . .

I want father to have some business or employment for me. I don't expect to work very hard at first, for I am not used to work, you know. Old Perkins and Murry are lying on the bunk making fun and laughing at me, and telling what they are going to do when they get home. We three boys have lived together for the last two years, and have never had a hard word. They are what I call bully boys. We will always remember each other, sure.

But I will close. Give my regards to all, and tell them that old Lute expects to call in and see them one of these fine days. Write soon and direct as before, and oblige your friends and brother.

Corp L.S. Moseley, Co B., 22nd Wis. Vol.

19. Lute's "hardest battle I ever fought" was saying goodbye to his family in Beloit and returning to military duty after taking "French leave" in May 1863.

∽

Raleigh, N.C. April 28th, 1865

My dear mother:-

On the 24th of this month, while we were lying here, anxiously waiting for peace to be confirmed from Washington, orders came for us to march in the morning. There was considerable speculation with us as to where we would go. In the morning we started after old Johnston again. So of course we knew that Johnston had not surrendered. We marched twelve miles that day. We expected to go on the next morning but Johnston came to his senses and surrendered all the Confederate forces unconditionally to little Wm. Sherman. Bully for us! I say. What say you?

We marched back to old camp this afternoon, in Raleigh. Tomorrow at eleven o'clock the last mail goes out—the last one from this city. We start Sunday the 30th for City Point. That is, we suppose we will go there. At any rate it is for some place towards *HOME*. We have already made twelve miles of our homeward trip. I shall not write again, probably, and you need not write again, for I would not get it. It is going to take some time to get home from here. There are so many to go and so few accommodations. I don't expect to be mustered out and home in less than two months.

You spoke about making shirts, etc. I think I shall get some all ready made. You have too much to do to make shirts for me. So don't do it, or any thing of the kind. I am coming home just as I am every day here—ragged, dirty and lousy, and will feel mighty glad to get home so I may write again but not without we are delayed somewhere. I received a letter from you dated the 16th. Bill got one dated the 20th today. But he isn't here so I don't know yet what the news is, but I will close.

As ever your boy, L.S.M.

∽

Camp near Richmond, Wed., May 10th, 1865

Dear home:-

The chaplain just came up and said if we wanted to write he would carry our letters to the city if we would have them ready in half an hour, so here goes for a note.

We started from Raleigh on the last day of April, and reached here on the eighth. It is, as near as I can calculate by the road we came, two hundred long miles. So you will see we have done some huge old marching. The roads were fine and the weather pretty cool, so old *Corp Ward* just more than lit out. He was in advance. We are now eight miles from Richmond. Tomorrow we pass thru the town on review before Gens Sherman, Halleck etc. We have to march to Washington and maybe farther.

It will be quite a while yet before we get home. The boys are all feeling well, only impatient at the delays, and mad that they march us so far when they might just as well transport us. It is mean, isn't it?

I will not write more this time. Write and direct to Washington.

Yours in love and respect, L.S. Moseley

 ∽

Camp 22nd Wis., near Washington, DC, May 25, 1865

Dear Parents:

A few lines from me will perhaps be acceptable. I will for lack of pen and ink, use a pencil, which I hope you will excuse.

The great question with me at this time is, when will I get home? It is hard to answer, or even to guess at an answer, but in all probability not before the middle or last of July. My pencil is inadequate to describe our feelings at this time. We volunteered to help put down the rebellion, which we have done. We did not volunteer to remain in the service as required to parade and make big shows to gratify the ambition of officers, and to be reviewed and rereviewed, and kept in the field when no human being can see the least bit of use for it. It is hard to the once free boys of Wisconsin at least. We have been marched from Raleigh to Richmond almost on a double quick. This we all stood like men, supposing it was to hasten our discharge, but come to find out it was only a race between the different corps commanders. We had some hope of being transported from there, but no,

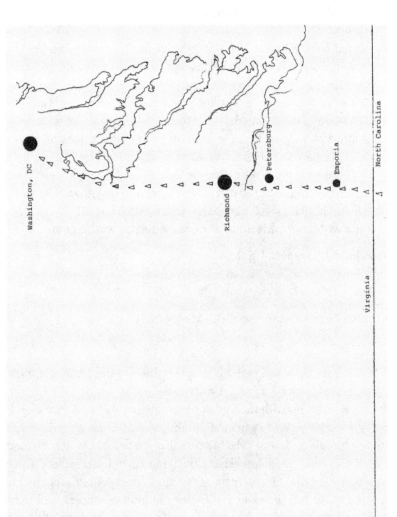

March to Washington, DC (courtesy of the Moseley family)

we march to Washington. Then a grand military display, a grand review. What benefit does the nation receive from it? The public are invited to attend. So we, who have faced bullets, are brot out and paraded around like a pair of fine horses, for a show. Who are the spectators? Let me tell you, principally the young dandies of the Northern cities that have managed some way to keep out of the army. The Chet Hodges, and the like: men who would scorn to speak to one of us—a soldier—only a soldier. He can't buy anything, or go any where without a pass. Now we are marched out some six miles and put in camp where we can't go to the city. As near as I can learn—to remain a month (at least I heard Col. Bloodgood say so) and eat up their hard tack and poor beef while the niggers and men imployed to care for horses and do other work around town, get their fill of soft bread, pork, potatoes etc. *Now is this using us right?*[20]

I ought to be ashamed, I suppose, for complaining thus, but I'm not. I believe I can stand all I have been thru, and a great deal more. In fact, we will have the easiest time now we have ever had. We will have no duty to do. It is only the suspence. We will get paid, but at the same time, we would all much rather go to our homes. At any rate, they ought to give us a little pay. Nine months is a good while to go without money. Nice things he wants so bad to eat, and cheap too.

Well now I will quit my growling, and tell you about the review. We were six miles from Washington. We were marched up there, and crossed the long bridge into Washington. Here we came to company front, and marched around the capital, down Pennsylvania avenue by the president's mansion, in front of which was the stand where all the big men were. We marched about two miles thru the town, and then came out here—some six miles to camp. The streets were filled with young fellows with their squinting glasses on their noses, laughing and tittering at us—besides lots of men, women and children. There were lots of mottoes hung out, but I didn't take much notice of them. I saw one welcoming the Potomac braves with the list of fights they had been in, ommitting Bull Run etc, Chancelorsville and others.[21]

Just day before yesterday we were notified to report forty-one recruits to our company, as on detached duty. What do they want of recruits now? I will tell you that too. You see Lieut Col Bloodgood had been carrying a Colonel's commission in his pocket for the last six months, and could not be mustered in as Colonel for there were not men enough in the regiment to allow one. So now *after the war is over*, it is filled up, and he is mustered in. At Goldsboro, when we were going out to chase Johnston, all thot there would be one big fight at least. He (Bloodgood) tried hard to go out of the service, but lucky for him, he failed. Now he is perfectly willing to stay any length of time for the big pay. I believe if we were paid up lots of the men would leave.

But I must close. I am feeling well and all right, only impatient to start home.

L.S. Moseley, Co. B. Write often.

∾

Camp near Washington, DC, Monday June 5th, 1865

Kind father and mother:

. . . I have nothing new to communicate, and had thot I would not write, as I had neither paper, envelopes, stamps or money to buy them with. But the Sanitary Commission furnished me with paper and envelopes, and I can send it without a stamp and I was at a loss to know how to spend the day.[22]

We have been very busy the last few days making out papers for our discharge, and hav'nt them all done yet. It is an awful job. There has been some talk that we would start for home (for Wisconsin) on the 6th. That is so near we all know better now. I say we won't leave here one minute before the 15th, and I know we won't for it will take two days before our papers are ready. Then it will take a whole week to go to Brigade, Division, Corps and Department headquarters to be approved, and then maybe they won't be right.[23]

Time hangs very heavy over our heads now. I was in hopes to get home before hot weather comes on. It is hot enough here now, I tell you. I have been feeling quite unwell the last three or four days, but am all right today.

Last night we marched over to fort Bunker Hill, where all the Wisconsin regiments near here came together, and the Hon. Ex Gov. Randall reviewed us and made a speech. It was a big imposition on us, to march men four or files miles in the dust on such a hot day to hear an old politician spout and tell about being in Italy, and that we had been fighting for a great cause. Who did'nt know that? I wonder if he thinks he could influence our votes in his favor by it. Why didn't he do as Gov. Lewis did: come around to us instead of marching us to have him look at us, but we won't have to stand it always, I hope.[24]

They have made out papers for the commutation on our rations while we were prisoners, amounting to $7. I wish they would pay it to us now.

The boys have gone down to the river to bathe. How strange it is; there have been three men drowned from our division since we have been here— more than I know of since we have been in the army. It seems hard to go thru so much danger, and then loose one's life so—just as they are about to go home.

I am in hopes to get a letter from you tonight when the mail comes. But I will close, as ever your son who is very anxious to get home to his ma.

L.S. Moseley

P.S. The mail has come, and no letter for L.S. Moseley. We may possibly leave before the 15th, as they have begun to send regiments from our division, and our papers are being hurried up. L.S.M.[25]

NOTES

20. Harvey Reid, Company A of the 22nd Wisconsin, also complained about the march to Washington by exhausted troops. Some felt they were being ill-used in a commanders' race to be the first to arrive in the nation's capital. Reid, *Uncommon Soldiers*, 247.

21. Walt Whitman, who served as an army orderly in the Washington, DC hospitals after nursing his wounded brother, wrote about the Grand Review of the Armies, a celebration of the Union victory ordered by the War Department. This military procession took place on May 23 and 24, 1865, celebrating the Union victory in the Civil War: "For two days now the broad spaces of Pennsylvania Avenue along to Treasury Hill, and so by detour around to the President's House (and so up to Georgetown and across the Aqueduct bridge) have been alive with a magnificent sight, the returning Armies. In their wide ranks stretching clear across the Avenue I watch them march or ride along at a brisk pace through two whole days—Infantry, Cavalry, Artillery—some 200,000 men." (Walt Whitman, *Civil War Poetry and Prose* [New York: Dover Publications, 1995], 56.)

22. The U.S. Sanitary Commission was organized by civilians in June 1861 to assist the army in improving sanitary conditions in the camps, caring for sick and wounded soldiers and aiding their dependents at home. The commission enlisted scores of physicians and hundreds of public-spirited men and women to provide wide-ranging services for the troops and their families. Commager, *Blue and the Gray*, "The Sanitary Commission to the Rescue," 773.

23. William H. McIntosh, Company F, 22nd Wisconsin, described final departure in his unpublished manuscript, *Annals of the 22d Wisconsin*, 248: "The time passed quickly till June 12th when the 22d Wisconsin Volunteer Infantry was discharged from the service of the United States after serving a period of two years, nine months and ten days. The welcome and familiar order to *prepare to march* was

quickly obeyed and the men marched with light knapsacks, empty cartridge boxes and yet lighter hearts from the wooded camp down to the depot in the valley where the novel experience of a ride in cars was anticipated—a ride homeward."

24. Chaplain George S. Bradley summarized the distances marched—and transported—by the 22nd Wisconsin during their service: By railroad—2,700 miles; by steamboat 1,400 miles; on foot 2,400 miles. Total 6,500 miles. Bradley, *Star Corps*, 282.

25. This letter from Lute to his family in Beloit was probably the last one he wrote before heading home. He was mustered out at Fort Lincoln—now Fort Lincoln Park in Northeast Washington, DC—on June 12, 1865, with an Honorable Discharge.

Afterword

Esther Baer Moseley

(December 25, 1919–March 12, 2009)

In the lean years following the war, Lucius S. Moseley worked at many different jobs. He and his friend Sam Goss, who had a horse-driven threshing machine, did threshing for farmers in the Beloit area during several seasons.

On December 15, 1869, Lute married Fannie Brittan, whose sister Cynthia had married Sam Goss, Lute's threshing partner. Lute and Fannie lived on rented farms until 1881, when they had finally, through great effort and considerable deprivation, saved enough for a down payment on eighty acres of farmland west of Beloit. Lute was 39 years old when his first child, a girl named Metta, was born. Later children were named Harry, Bert, Jessie, and Florence.

Hard work and "unfair usage in business" took a heavy toll on Lute's naturally cheerful and affectionate spirit. He soon became quite serious. His temper was quick, but he was unfailingly honest and good to his family. Besides taking care of his farm, he did carpentry work in town to support his family. The children later reported many happy memories.

On September 2, each year for twenty-one years (1885–1906), the veterans of Company B and their families held reunions at Lute Moseley's farm. The date was chosen to commemorate the organization of the 22nd Wisconsin Volunteer Infantry Regiment at Camp Utley in Racine, which had taken place on September 2, 1862. Veterans greeted each other with affection, remembering the hardships and the victories they had shared. Many still lived in or near Beloit; others traveled long distances to attend the reunions that had become healing events for them. Most felt reluctant to talk freely of the war except with others who had lived through it.

Lucius S. Moseley died on January 5, 1923, a few weeks before his 80th birthday. He is buried in Oakwood Cemetery, in Beloit, Wisconsin.

Lucius S. Moseley in later life (courtesy of the Moseley family)

Obituary of
Lucius S. Moseley

Obituary from *Beloit Daily News*, Beloit, Wisconsin, January 6, 1923; final paragraph from Frank L. Klement, *Wisconsin in the Civil War*, 123, 124.

LUCIUS MOSELEY, RESIDENT HERE 80 YEARS, DEAD

Civil War Vet Succumbs After Long Illness—Funeral 2:30 Monday

Had Interesting War Record—Prominent in G.A.R. Circles for a Number of Years

Lucius S. Moseley, for 80 years a resident of the city and township of Beloit and the father of Assemblyman H. B. Moseley, died at the Beloit hospital early last night after an illness of several months. Except for the period of his active service in the 22nd Wisconsin infantry during the Civil War, he had lived continuously in Beloit township and city since the spring of 1843 when he was brought here as a babe in arms by his parents.

Surviving Mr. Moseley are three daughters, Metta and Jessie, of this city, and Mrs. Robert I. Riggs of Oshe, South Dakota, and two sons, Harry L. Moseley and Hubert B. Moseley, both of the town of Beloit. Moseley's wife, who was Miss Fannie Brittan before her marriage, died in 1908.

Mr. Moseley had an unusually interesting Civil War record and, following his return to civilian life, he was prominent for many years in G.A.R. circles and in Republican political affairs. He was known to many hundreds of public school pupils for his frequent addresses on patriotic subjects. He was one of the organizers and for many years an officer of the 22nd Wisconsin infantry association, and for many years he was host to comrades of his company at their annual meetings at his farm home.

Beloit was a hamlet of only a few hundred population when Mr. Moseley was a boy here. It was a pioneer settlement with few buildings and streets and no bridges. At the outbreak of the Civil War, Mr. Moseley was a student in the old Beloit academy. He dropped his studies to enlist in Company B of the 22nd Wisconsin infantry, recruited and commanded by Captain Thomas P. Northrop. After being mustered into federal service at Racine, the regiment moved south and engaged in its first battle at Thompson's Station, near Nashville, Tenn.

The Beloit man's service record showed that while the Confederates were forming for the attack on the Union forces, Mr. Moseley, who was standing near Colonel Utley, asked and was given permission to fire upon the enemy. His shot was the opening one of the engagement and for his action he was promoted to the rank of corporal on the field. In this engagement the Confederates overwhelmed the Wisconsin regiment, and Mr. Moseley and most of his comrades were taken captive. The Badgers were marched by the Confederates to the notorious Libby Prison where Mr. Moseley was incarcerated for a month before being transferred.

When it became known that he was to be removed from Libby, an Orfordville man, whose name was Tanberg, pleaded with Moseley to take out a message from him to his family. Although knowing that should he be found in possession of the message it would mean death for him, the Beloit man yielded to Tanberg's supplication, and the message was sewed between two shirts Mr. Moseley wore for warmth. He was searched by Confederate guards, but the message escaped detection and, once free to do so, Mr. Moseley sent it northward. For many years afterward, Tanberg acknowledged—in a public statement at a patriotic rally held in Janesville—the hazardous service rendered him by Moseley.

After leaving Libby Prison, Mr. Moseley was sent to barracks at St. Louis, Mo. Captivity becoming irksome, he fled the camp with another Beloit man, Osa Freeman, and the two made their way back to Beloit, traveling by night and hiding by day in enemy territory in order to elude Confederate outposts and scouting parties.

After reaching home, Mr. Moseley immediately rejoined his regiment and served until the end of the war. He was with Sherman on the march from Atlanta to the sea. During long months of the war, the Beloit man was in charge of a part of Federal foragers, and he had frequent escapes from capture and death on this hazardous service. He marched with his regiment in the Grand Review held in Washington after the war.

After his return to Beloit, the young veteran engaged in farming. Forty-one years ago he purchased a farm a short distance west of Beloit on the Monroe road, and he lived there for 32 years before retiring and moving into Beloit. He was a leading citizen of the township of Beloit and held all public offices in the township.

He was perhaps more widely known for the intense and active interest he took in Grand Army of the Republic affairs. He was for several terms commander of L.H.D. Crane post, G.A.R. of Beloit, and occupied important departmental posts, serving for several years as an aide-de-camp with the rank of colonel on the staff of General Rosecrans, commander-in-chief of the G.A.R. For 26 consecutive years he entertained his comrades of Company B at annual reunions at his farm home. He also was president of the Rock County Old Soldiers' and Sailors' association, and he served the Rock River Valley Old Settlers' association as president for two years. He was a member of and active in the affairs of the Beloit lodge of Knights of Pythias.

Lucius S. Moseley's gravestone, Oakwood Cemetery, Beloit, Wisconsin (photo by Fred Burwell)

Civil War soldiers' monument, Oakwood Cemetery, Beloit, Wisconsin (photo by Fred Burwell)

Mr. Moseley had a remarkable memory and had made a devoted study of Civil War history. He had a delightful way of telling his war experiences and, as a patriotic instructor of the G.A.R., he appeared many times in public schools to deliver a message of patriotism to the pupils.

One of his prized possessions was a remarkable scrapbook filled with clippings of local and patriotic history. He often told his friends he "wouldn't take a thousand dollars for the book."

In his inaugural address of January 3, 1866, the one-armed Lucius C. Fairchild, elected as Wisconsin's governor in November 1865, spoke of the peaceful transformation. As a former Union general and diplomat, wounded in the battle at Gettysburg, his words carried great significance to all who had sacrificed. "A million of men have returned from the war, been disbanded in our midst, and resumed their former occupations . . . The transition from the citizen to the soldier was not half so rapid, not half so wonderful, as had been the transition from the soldier to the citizen." He reported on the heavy financial burden carried by the citizens of the state, and the heavier cost in lives that could not be recovered. A total of 10,752 Wisconsin soldiers—about one in every eight—had died while in the service of their country.

"Cover Them Over with Beautiful Flowers"

E. F. Stewart, Published by Lee & Walker, Philadelphia, 1874.

Library of Congress, Music Division, https://www.loc.gov/item/sm1874.0472/.

Cover them over with beautiful flowers,
Deck them with garlands, those brothers of ours,
Lying so silent by night and by day,
Sleeping the years of their manhood away.
Give them the meed they have won in the past;
Give them the honors their future forecast;
Give them the chaplets they won in the strife;
Give them the laurels they lost with their life.

Cover them over, yes, cover them over,
Parent, and husband, brother and lover;
Crown in your hearts those dead heroes of ours,
Cover them over with beautiful flowers.

Appendix A

Roster, 22nd Wisconsin Officers and Staff;
Company B Infantry

Twenty-Second Regiment Infantry; Field and Staff; Company B Officers and Enlisted Men

Wisconsin Adjutant General's Office, 1886; digital publication by Wisconsin Historical Society, https://content.wisconsinhistory.org/digital/collection/quiner/id/50026/, pp. 201, 202, 205, 206, 207.

TWENTY-SECOND REGIMENT INFANTRY.

FIELD AND STAFF.

NAME.	RESIDENCE.	DATE.	REMARKS.
OFFICERS.			
Colonels.		*Rank from.*	
William L. Utley......	Racine	July 17, '62..	Res. Jrly 5, '64, disability.
Edward Bloodgood....	Milwaukee	Aug. 17, '64..	Lieut. Col., July 22, '62; M. O. July 12, '65.
Majors.			
Edward D. Murray....	Beloit	Sept. 1, '62..	Res. Feb. 4, '63.
Charles W. Smith	Geneva........	Feb. 4, '63..	From Capt. Co. C; Lieut. Col., Sept. 24, '64, not mustered; det. at Draft Rendezvous, Madison, Wis., From Dec. 23, '63, till Aug. 1, '65; M. O. Aug. 1, '65.
Adjutants.			
William Bones	Caledonia	July 22, '62..	Wnd. and pris. Thomson's Station; prom. Capt. Co. K, June 8, '63.
J. Oscar Conrick	Delavan	Nov. 11, '63..	From 2nd Lieut. Co. D; res. Mar. 1, '64.
John C. Durgin	Beloit	Mar. 21, '64..	From Sergt. Major; M. O. June 12, '65.
Quartermasters.			
John E. Holmes.......	Jefferson	July 18, '62..	Pris. Mar., '63; died June 8, '63, Annapolis, Md., disease.
Jesse L. Berch.........	Racine	June 5, '63..	From Q. M. Sergt.; M. O. June 12, '65.
Surgeons.			
George W. Bicknell....	Beloit	July 29, '62..	Res. Feb. 12, '63, disability.
Henry W. Cansdell....	Whitewater ...	May 20, '63..	Res. Mar. 18, '64, disability.
Thomas Hatchard	Milwaukee ...	Apr. 2, '64..	1st Asst. Surgeon, Sept. 21, '63; M. O. June 12, '65.
First Asst. Surgeons.			
Caleb S. Blanchard ...	East Troy	Aug. 5, '62..	Res. July 31, '63, disability.
Jerome Burbank	Whitewater ...	July 31, '63..	2nd Asst. Surgeon, Aug. 25, '62; res. Sept. 7, '63, disability.
James E. Coakley.....	Lima Center ..	Apr. 2, '64..	M. O. June 12, '65.
Chaplain.			
Caleb D. Pillsbury	Beloit	Sept. 13, '62..	Res. July 27, '63, disability.
George S. Bradley	Mt. Pleasant ..	Feb. 10, '64..	M. O. June 12, '65.
NON-COMMISSIONED OFFICERS.			
Sergeant Majors.		*Appointed.*	
Francis N. Keeley.....	Watertown....	Sept. 1, '62..	Prom. 2nd Lieut. Co. E, Dec. 27, '62.
James J. Hinds........	Racine	Jan. 1, '63..	From Corp. Co. A; wnd. Thomson's Station; died Mar. 10, '63, Franklin, Tenn., wnds.
Evan O. Jones.........	Racine	May 1, '63..	From 1st Sergt., Co. F; disch. Sept. 7, '63, disability.
John C. Durgin	Beloit	. Sept. 7, '63..	From 1st Sergt. Co. I; prom. Adjutant Mar. 21, '64.
Judson A. Mitchell ...	Spring Grove..	Apr. 6, '64..	From Sergt. Co. K; M. O. June 12, '65.

Roster pages (courtesy of Wisconsin Historical Society)

202   ROSTER WISCONSIN VOLUNTEERS.

NAME.	RESIDENCE.	DATE.	REMARKS.
Quartermaster Sergts.			
Jesse L. Berch	Racine	Sept. 1, '62..	From Sergt. Co. A; prom. Q. M., June 5, '63.
Horatio G. Billings...	Racine	June 16, '63..	From Corp. Co. F; prom. June 2nd Lieut. Co. E, 1st Wis. H. Art., Sept. 13, '64.
Heman S. McKenzie...	Janesville	Sept. 22, '64..	From Com. Sergt.; M. O. June 12, '65.
Commissary Sergts.			
Theodore D. W. Manchester.	Caledonia	Sept. 1, '62..	Enl. Aug. 14, '62; reduced and trans. to Co. H, Mar. 23, '63.
Heman S. McKenzie...	Janesville	Nov. 12, '62..	From Co. E; prom. Q. M. Sergt., Sept. 22, '64.
George T. Belding. ...	Richmond......	Sept. 22, '64..	From Sergt. Co. D; M. O. June 12, '65.
Hospital Stewards.			
Charles J. Cooper.....	Beloit.........	Sept. 1, '62..	From Co. I; disch. July 1, '63, disability.
Christopher Tochterman.	Clarno.........	July 1, '63..	From Corp. Co. G; ret. to Co., Sept. —, '63; re-appt'd Jan. 25, '64; prom. 2nd Asst. Surg. 35th Wis. Inf., Nov. 29, '64.
Proctor D. Scofield....	Janesville	Dec. 24, '64..	From Sergt. Co. E; M. O. June 12, '65.
Principal Musicians.			
John M. James......	Racine	Sept. 1, '62..	From Co. F; M. O. June 12, '65.
Martin Rice...........	Rock...	Sept. 1, '62..	From Co. E; disch. Jan. 25, '63, disability.
John J. Cone..........	Lynn	Feb. 13, '63..	From Co. C; M. O. June 12, '65.

ROSTER OF COMPANY "B."

NAME.	RESIDENCE.	DATE.	REMARKS.
OFFICERS.			
Captains.		*Rank from.*	
Thomas P. Northrop..	Beloit	Aug. 26, '62..	Res. Jan. 23, '63.
George H. Brown	Geneva........	Jan. 23, '63..	1st Lieut., Sept. 1, '62; wnd. Dallas; res. Apr. 1, '65.
First Lieutenant.			
Ira P. Nye............	Beloit	Jan. 23, '63..	Enl. Aug. 13, '62; Sergt.; 2nd Lieut., Jan. 12, '63; detach. Top. Eng. Corps, from Mar. 17, '64, till June 8, '65; M. O. June 12, '65.
Second Lieutenants.			
William H. Calvert....	Beloit	Aug. 26, '62..	Res. Jan. 12, '63.
James W. Crandall....	Beloit	Jan. 23, '63..	Enl. Aug. 15, '62; Sergt.; wnd. and pris. Thomson's Station; res. Nov. 21, '63.
ENLISTED MEN.		*Enlisted.*	
Adams, Rollin L.......	Beloit	Aug. 14, '62..	M. O. June 12, '65.
Anderson, Alexander..	Beloit	Aug. 15, '62..	Sergt.; wnd. Thomson's Station; died Mar. 28, '63, wnds.
Anderson, Edward	Hudson	Aug. 15, '62..	M. O. June 12, '65.
Bailey, George W	Beloit.........	Aug. 14, '62..	M. O. June 12, '65.
Bailey, James	Geneva........	Aug. 15, '62..	Pris. Brentwood; absent sick at M. O. of Regt.
Baker, Clarence W....	Janesville	Aug. 21, '62..	Disch. Oct. 31, '63, to accept Com. in U. S. C. T.
Bibbins, Silas L.......	Beloit.........	Aug. 14, '62..	Corp.; M. O. June 12, '65.
Bibbins, Adney F.....	Beloit	Aug. 15, '62..	Died Jan. 2, '63, Danville, Ky., disease.
Bicknell, Otis P.......	Beloit	Aug. 15, '62..	Disch. Oct. 10, '63, disability.
Block, Lewis	Cross Plains...	Aug. 22, '64..	M. O. June 12, '65.
Bond, Alfred	Bloomfield	Aug. 15, '62..	Corp.; wnd. Dallas; M. O. June 12, '65.
Bradt, Abram	Farmington ...	Aug. 14, '62..	Trans. to V. R. C., Sept. 30, '63; M. O. May 22, '65.
Brownell, David E.....	Beloit	Aug. 14, '62..	Disch. Jan. 15, '63, disability.
Bullock, Calvin H	Beloit	Aug. 10, '62..	1st Sergt.; 2nd Lieut., June 2, '65, not mustered; M. O. June 12, '65.
Bullock, Albert W	Beloit	Aug. 10, '62..	Wnd. Thomson's Station and Atlanta; M. O. May 23, '65.
Capron, Orange V.....	Newark........	Aug. 15, '62..	M. O. June 12, '65.
Clark, George C.......	Afton...... ...	Aug. 14, '62..	M. O. June 12, '65.
Cook, Daniel	Harrison	Aug. 15, '62..	Pris.; absent sick at M. O. of Regt.
Court, Thomas........	Lyons.........	Aug. 15, '62..	Wnd. Peach Tree Creek; M. O. May 19, '65.
Crist, Charles H......	Beloit	Aug. 14, '63..	M. O. June 12, '65.
Cullen, Martin	Linn...........	Aug. 15, '62..	Died Jan. 15, '63, Lexington, Ky, disease.

NAME.	RESIDENCE.	DATE.	REMARKS.
Darling, Josiah	Rock	Aug. 14, '62	M. O. June 12, '65.
Dates, George W	Beloit	Aug. 14, '62	Disch. Jan. 18, '63, disability.
Dawson, William A	Beloit	Aug. 14, '62	M. O. June 9, '65.
Dwyer, James	Beloit	Aug. 13, '62	Deserted Dec. 20, '62.
Ellingson, Hiram	Beloit	Aug. 15, '62	Disch. May 4, '63, disability.
Elliott, James P	Jefferson	Aug. 15, '62	Wnd. Dallas; M. O. June 12, '65.
Fairbanks, Edwin S	Rockton, Ills	Aug. 15, '62	M. O. June 12, '65.
Fairservice, Marshall L	Summit	Aug. 15, '62	Sergt.; prom. 2nd Lieut. Co. A, 46th Wis. Inf., Feb. 17, '65.
Farr, Edgar A	Beloit	Aug. 15, '62	Corp.; M. O. June 12, '65.
Fay, John	Geneva	Aug. 14, '62	Trans. to V. R. C., Apr. 10, '64.
Fleming, James	Bloomfield	Aug. 20, '62	M. O. May 13, '65.
Fountain, Charles	Beloit	Aug. 15, '62	M. O. June 12, '65.
Getten, Albert C	Beloit	Aug. 15, '62	Corp., Sergt.; M. O. June 12, '65.
Gullickson, Ole	Newark	Aug. 13, '62	Disch. Aug. 10, '64, disability.
Hackett, Joseph	Beloit	Aug. 13, '62	Died Apr. 23, '63, Annapolis, Md., disease.
Harrison, Joseph A	Beloit	Aug. 15, '62	Disch. Jan. 20, '63, accidental wnds.
Harwood, George W	Beloit	Aug. 15, '62	Died Jan. 20, '63, Danville, Ky., disease.
Haskell, Jeremiah	Geneva	Aug. 20, '62	Died Dec. 20, '62, Nicholasville, Ky., disease.
Herrick, Sophronius S.	Beloit	Aug. 15, '62	Corp., Sergt.; M. O. June 12, '65.
Herring, Benjamin	Jefferson	Aug. 12, '62	Disch. Mar. 24, '65, disability.
Hodge, Henry A	Beloit	Aug. 15, '62	Corp.; disch. June 12, '65, disability.
Hood, Wilson	Spring Green	Jan. 23, '65	Trans. to 3rd Wis. Inf., June 10, '65.
Hosier, John C	Rock	Aug. 17, '62	Trans. to V. R. C., Mar. 13, '65; M. O. July 8, '65.
Jacobson, John	Plymouth	Aug. 14, '62	Killed July 20, '64, Peach Tree Creek, Ga.
Johnson, John F	Milwaukee	Sept. 21, '64	Drafted; M. O. May 17, '65.
Johnson, William H	Milwaukee	Oct. 7, '64	Trans. to 3rd Wis. Inf., June 10, '65.
Kadow, John	Montello	Sept. 5, '64	M. O. June 12, '65.
Kelley, Frank H	Beloit	Aug. 14, '62	Corp., Sergt.; M. O. June 12, '65.
Kelsey, Dennis	Wonewoc	Sept. 19, '64	Drafted; M. O. May 17, '65.
Kelsey, Morgan	Hortonia	Mar. 8, '65	Drafted; trans. to 3rd Wis. Inf., June 10, '65.
Kendall, Richard A	Beloit	Aug. 12, '62	Trans. to V. R. C., Mar. 15, '65; M. O. June 30, '65.
Kendall, John S	Beloit	Aug. 15, '62	Corp.; prom. 2nd Lieut. Co. C, 48th Wis. Inf., Mar. 16, '65.
Kenney, Thomas	Mt. Pleasant	Mar. 22, '65	Trans. to 3rd Wis. Inf., June 10, '65.
King, James	Beloit	Aug. 14, '62	Wnd. Brentwood; disch. July 31, '63, wnds.
Kline, Benjamin	Beloit	Aug. 15, '62	M. O. June 12, '65.
Kneeland, John	Ridgeway	Apr. 1, '65	Trans. to 3rd Wis. Inf., June 10, '65.
Kober, Herman	East Troy	Sept. 24, '64	Drafted; M. O. May 17, '65.
Kopp, Gustave	Milwaukee	Sept. 21, '64	Drafted; M. O. May 17, '65.
Kuntz, William	Green Bay	Mar. 10, '65	Trans. to 3rd Wis. Inf., June 10, '65.
Langenberg, Conrad	Herman	Oct. 18, '64	Drafted; trans to 3rd Wis. Inf., June 10, '65.
Lawton, John	Wyocena	Sept. 21, '64	Drafted; M. O. May 17, '65.
Leighton, Lowell E	Shields	Nov. 1, '64	Drafted; trans. to 3rd Wis. Inf., June 10, '65.
Le Marsh, Frank	Herman	Nov. 14, '64	Trans. to 3rd Wis. Inf., June 10, '65.
Link, Peter	Milwaukee	Nov. 25, '64	Drafted; trans. to 3rd Wis. Inf., June 10, '65.
Luck, Frederick	Milwaukee	Sept. 21, '64	Drafted; M. O. May 17, '65.
Luhring, Frederick	Milwaukee	Sept. 21, '64	Drafted; M. O. May 17, '65.
Moeller, Frederick	Milwaukee	Nov. 14, '64	Drafted; trans. to 3rd Wis. Inf., June 10, '65.
Mark, August	Milwaukee	Nov. 25, '64	Drafted; trans. to 3rd Wis. Inf., June 10, '65.
Maxworthy, Albert	Beloit	Aug. 15, '62	Deserted Feb. 28, '63.
Mengel, Frederick	Milwaukee	Nov. 16, '64	Drafted; trans. to 3rd Wis. Inf., June 10, '65.
Merriman, Amasa H	Beloit	Aug. 13, '62	M. O. June 12, '65.
Messersmith, Ernst	Berry	Jan. 18, '65	Trans. to 3rd Wis. Inf., June 10, '65.
Miles, William S	Madison	Aug. 12, '64	Trans. to 3rd Wis. Inf., June 10, '65.
Miller, Sanford L	Beloit	Aug. 11, '62	Corp.; absent sick at M. O. of Regt.
Minot, William H. H	Beloit	Aug. 14, '62	Corp.; wnd. Thomson's Station; M. O. June 12, '65.
Minot, Charles A	Beloit	Aug. 14, '62	Disch. Dec. 29, '63, disability.
Moseley, Lucius S	Beloit	Aug. 13, '62	Corp.; M. O. June 12, '65.
Murphy, Cornelius J	Glenmore	Dec. 28, '64	Drafted; trans. to 3rd Wis. Inf., June 10, '65.
Murray, Charles P	Beloit	Aug. 15, '62	Corp., Sergt.; M. O. June 12, '65.
Neal, William F	Beloit	Aug. 15, '62	Deserted May 12, '63.
Nelson, Sumner	Bloomfield	Aug. 13, '62	Wnd. Peach Tree Creek, leg amputated; absent wnd. at M. O. of Regt.
Nelson, John	Newark	Aug. 15, '62	M. O. June 12, '65.
Newman, John	Bradford	Aug. 15, '62	M. O. June 12, '65.
Norris, Joseph	Dayton	Sept. 26, '64	Drafted; M. O. May 17, '65.
Northrop, Frederick J.	Beloit	Aug. 10, '62	Sergt.; disch. May 25, '63, disability.

NAME.	RESIDENCE.	DATE.	REMARKS.
Olmstead, Clarence S..	Rockton, Ills..	Aug. 18, '62..	Trans. to V. R. C., Oct. 31, '63; M. O. June 29, '65.
Olson, John	Beloit	Aug. 15, '62..	Died Jan. 30, '63, Danville, Ky., disease.
Olson, John..........	Clyde.........	Nov. 19, '64..	Drafted; trans. to 3rd Wis. Inf., June 10, '65.
Ormsby, Horace.......	Beloit	Aug. 14, '62..	Musician; disch. June 12, '63, disability.
Orr, John.............	Rock	Aug. 14, '62..	M. O. June 14, '65.
Orr, William C......	Rock	Aug. 14, '62..	Wnd. Peach Tree Creek; disch. May 29, '65, disability.
Perkins, George M.....	Turtle	Aug. 15, '62..	M. O. June 12, '65.
Perry, Napoleon B....	Beloit	Aug. 14, '62..	Wnd. Dallas; M. O. June 3, '65.
Phillips, William T...	Dodgeville ...	Oct. 3, '64..	Trans. to 3rd Wis. Inf., June 10, '65.
Pomeroy, John M....	Beloit	Aug. 14, '62..	Wnd. Thomson's Station; M. O. June 12, '65.
Pope, Alexander	Geneva	Aug. 15, '62..	Absent sick at M. O. of Regt.
Pope, Benjamin F....	Elkhorn	Nov. 23, '63..	Trans. to 3rd Wis. Inf., June 10, '65.
Pryce, John D.........	Ellington.....	Nov. 29, '64..	Trans. to 3rd Wis. Inf.. June 10, '65.
Pung, Paul	Preble	Dec. 28, '64..	Drafted; trans. to 3rd Wis. Inf., June 10, '65.
Radway, Richard M..	Clinton.......	Aug. 18, '62..	M. O. June 12, '65.
Ranney, William O....	Plymouth	Aug. 15, '62..	Wagoner; M. O. June 12, '65.
Reinhart, George.....	Watertown ..	Nov. 15, '64..	Drafted; trans. to 3rd Wis. Inf., June 10, '65.
Robinson, William F..	Dayton	Sept. 26, '64..	Drafted; M. O. May 17, '65.
Rose, George W.......	Beloit	Aug. 11, '62..	Disch. Jan. 25, '63, disability.
Rose, Leonard M.....	Beloit	Aug. 13, '62..	M. O. June 12, '65.
Ross, James E... ...	Beloit	Aug. 13, '62..	Corp., Sergt.; wnd. Dallas; disch. Oct. 1, '64, to accept com. in U. S. C. T.
Russell, John D........	Clinton.......	Aug. 15, '62..	Disch. Oct. 3, '63, disability.
Sage, Simon M	Beloit	Aug. 15, '62..	Corp.; M. O. June 12, '65.
Salisbury, Nelson......	Magnolia	Aug. 14, '62..	Wnd. Peach Tree Creek; M. O. June 12, '65.
Schard, Joseph.......	Milwaukee	Nov. 25, '64..	Drafted; trans. to 3rd Wis. Inf., June 10, '65.
Schilling, Henry.......	Milwaukee ..	Sept. 20, '64..	Drafted; M. O. May 17, '65.
Schmitz, Hubert.......	Milwaukee ..	Sept. 20, '64..	Drafted; M. O. May 17, '65.
Schoening, Weaver F..	Rock	Aug. 13, '62..	Corp., Sergt.; wnd. Peach Tree Creek; M. O. June 12, '65.
Schugg, Casper........	Menomonie ...	Dec. 1, '64..	Drafted; trans. to 3rd Wis. Inf., June 10, '65.
Scott, J. G............	Ellington.....	Mar. 7, '65..	Drafted; trans. to 3rd Wis. Inf., June 10, '65.
Selleck, Benjamin.....	Beloit	Aug. 15, '62..	Disch. Mar. 15, '64, to accept prom. as Hosp. Steward, U. S. A.
Simonson, Thomas ...	Spring Valley.	Aug. 15, '62..	M. O. June 12, '65.
Smith, Austin E.......	Beloit	Aug. 14, '62..	M. O. June 12, '65.
Smith, Frank H.......	Beloit	Aug. 15, '62..	Absent sick at M. O. of Regt.
Smith, Harvey C......	Beloit	Aug. 15, '62..	Disch. July 8, '63, disability.
Smith, James O.......	Cato.........	Sept. 30, '64..	Drafted; M. O. May 17, '65.
Snyder, Washington...	Plymouth	Mar. 17, '65..	Trans. to 3rd Wis. Inf., June 10, '65.
Spencer, Rudolph A...	Magnolia......	Aug. 14, '62..	Wnd. Thomson's Station; absent sick at M.O. of Regt.
Stahl, Ernst	Herman......	Dec. 2, '64..	Drafted; trans. to 3rd Wis. Inf., June 10, '65.
Stewart, Silas.........	Granville	Mar. 23, '65..	Trans. to 3rd Wis. Inf., June 10, '65.
Stott, Joseph B.......	Turtle	Aug. 23, '64..	M. O. June 24, '65.
Straw, Josiah.........	Cato.........	Sept. 30, '64..	Drafted; M. O. May 17, '65.
Teague, John.........	Newark	Aug. 15, '62..	Died May 20, '63, Beloit, Wis., disease.
Thomas, George H....	Dekorra	Sept. 21, '64..	Drafted; M. O. May 17, '65.
Traver, Rauaf W......	Walworth	Sept. 1, '62..	Corp.; wnd. Thomson's Station; M. O. June 12, '65.
Underwood, William P	Geneva	Aug. 28, '62..	M. O. June 12, '65.
Wachter, Jacob.......	Geneva	Aug. 13, '62..	Drowned in Cumberland River, Feb. 2, '63.
Walker, John D.......	Racine	Sept. 1, '62..	Musician; disch. Dec. 28, '63, disability.
Walsh, Thomas	Linn..........	Aug. 15, '62..	Deserted May 12, '63.
West, George W.......	Beloit	Aug. 15, '62..	Corp.; trans. to V. R. C., Jan. 15, '64; M. O. May 29, '65.
West, Salvin C	Kenosha......	Aug. 15, '62..	Disch. Jan. 20, '63, disability.
Wright, Silas	Turtle	Aug. 14, '62..	Wnd. New Hope Church; M. O. May 16, '65.

Appendix B

Colonel John Coburn's
Farewell Address to His Troops

John R. McBride, *History of the Thirty-Third Indiana Veteran Volunteer Infantry*
(Indianapolis: William B. Burford, Printer and Binder, 1900), 146.

Headquarters Second Brigade, Third Division, Twentieth Army Corps

Atlanta, Georgia, September 20, 1864

Soldiers of the Second Brigade:

My term of service has expired and I am about to be separated from
you. We have been associated as a brigade almost two years. We have borne
in that time all the burdens and endured all the trials and hardships of war
together. This experience has made us friends—such friends as only suffering and toil together can make. In that time you have shared an eventful
part in the great struggle of the age. In Tennessee, Kentucky, and Georgia
you have nobly illustrated the history of your own states of Indiana, Michigan, and Wisconsin. That history cannot be written without a record of your
calm patience, disciplined courage, and heroic daring. The bloody and desperate battle at Thompson Station and the successful fights at Franklin in
Tennessee gave early proof of your valor. While in the past campaign, at
Resaca, Cassville, New Hope Church, Culps's Farm, Peachtree Creek, and
Atlanta you have, in the front of the fight, borne straight onward your victorious banners. At Resaca your flags were the first to wave on the enemy's
ramparts, at New Hope Church the fury of your onset redeemed the day's
disaster, at Peachtree Creek your charge rivaled the most famous feats of

arms in the annals of war, and at Atlanta your ranks were the first to climb the works and take possession of that renowned city.

The Thirty-Third Indiana at Wild Cat fought the first battle and won the first victory gained by the Army of the Cumberland, and the united brigade fired the last shot at the flying foe as he fled from his stronghold in Atlanta.

But not alone in the stormy and fiery fight have you been tried. You have by long marches, by herculean labors upon fieldworks, by cheerful obedience, by watching what knew no surprise, and by toil that knew no rest or weariness, eclipsed the fame of your daring in battle and place high above the glitter of victorious arms the steady light of your solid virtues.

We have lived together as brethren in a great common cause. We part, our hearts glowing with the same patriotic ardor, and hereafter, when the war is over and the light of home is smiling around you, you will have no prouder memories than those associated with this brigade.

Your comrades in arms are sleeping beneath the clods of the valley from Ohio to Atlanta, and from Atlanta to Richmond. Faithful, patient, and brave, they have given to their country and God whatever martyrs and heroes can give, as one by one they fell out from your glorious ranks they have added new testimony to the sacredness of your cause.

My friends and soldiers, farewell.

John Coburn, Colonel

Thirty-Third Indiana Volunteers, Commanding Brigade

Appendix C

22nd Wisconsin Chronology of Service
and Regimental Statistics

As recorded in E. B. Quiner's *Military History of Wisconsin* (Chicago, 1866), chap. 36, p. 706

Original Strength	1009
Gained by recruits in 1864	139
Gained by recruits in 1865	4
Gained by substitutes	130
Gained by draft in 1865	223
Total numbers	1505
Losses by death	226
Losses by desertion	46
Transferred	31
Discharged	106
Mustered out	1,006

Another set of statistics for the 22nd Wisconsin is found in Groves, *Blooding the Regiment*, 330.

Enlisted on September 2, 1862	1,009
Enlisted/drafted subsequently	496
Total served	1,505
Killed in action or died of wounds	79
Died of disease	163
Died accidentally	6

Total loss	248
Death rate	16.478%
Engagements	13

In his epilogue, p. 326, Richard Groves wrote that following the Grand Review in Washington, DC, the men of Wisconsin's 22nd Regiment headed westward to Milwaukee, where they were discharged by the state. They marched through downtown Racine to a tumultuous welcome home. Then, as best they could, they returned to peaceful pursuits.

Index